QA 66 KIN

1

Theory of Computing

A Gentle Introduction

Theory of Computing
A Gentle Introduction

Efim Kinber
Sacred Heart University

Carl Smith
University of Maryland

PRENTICE HALL, Upper Saddle River, New Jersey 07458

Library of Congress Cataloging-in-Publication Data

Kinber, Efim
   Theory of computing: a gentle introduction / Carl Smith, Efim Kinber,
     p. cm.
  Includes bibliological references and index.
  ISBN: 0-13-027961-7
  1. Electronic data processing. I. Smith, Carl, 1950 April 25 - II. Title.

QA76 .K475   2001
004—dc21   00-024617

Acquisition Editor: *Petra J. Recter*
Editorial Assistant: *Sarah Burrows*
Vice President and Editorial Director of Engineering and Computer Science: *Marcia Horton*
Assistant Vice President and Director of Production and Manufacturing, ESM: *David W. Riccardi*
Editorial/Production Supervision: *Barbara A. Till*
Managing Editor: *David A. George*
Executive Managing Editor: *Vince O'Brien*
Manufacturing Buyer: *Pat Brown*
Manufacturing Manager: *Trudy Pisciotti*
Senior Marketing Manager: *Jennie Burger*
Marketing Assistant: *Cynthia Szollose*
Creative Director: *Paul Belfanti*
Art Director: *Jayne Conte*
Cover Designer: *Bruce Kenselaar*

© 2001 by Prentice-Hall, Inc.
Upper Saddle River, New Jersey 07458

The author and publisher of this book have used their best efforts in preparing this book. These efforts include the development, research, and testing of the theories and programs to determine their effectiveness. The author and publisher make no warranty of any kind, expressed or implied, with regard to these programs or the documentation contained in this book. The author and publisher shall not be liable in any event for incidental or consequential damages in connection with, or arising out of, the furnishing, performance, or use of these programs.

Printed in the United States of America

10 9 8 7 6 5 4 3 2

0-13-027961-7

Prentice-Hall International (UK) Limited, London
Prentice-Hall of Australia Pty. Limited, Sydney
Prentice-Hall Canada Inc., Toronto
Prentice-Hall Hispanoamericana, S.A., Mexico
Prentice-Hall of India Private. Limited, New Delhi
Prentice-Hall of Japan, Inc.,Tokyo
Pearson Education Asia Pte. Ltd.
Editora Prentice-Hall do Brasil, Ltda., Rio de Janeiro

*Dedicated to those who created the material herein
and to those who taught it to us.*

Contents

List of Figures

Preface

The theory of computing provides students with a background in the fundamentals of computing with which to achieve a deeper understanding of contemporary computing systems. Computers are evolving and developing at a dizzying rate. Yet, the fundamentals of pattern matching and programming language design and implementation have remained unchanged. In this book, we present a perspective on computing that will always apply since it addresses only the fundamental issues. In this way, mastery of the topics in this book will give the reader a perspective from which to understand all computers, not just the ones in use today.

We cover the automata and regular languages that serve as the basis for pattern-matching algorithms, communication protocols, control mechanisms, sequential circuit design, and a host of other ubiquitous applications. The basic principles behind the parsing of computer languages are also presented as well as a simple, yet general, model of all computation. This leads to some important distinctions. Some problems of interest turn out to be unsolvable. That is, not only can they not be solved by today's computers, but they will also never be solved by any future computer. Some problems that are solvable are nonetheless so difficult that they are called intractable. These intractable problems cannot be solved *efficiently* by any current computer. Furthermore, advances in the design of computers will not make a significant difference.

The collection of intractable problems includes several that must be solved in some way every day. The "solutions" to these problems are generally approximations. Such problems are ubiquitous in everyday life. Consider the shirt you are wearing. The cloth with which it was made was delivered to the clothing manufacturer in a bolt of cloth. The bolt of cloth is a large roll, perhaps two meters wide and hundreds of meters in length. The manufacturer must cut this cloth into pieces of different sizes for different size shirts and for other garments that use the same material. Some of the material will naturally be wasted — scraps will be left over since the pieces that are cut do not form perfect rectangles, two meters per side. How to cut this cloth so as to minimize the leftover useless scraps is a provably intractable problem. Imagine how much cloth could be wasted in an attempt to find the best solution! Such problems occur frequently in computing. It is vital for any computer professional to be able to recognize an intractable or unsolvable problem when confronted with one. Our intent is to impart such knowledge to the student.

All of the above requires some analysis, and hence some mathematics. The material can become very difficult for students. We soften the material by taking a more "how to" approach as opposed to a "how come" one. Many Colleges and Universities choose to cover the material in two or more courses. We have sacrificed some depth to create a book for a one semester course primarily intended for use at institutions that have only one upper level course in the theory of computing. However, this book can be, and has been, used to teach a traditional automata theory course. For this purpose, the final chapter is omitted, the material on Turing Machines is abbreviated and the remaining topics are covered in more depth. This extra depth can be achieved by working through the detailed proofs that we relegate to the exercises.

For the student, we give dozens of detailed examples, numerous figures, and hundreds of exercises. The exercises are graded according to difficulty. More challenging exercises are marked with a ◆ and the most challenging exercises are marked with ◆◆. Preliminary versions of this text were tested in the classroom by both authors. Reviewers Diane Cook and Piotr Gmytrasiewicz of the University of Texas at Arlington and Guo-Qiang Zang of the University of Georgia imporved the exposition with their comments. We wish to thank our colleagues William Gasarch, Vincenzo Liberatore, and Raymond Miller for suggesting several changes. Preliminary versions were tested in the classroom with resultant textual improvements. A web page with the latest news, errata, etc., for the book is maintained at `http://www.cs.umd.edu/~smith/TCGI.html` An *Instructor's Manual*, containing the solutions to all the exercises in the book, is available from the publisher.

Theory of Computing
A Gentle Introduction

Chapter 1

Introduction

Chapter 1

Introduction

1.1   Why Study the Theory of Computing?

Computers are changing our world and the way people think. New models appear on the market almost every month. Some televisions are taking on the functionality of what we call computers, blurring the distinction of what is and what is not a computer. How can you tell the difference?

The consumer is hit with a mind-boggling array of products to choose from. How do you decide which computer to buy when the salespeople themselves often don't really understand the differences between the machines? They usually characterize the machines based on what software they run or confuse the consumer with buzzwords like 500 megahertz, 16-meg RAM, multipurpose ports, and so on.

While model numbers, and software change, the theory is fixed. It can be used to recognize computation in all its forms and disguises. For example, the ubiquitous vending machines that dispense products from canned soft drinks and juices, to snacks, train tickets, and cash are all really a type of computer called an **automaton**. This same type of computer is at the heart of the search engines that ply the Internet to help Web surfers find new pages to explore.

When you study the theory of computation, you develop an understanding of what computation is. The viewpoint presented in this book will not vary with the next new model of computer. A firm knowledge of the theoretical basis for computation will give you a stable platform from which to observe and understand the dazzling progress being made in the production of new computers and software.

1.2   What Is Computation?

A simple working definition of computation is that **computation is the movement, and perhaps alteration during transit, of data**. Let's work through some examples. Consider a vending machine dispensing soft drinks. The input to the computation, the original data, is the coins you put in the slot and buttons(s) you press to select the product. The coins are moved to a holding area and some electronic impulses are generated. The coins have been altered into electronic impulses that are now moving through wires. The data now contain information about how many coins you entered and which denominations. These impulses are transformed into signals that trigger the gate that lets the product you selected move to the area of the machine where it can be collected. So, the impulses encoding your selection and the coins entered are changed into a product, and perhaps some change in another area of the machine.

When you use an automatic teller machine, another sequence of events happens that looks like a computation. You insert your card and then use a keypad to input more data. Sometimes the keypad is organized around a display and you must make several selections. As the display changes, so does the meaning of each button. Nonetheless, you are still inputting data to the machine. After a while, you get some cash as output and maybe a transaction receipt as well. So, according to our working definition, a computation has taken place. A more detailed analysis reveals even more computations. After you have entered all the data, such as pin codes and transaction type, the bank machine contacts another computer holding your account information. This connection may be complicated depending on how far away the bank machine you are using is from the location of the computer holding the needed information. It is not unusual for such connections to cross state and even country borders. The computer with the account information does what is typically considered a computation and sends some information, like an authorization number, back to the bank machine you are using. Few data are being transfered between the computer and the bank machine, but the amount of withdrawal and account number information is transformed into an authorization to dispense cash.

Another computation that has layers and layers happens every time you use a computer. At the outermost level, the keystrokes and mouse movements you enter are transformed into the display on the screen. At the next level, the keystrokes activate some program which runs on the computer. One level deeper, the program is meticulously telling the computer to get data from memory and move them into the processing chip where they are transformed into commands for the display chip(s). There is another level, what happens inside the chip, but we won't get that detailed. The basic idea of computation as movement and transformation of data should be clear.

1.3   The Contents of This Book

In Chapter 2, we study finite automata. These simple devices serve as the basis for all pattern-matching algorithms. All the World Wide Web search engines use pattern matching as a host of other applications. Interacting automata, not considered in this text, are the basis for all communication protocols used in computer networks of all kinds.

In Chapter 3 we study context-free languages which are used to describe all contemporary programming languages. Topics such as parsing are discussed. A fully general model of computers is presented in Chapter 4. The limitations of this model are revealed in Chapter 5. Finally, in Chapter 6, we consider the limitations of feasible computation.

1.4 Mathematical Preliminaries

This is a technical book. We have tried to make the presentation as intuitive as possible, often deviating from the traditional presentation of iterating definition, theorem, and proof. However, we must rely on some mathematical notation to make our presentation clear and precise. We anticipate that every student using this book will have seen all the concepts in this section before. They are presented mainly for review and to establish notational conventions.

Computers typically deal with numbers and strings. We will do so as well. The only numbers that we will consider are the natural numbers, 0, 1, 2, ... which we denote by N. Actually, the natural numbers can be pulled, more or less, from thin air by the operation of *collection*. For example, even though we start with no numbers, we can still collect what we have. Visually, this collection of nothing appears as { }. Call this representation zero. Now we have something, so we can collect our zero: {{ }}. Call this one. Now we have two things to collect: {{ }, {{ }}}. This last collection, call it two, is the collection of two items:

- The collection of nothing, and

- The collection of the collection of nothing.

Now we have three objects to collect and the process continues, defining representations for all the natural numbers in terms of the operation of collection. Please note that this definition of natural numbers is an **inductive definition**. In this style of definition a *base object* is specified (in this case, the empty object) and an operation to produce new objects from previously defined objects is specified (in this case, collection).

Once we have natural numbers, we can collect those as well forming **sets**. For example, the set of prime numbers less than 10 is denoted by $\{2, 3, 7\}$. Set membership is denoted by the symbol "$\in$," so $2 \in \{2, 3, 7\}$. Nonmembership is denoted by "$\notin$." For example, $4 \notin \{2, 3, 7\}$. Larger sets, like all the numbers between 1 and 100 are denoted as $\{1, 2, \ldots, 100\}$. If all the elements of one set are contained in some other set, then we say the first set is a subset of the second set and use the symbol "$\subseteq$" to denote this. So, for example, $\{2, 3, 7\} \subseteq \{1, 2, \ldots, 100\}$. For a finite set of numbers, the largest element in set is called the *max* and is denoted by $\max\{\ldots\}$. Infinite sets, like the set of even numbers, can be represented as $\{0, 2, \ldots\}$ or in closed form as $\{2n | n \in N\}$.

A common way to form one set from another is to take away some elements. The "−" operator is used to denote set difference. For example, $N - \{0\}$ denotes the set of positive natural numbers and $N - E$ denotes the set of odd numbers. Sets can also be formed by joining two existing sets. For example, if you are making sandwiches for a picnic and you like sandwiches in the set

$$A = \{\text{peanut butter and jelly, tuna fish}\}$$

and your friend likes sandwiches in the set

$$B = \{\text{tofu ginger, pastrami}\}$$

you would want to pack sandwiches of all four types. Mathematically, you would take the **union** of the two sets, written as $A \cup B$.

On the other hand, you might be ordering a pizza. If you like the toppings

$$A = \{\text{pepperoni, sausage, peppers, mushrooms, anchovies}\}$$

and your friend likes

$$B = \{\text{olives, mushrooms, pineapple, peppers}\}$$

and you want to please everyone, you will order a mushroom and pepper pizza. To decide this, you took all the elements common to both sets of preferred pizza toppings. Mathematically, you took the **intersection** of the two sets, written as $A \cap B$.

Another way to form new sets from old sets is to take all the pairs of elements, one chosen from each set. Formally, given two sets, R and S, the *Cartesian product* of R and S, written as $R \times S$, is the set of pairs that includes all combination of something from R and something from S. So, for example, if $R = \{0, 1, 2\}$ and $S = \{a, b\}$, then

$$R \times S = \{(0, a), (0, b), (1, a), (1, b), (2, a), (2, b)\}$$

For example, if S is the set of students at your college, and C is the list of courses offered, then the set of pairs (s, c) such that student s is taking course c is a subset of the Cartesian product $S \times C$. In symbols we write

$$\{(s, c)|\ \text{student } s \text{ takes course } c\} \subset S \times C$$

Computers store numbers in a binary representation using only 0's and 1's. Alphabetic symbols are stored in a computer as a fixed-length sequence of 0's and 1's. Similarly, words are just sequences of the symbols representing the letters of the Latin alphabet, a, b, c, ..., z, A, B, ..., Z. Continuing, we find that sentences, like this one, are just longer sequences of symbols that alternate between the symbols for a word and a blank symbol, or some other punctuation symbol, like the period at the end of a sentence. If we admit symbols that do not appear but cause other effects, like *newline* and *newpage*, we can describe this entire book as a sequence of symbols. Notice that standard terminology gives up notions of levels. Sequences of bits form words, sequences of words form sentences, and sequences of sentences form books. However, this book really is just a sequence of suitable chosen symbols (about a half million of them). Some of these symbols we haven't talked about, they format the mathematical symbols, and the like.

Rather than use a jumble of terminology, we will simply discuss **strings** which are just finite sequences of symbols where each symbol is chosen from a fixed **alphabet**. Sometimes we call strings *words*. An alphabet is just some finite set of symbols, like the binary alphabet $\{0, 1\}$ or the lowercase Latin alphabet $\{a, b, c, \ldots, z\}$. The empty word, the unique string with no symbols, is denoted by e. The *length* of a word w is the number of symbols in the word and is denoted by $|w|$. Since the empty word has no symbols, $|e| = 0$. If w is a word, w^R denotes the *reverse* of w. So, if w is 011, then w^R is 110. A word w such that $w = w^R$ is called a *palindrome*. A set of words is called a *language*. These terms are meant to conjure images of their standard usage. We will use them to discuss the nature of computation, where the input and output are given as strings of symbols. Even the display on your computer screen is a sequence of symbols (a string) to a particular device (the monitor).

We often have need to manipulate sets of numbers and strings. Here we review some common operations on sets. If S is a set, then $\bar{S}$ denotes the *complement* of S. The complement of a set is always taken with respect to some larger, often only implicitly specified, set. For example, if E is the set of even numbers, then $\bar{E}$ is the set of all numbers that are not even, that is the odd numbers. If S is a set of words, then $\bar{S}$ is the set of all words that can be formed using the same alphabet as was used to construct S that are not in S. So for example, for the alphabet $\{a, b\}$, if S is the set of words with only a's, $\{a, aa, aaa, \ldots\}$ then $\bar{S}$ is the set of words with a's and at least one b, maybe more.

Often, we need to count and sort things. If you are trying to place n items into m slots and $n > m$, then one slot will have more than one item in it, no matter what you do. This is called the *pigeonhole principle*.

Relations between objects are often crucial. Mathematically, a relation is represented as a subset of some Cartesian product. For example, "$<$" is a relation on $N \times N$. It contains all the pairs of natural numbers (x, y) such that $x < y$. The "less than" relation is so common we have a special symbol for it. In less common cases, when we have no special symbol, we give the relation explicitly as a subset of a Cartesian product. Doing this formally with the "$<$" relation, we would define

$$R = \{(x, y) | x \in N, y \in N \text{ and } x < y\}$$

Then $(2, 3) \in R$ and $(3, 2) \notin R$.

There are several common properties that a relation may or may not have. For example, if R is a relation on $S \times S$, then R is **reflexive** if $(a, a) \in R$ for each

$a \in S$. For example, let S be the set $\{a, b, c\}$. Then any subset of $S \times S$ is a relation. Consider $\hat{R} = \{(a, a), (a, b), (b, b)\}$. Then R is NOT a reflexive relation. However, $\hat{R} \cup \{(c, c)\}$ is reflexive. We say that R is **symmetric** if $(a, b) \in R$ whenever $(b, a) \in R$. Using the same relation $\hat{R}$, we see that it is not symmetric either, but $\hat{R} \cup \{(b, a)\}$ is. A **transitive** relation is one such that if $(a, b) \in R$ and $(b, c) \in R$, then $(a, c) \in R$. Notice that $\hat{R}$ is transitive, but $\hat{R} \cup \{(b, c)\}$ is not. This is because $(a, b) \in \hat{R} \cup \{(b, c)\}$, $(b, c) \in \hat{R} \cup \{(b, c)\}$, but $(a, c) \notin \hat{R} \cup \{(b, c)\}$. An **equivalence relation** is a reflexive, symmetric, and transitive relation.

Equivalence relations give rise to **equivalence classes** where each such class contains all and only the members of the underlying set that relate to each other. For example, unless you are fortunate to be reading this book outside in a sunny place, you are using some sort of artificial light source to see the words on this page. The power of the artificial lights, whether they are incandescent, fluorescent, or halogen, is usually measured in watts. Define a relation of the set of light bulbs, of all types, sizes and shapes, by saying that two light bulbs relate to each other if they are of the same power (wattage). This relation is reflexive, since every bulb has the same power as itself. It is also symmetric, since if bulb A has the same wattage as bulb B, then bulb B has the same wattage as bulb A. Finally, this relation is transitive, since if bulb A has the same wattage as bulb B and bulb B has the same wattage as bulb C, then bulbs A and C must have the same wattage. So, equivalence classes arise, where, for example, there is one equivalence class for 40-watt bulbs. It contains all the 40-watt bulbs of all types, shapes, and sizes, but no bulbs of any other wattage.

Suppose R is a relation over a set S such that for each $a \in S$ there is at most one $b \in S$ such that $(a, b) \in R$. Thus we say that R is a **function**. We will use the more familiar notation $f : R \rightarrow S$ to indicate a function that takes inputs from the set R and returns elements from the set S. More formally, $f \subseteq R \times S$ and for each $x \in R$ there is at most one $y \in S$ such that $f(x) = y$, that is, (x, y) is in the relation. See Figure 1.1.

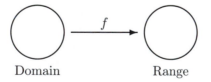

Domain   Range

Figure 1.1 A Function

A function from R to S can be considered as a *mapping* from R to S, or as a transformation of elements of R into elements of S. We call the set R the **domain** of the function f. When the relation that forms the function f is not explicitly formalized and we need to talk about its domain, we will write $Dom(f)$. A function f is one-to-one, also called a **bijection**, if for each y there is exactly one $x \in Dom(f)$ such that $f(x) = y$. Bijective functions have an **inverse**. Suppose that f is a bijective function. Then the inverse function, f^{-1}, is such that $f^{-1}(y) = x$ if and only if $f(x) = y$.

Exercises

───────   **Section 1.4**   ───────

Exercise 1.1 Give the notation for a set that contains only the page number of this exercise.

Exercise 1.2 True or false:

a) $\{2, 4, 5\} \subseteq \{2n | n \in N\}$

b) $\{e, i, t, c\} \subseteq \{a, \dots, z\}$

c) $\{2n | \bar{n} \in N\} = \{2n + 1 | n \in N\}$

d) $\{1, 2, 3, 4, 5\} = \{1, \dots, 5\}$

Exercise 1.3 Give a representation for the odd natural numbers.

Exercise 1.4 For each of the strings w below, exhibit both $|w|$ and w^R:

a) dooGyreV

b) kaerBAekaT

c) kcanSAevaH

d) ysaEooTsIsihT

Exercise 1.5 Let $A = \{1, 2, \dots, 100\}$ and $B = \{a, b, c, d\}$. How large is $A \times B$?

Exercise 1.6 Let $R = \{a, b, c, d\}$ and $S = \{0, 1\}$. What is $R \times S$?

Exercise 1.7 Define a relation R on $N \times N$ by

$$R = \{(x, y) | x \in N, y \in N \text{ and } x + y \text{ is even}\}$$

Prove or disprove: R is an equivalence relation.

Chapter 2

Finite Automata

Chapter 2

Finite Automata

2.1 Deterministic Finite Automata

We start by considering two simple problems. Despite their simplicity, these problems, or ones very similar to them, arise frequently in the everyday practice of computing.

Problem 2.1.1 *Design a computer program that, for any input word, outputs 1 if the word is of the length $4n, n = 0, 1, 2, \ldots$, and outputs 0, otherwise.*

Problem 2.1.2 *Design a computer program that sorts (in ascending order) and outputs the result for any input sequence $a_1, a_2, \ldots, a_n$, where n is any number in N.*

Anyone who has ever been exposed to computer programming can probably easily design many different computer programs solving these two problems. For our purposes, the choice of programming language does not matter. There is also no doubt that the second problem requires a more complex program solution than the first one. How can we measure the complexity of the programs in question (or any other programs)? A possible way is to measure their **running time**, which, roughly speaking, is the number of program instructions being executed before the program terminates. This measure of program complexity will be addressed in Chapter 6. Another measure of program complexity is the amount of memory required to execute the program. Every computer has a small memory in its central processing unit (registers) and main memory (e.g., RAM on PCs), which is sometimes is referred to as **auxiliary** memory. Registers are usually being used for the internal needs of program execution. Thus, it is natural to measure the amount of main memory that stores the input, results of computations, and output. From this point of view, there is an obvious difference between the solutions to Problem 2.1.1 and Problem 2.1.2. Any reasonable program that solves Problem 2.1.1 will use its main memory to store just the numbers 0 through 3 to memorize the length of the input modulo

4; this requires a constant amount of memory **regardless** of the input length. On the other hand, any program that solves Problem 2.1.2 must memorize the entire input list, and that can be of any **arbitrary** length. Hence, the amount of memory used by any program that solves Problem 2.1.2 cannot be bound by any constant.

The programs that use a constant amount of auxiliary memory regardless of the input form the simplest class of programs as far as the amount of auxiliary memory is concerned. In order to explore the power and limitations of the programs in this class, we introduce a theoretical model for this kind of program called a **finite automaton**. As the programs in question use at most a constant amount of auxiliary memory, this memory can be moved to the central processing unit. Thus, a finite automaton is a device that has a processing unit with limited memory capacity and has no auxiliary (main) memory at all. It receives input on a special input tape and reads it, one character at a time, using its reading head connected to the processing unit. Reading a character results in changing the **state** of the automaton and moving the head one position to the right; the set of states is its "finite control" (see Figure 2.1). If the head reaches beyond all the input string (after having read the last input character), it halts. The automaton has no means to deliver output; however, some states can be designated as **favorable**, and if a favorable state is reached while reading some input word w, this can be regarded as indication of acceptance of the word w by the device. Thus, even though an automaton does not produce any physical output, it still can be used as a **recognition** device. Sometimes, we will call the favorable states **accepting** states.

Formally, a **Deterministic Finite Automaton** (DFA) is denoted by a quintuple $A = (Q, \Sigma, \delta, s, F)$ where

> Q is a finite set of **states**;
> Σ is a finite input alphabet;
> δ is a **transition function** from $Q \times \Sigma$ to Q;
> $s \in Q$ is the **initial state** of the automaton;
> $F \subseteq Q$ is the set of **favorable states**.

We use the term **deterministic** in this definition, as every move of a finite automaton is completely determined by the input and its current state.

A finite automaton can be visualised as a device that gets its input from the **input tape**. The input tape is divided into cells; each cell may contain one input character. The automaton reads the input using its movable **reading head**. Initially, the reading head is positioned on the leftmost cell of the input tape containing the first character of the input word. The main part of the automaton is its **finite control device** that at any moment can be in any one of the states $q \in Q$. Initially, the finite control device is in state s. At regular time intervals, the automaton reads one character from the input tape, moves the reading head one cell to the right, and changes its state. The new state is defined by the function δ. If the automaton, being in the state q, has read the symbol $a \in \Sigma$, it enters state $q' = \delta(q, a)$. Thus the new state is completely determined by the content of the cell and the internal state of the automaton. At some moment the reading head reaches the end of the input word (the next cell contains a blank). If at this moment the automaton is in a favorable state $q \in F$, the input word is said to be **accepted** by the automaton. Otherwise, the input word is not accepted. The set of all input words accepted by the automaton A is called the **language** accepted by A. We denote this language by $L(A)$.

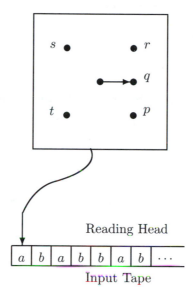

Figure 2.1 A Finite Automaton

A convenient way to represent finite automata is a **finite state diagram**. The finite state diagram is a directed graph, where nodes represent states and arrows are labeled with characters from the input alphabet. If in state q and reading input character a the automaton changes its state to q' [that is, $\delta(q, a) = q'$], the arrow from state q to the state q' is labeled by a (Figure 2.2). Favorable states are circled, and the initial state is indicated by $>$. Thus, the automaton of Figure 2.2 accepts the language containing all the strings $a^n b^m$ for $n = 0, 1, 2, \ldots$ and $m = 1, 2, \ldots$.

Example 2.1.1 The automaton in Figure 2.3 accepts all strings that have two consecutive a's. While the automaton has not read two consecutive a's, it returns back to state s. Once it has reached the accepting state r, it stays there forever, no matter what suffix the input string has. One might call r a **trap** state, as there is no way out of it.

End Example

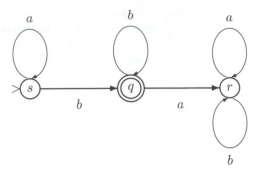

Figure 2.2 State Transition Diagram

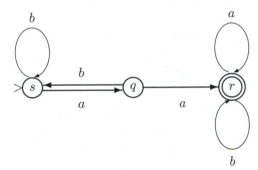

Figure 2.3 Recognizing Two Consecutive a's

Example 2.1.2 Another example of a finite automaton is represented by the diagram of Figure 2.4. The difference between the automata of Figure 2.3 and Figure 2.4 is in the set of favorable states. In Figure 2.4 all the states except the trap one are favorable states. The automaton accepts the language that complements the one in the previous example: all the strings that do not contain two consecutive a's. This time the trap state can be called a ***dead*** state, as from this state no further input string read by the automaton can bring it to another state. Hence, the automaton can never reach a favorable state.

> End Example

We suggest that the reader attempt to describe the set of strings recognized by the automaton of Figure 2.5 (*Hint*: Run the automaton on strings $ababab$, $ababa$, $ababb$, ba) and the set of strings recognized by the automaton of Figure 2.6 (*Hint*: run the automaton on strings $abbaba$, $baba$, $bbaa$).

Example 2.1.3 This example is an automaton that recognizes the language of all strings that contain an even number of a's and an odd number of b's. This

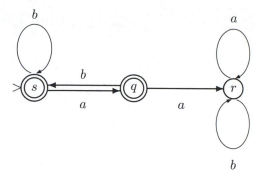

Figure 2.4 Recognizing the Complement

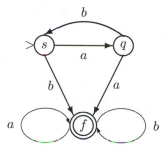

Figure 2.5 Mystery Automaton 1

automaton has four states (Figure 2.7). The initial state s "memorizes" the fact that the prefix of the input seen so far has an even number of a's and an even number of b's (in particular, this is the case when the automaton is about to start its operation). If the number of a's in the prefix read so far reaches an odd number and the number of b's is even, then the automaton enters state q. When both numbers are odd, it enters state r. If the number of b's in the prefix seen so far reaches an odd number and the number of a's is even, the automaton enters state t. The favorable state t "indicates" the fact that the input string satisfies the required condition.

> End Example

Now we are going to formally define what a computation by a deterministic finite automaton is and what acceptance by a deterministic finite automaton is. In the center of this definition is the notion of **configuration** that is a composite of finite control (state), position of the reading head, and the input to be read. Suppose, for example, that, having read the prefix aaa of the string $aaaabba$, a finite automaton A has reached state q. Since A cannot move the reading head

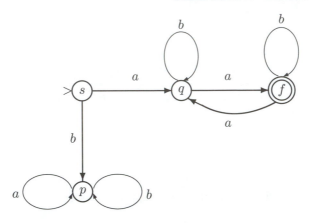

Figure 2.6 Mystery Automaton 2

back, its further processing is fully specified by state q and the suffix *abba*. We call the ordered pair $(q, abba)$ a configuration of the automaton A. Formally, a configuration of an automaton $A = (Q, \Sigma, \delta, s, F)$ is any element of $Q \times \Sigma^*$. If, being in the configuration (q, w), the automaton moves to the configuration (q', w') (this means that $w = \sigma w'$ for some symbol $\sigma \in \Sigma$ and $\delta(q, \sigma) = q'$), we say that the configuration (q, w) **yields** the configuration (q', w') **in one step**. (q, w) **yields** (q', w') if there exists a sequence of configurations

$$(q_1, w_1), (q_2, w_2), \ldots, (q_k, w_k)$$

such that $(q_1, w_1) = (q, w)$, $(q_k, w_k) = (q', w')$ and every (q_i, w_i) yields the configuration (q_{i+1}, w_{i+1}) in one step. As the finite automaton is deterministic, every configuration uniquely determines all the configurations that it yields. We say that a string w is **accepted** by the automaton A if the initial configuration (s, w) yields the configuration (q, e) for some favorable state q. In other words, being fed the string w, the automaton A reaches a favorable state having read the entire input word. This definition is apparently in compliance with the informal notion of acceptance that we introduced in the beginning of this section.

An important property of every deterministic finite automaton is that its transition function δ is defined for every state and every input character. In terms of finite state diagrams this means that for every state s and every character $\sigma \in \Sigma$ there exists one and only one arrow labeled by σ coming out of this state.

As an example of a practical application of finite automata, we now present the diagram of a finite automaton simulating a newspaper vending machine (see Figure 2.8). Our machine accepts nickels, dimes, and quarters. When the total of coins input reaches 25 cents, the machine releases the cover, and the user can pick a newspaper. If the total exceeds 25 cents, the machine does not return change.

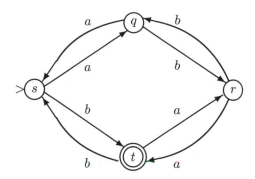

Figure 2.7 Recognizing an Even Number of a's and Odd Number of b's

The memory of the machine is represented by a finite number of states. When, say, 15 cents are entered, the machine "memorizes" this fact by the state that requires 10 additional cents to unlatch the cover. The accepting state represents the release of the cover. The following six states fully describe the behavior of the desired automaton:

s is the **initial** state (needs 25 cents);

20 is the state after the first nickel has been entered (needs 20 cents);

15 is the state after two nickels or a dime have been entered (needs 15 cents);

10 is the state after three nickels or a dime and a nickel have been entered (needs 10 cents);

5 is the state after four nickels, or a dime and two nickels, or two dimes have been entered (needs a nickel);

a is the **accepting** state after the total of at least 25 cents have been input.

The input alphabet Σ is n (for nickel), d (for dime), and q (for quarter).

We call finite automata a type of **program**. They hardly look like programs in any conventional programming language. On the other hand, the reader probably has no doubt that they can be simulated by software programs. As our vending machine example shows, they can also be directly implemented on the hardware level.

At first glance, the finite automata do not seem to deserve serious study. However, as we have seen, though yet in a rudimentary form, they incorporate all the major concepts of imperative programming: sequences, branching, and loops. Furthermore, all pattern matching, such as the kind used by World Wide Web search

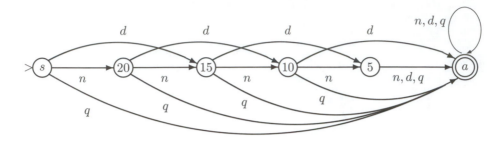

Figure 2.8 The Finite State Diagram of a Newspaper Vending Machine

engines, can be described in terms of finite automata. The advantage of finite automata is that these concepts and relationships among them can be studied in their pure form. This results in an elegant, thoroughly developed theory that completely describes the computational power of this somewhat primitive programming language. From this comes a better understanding of how the use of a potentially unlimited auxiliary memory may enhance computational potential.

While being interesting on their own, finite automata are also used in several areas of algorithm and software design. A popular example is the lexical analysis in the process of compilation: The algorithms that perform lexical analysis often simulate finite automata. Finite state machines, a version of finite automata, are widely used for software specification and design.

2.2   Nondeterministic Finite Automata

In Section 2.1 we observed an automaton accepting all the strings that had two consecutive a's. This automaton can easily be transformed into an automaton that accepts all the strings that have two consecutive b's. Now, can we design a deterministic finite automaton that accepts the union of those two languages, in other words, all the strings that have two consecutive a's or two consecutive b's? Since we already have the "programs" that solve the problem for aa's and, respectively, bb's, an obvious idea would be to design a "program" that would just "call" the given programs as "subprograms." How do we express this idea in the form of a finite state diagram? A possible solution would be to combine initial states of the automaton in Figure 2.2 and its counterpart that accepts the strings containing bb's (see Figure 2.9).

However, the diagram no longer represents a deterministic finite automaton, as there is more than one arrow coming out of the initial state with identical labels (say, a). In the next section we will show that there is a deterministic finite automaton that accepts the language in question, but we are not going to give up the approach that has led us to the diagram of Figure 2.9; we will see that this approach results

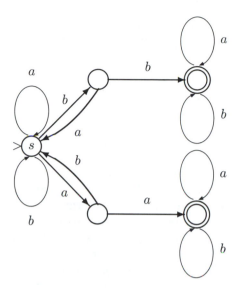

Figure 2.9 Combining Two Automata

in a powerful tool for building "programs" from "subprograms." The diagram of Figure 2.9 represents an example of a **nondeterministic** finite automaton, where **several** next states can be reached from the combination of a state and input symbol. A useful interpretation of the automaton's behavior on any input string w is as a thread of execution. Different threads can end in different states. We say that this automaton is nondeterministic, because the device now has a choice: It can choose where to go from the whole **set** of next states. What can affect this choice? We can assume that the automaton "strives" to accept an input word. Thus, it may try to "guess" which way will lead it to a favorable state. One can argue that a real computational device cannot "guess." This argument can hardly be refuted. However, we will establish two facts that fully justify this variant of finite automata:

1) Nondeterminism does not increase computational power of finite automata (that is, deterministic automata do whatever can be done by nondeterministic ones);

2) Nondeterministic finite automata are much easier to design.

Given these two facts, a "programmer" can proceed as follows: Design a nondeterministic finite automaton, and then, applying a general method, transform it into a deterministic one.

Now we proceed with the formal definition of nondeterministic finite automata. A **Nondeterministic Finite Automaton** (NFA) is a quintuple $A = (Q, \Sigma, \Delta, s, F)$, where

> Q is a finite set of **states**;
> Σ is an input alphabet;
> $s \in Q$ is the **initial** state;
> $F \subseteq Q$ is the set of **favorable** states;
> $\Delta \subseteq Q \times (\Sigma \cup \{e\}) \times Q$ is the **transition relation**.

Every triple (q, a, p) in Δ is represented by an arrow connecting the states q and p and labeled a in the state diagram of A. Note that an arrow can be labeled by the empty string e; this is very different from the deterministic version of an automaton. To understand the meaning of an arrow from q to p labeled by the empty string, imagine that the automaton can "jump" from state q to p if it wants to. Another difference is that some states may have no arrows coming out of them labeled by some symbols $a \in \Sigma$. For example, Figure 2.10 shows a finite automaton that accepts the language that contains all strings of a's and all strings of b's. While Σ

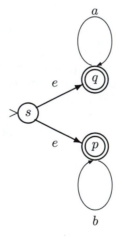

Figure 2.10 Accepting All a's or All b's

contains symbols a and b, there is no arrow labeled by b coming out of state q. If the automaton enters state q and then next symbol is a b and there are no jumps out of state q via an arrow labeled with an e, then the automaton is stuck. This represents a computation that cannot lead to an accepting state. In particular, now there is no need for a trap state. These new opportunities can significantly simplify programming as we will see below.

The computation by a nondeterministic finite automaton can be defined very similarly to a computation by a deterministic automaton. However, now a configuration (q, w) can yield many different configurations (q', e). The string w is accepted if $q = s$, and, among all the configurations (q', e) that (s, w) yields, at least one configuration (q', e) contains a favorable state q'.

An example of a nondeterministic finite automaton is given in Figure 2.11.

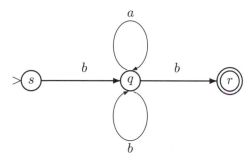

Figure 2.11 Start and End with a b

This automaton accepts strings over the alphabet $\{a, b\}$ that begin and end with the letter b (we assume that every string contains at least 2 b's). The automaton of Figure 2.11 naturally implements the specifications. Consider the automaton's behavior on the string $bbbb$. One possible computation is

Another possible computation is

Still, the string $bbbb$ is accepted, since at least one computation ends in a favorable state. Compare the nondeterministic automaton of Figure 2.11 with the deterministic automaton of Figure 2.12 that accepts the same language and contains somewhat redundant states and arrows.

2.3 Determinism versus Nondeterminism

In this section we show that although nondeterministic automata seem to be much more flexible and versatile, their computational power does not exceed the power of deterministic automata. Automata A and A' that accept the same language L are said to be **equivalent**. We are going to show that, for every nondeterministic finite automaton there exists an equivalent deterministic one. Moreover, we will design an algorithm that carries out conversion from a nondeterministic automaton to its deterministic equivalent.

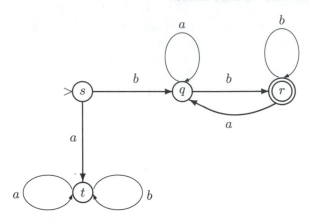

Figure 2.12 With Extra States

Theorem 2.3.1 *For each nondeterministic finite automaton A, there exists a deterministic finite automaton A' equivalent to A.*

Proof: (We give just a sketch.) Let $A = (Q, \Sigma, \Delta, s, F)$ be a nondeterministic finite automaton. The conversion of A to a deterministic automaton A' implements the following idea. From any state q, reading any character $a \in \Sigma$, the automaton A can make a transition to any state q_i in some set $\{q_1, q_2, \ldots, q_n\}$, see Figure 2.13. We make the **whole set** $\{q_1, q_2, \ldots, q_n\}$ a state of the new automaton A'. Then the

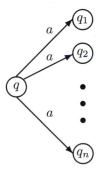

Figure 2.13 Multiple Possible Transitions

set of transitions from Figure 2.13 can be replaced by the single transition of Figure 2.14 which eliminates nondeterminism present in the diagram of Figure 2.13.

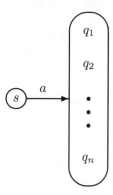

Figure 2.14 Replacement Transition

An important question is if the new set $\{q_1, q_2, \ldots, q_n\}$ should be a favorable state. If any of the states $q_1, q_2, \ldots, q_n$ is a favorable state of A, then the symbol a can drive A from the state s to a favorable state. If as in the new diagram $\{q_1, q_2, \ldots, q_n\}$ is the only state that can be reached from q by reading a, we have to make it a favorable state. If no state $q_1, q_2, \ldots, q_n$ is favorable, then naturally the corresponding state in the new diagram will not be favorable.

More generally, if S and P are two arbitrary subsets of Q, we draw an arrow in the diagram of A' labeled by a from state S to state P if there is at least one arrow in A labeled by a that connects a state in Q with a state in P, see Figure 2.15.

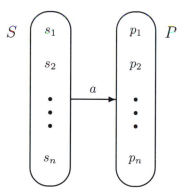

Figure 2.15 A New Connection

In fact, instead of connecting S to an arbitrary P, we can choose the set $P(S, a)$ that contains **all** the states that are reachable from **all** the states in S by reading the symbol a. This way we can eliminate many redundant states in diagram A'.

However, still there is a technical problem that must be resolved. Some arrows in diagram A may be labeled by the empty symbol e. Such arrows cannot be permitted in a deterministic diagram. In order to eliminate arrows of this kind, we will extend the set $P(S, a)$, adding to it the set $P'(P(S, a), e)$ of the states in A that can be reached from $P(S, a)$ by "reading" one or more symbols e (in fact, merely by "jumping"); see Figure 2.16. Thus, the arrow labeled by a will connect the state

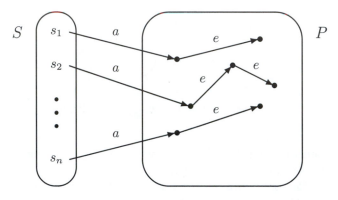

Figure 2.16 An e-Move

S in A' with the state $P(S, a) \cup P'(P(S, a), e)$; see Figure 2.17. For example, if

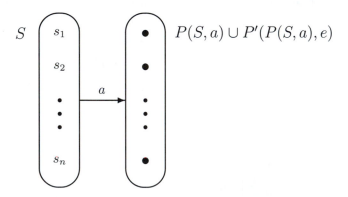

Figure 2.17 An e-Move Eliminated

Figure 2.18 represents a segment of a nondeterministic finite automaton, then it is converted to the deterministic segment shown in Figure 2.19. To complete diagram A' we must make sure that for **every** symbol $a \in \Sigma$ there is an arrow labeled by this symbol that comes out of any state S (some of them could have been missing

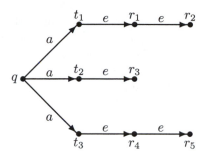

Figure 2.18 Segment of a Nondeterministic Finite Automaton

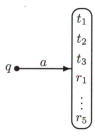

Figure 2.19 Corresponding Deterministic Segment

in the original nondeterministic diagram A). This can easily be achieved by adding the trap state T to the diagram and directing all the necessary arrows to this state. Formally, the trap state is represented by the empty set of states in A.

Thus, given a nondeterministic automaton A, we form the initial state of the corresponding deterministic automaton using the initial state s of A and all states $s_1, \ldots, s_k$ in A that can be reached from s just by one or more "jumps" (e-arrows); thus $\{s, s_1, \ldots, s_k\}$ becomes the initial state of the desired deterministic finite automaton. Now, we find all states $t_1, \ldots, t_i$ in A that can be reached from $s, s_1, \ldots, s_k$ reading the symbol a and then all the states $r_1, \ldots, r_j$ that can be reached from $t_1, \ldots, t_i$ by "jumps" (e-arrows); the arrow a connects the initial state $s, s_1, \ldots, s_k$ with the state $\{t_1, \ldots, t_i, r_1, \ldots, r_j\}$, and so on.

We leave technical details of the construction to the reader. The formal proof of the equivalence of A and A' can be carried out by induction on the length $|w|$ of any string $w \in \Sigma^*$. It is suggested in Exercise 2.13.

The diagrams of Figures 2.20 and 2.21 present an example of a nondeterministic automaton and the result of conversion to an equivalent deterministic automaton. We start building the deterministic automaton with the set containing the initial state s. Since no state can be reached from s by "jumping" (that is, reading the empty character), the initial state of our deterministic automaton will be the set containing just s. Now, from s, reading a and making few "jumps," we can reach the states q, r, t. Thus, the initial state $\{s\}$ in the deterministic diagram connects to the state $\{q, r, t\}$ by the arrow labeled by a. Similarly, the arrow labeled by b will connect $\{s\}$ with $\{r, t\}$. An arrow labeled by a connects r and t, and an arrow labeled by b connects t with itself in the nondeterministic diagram; thus $\{r, t\}$ gets connected with $\{t\}$ in the deterministic diagram, as no "jumps" from t are possible. Other arrows can be obtained similarly. As there is no arrow labeled by a coming out of t, state $\{t\}$ connects by an arrow labeled by a to the trap state $\emptyset$. All the states that contain t, the sole accepting state in the nondeterministic diagram, become accepting states in the deterministic one.

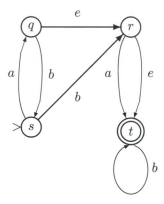

Figure 2.20 Untransformed Automaton

How practical is the conversion algorithm of Theorem 2.3.1? It turns out that in the worst case it can be very slow: If n is the number of states of the input nondeterministic finite automaton, the resulting deterministic finite automata may have 2^n states.

Nondeterministic finite automata are useful tools in solving **pattern matching**, a very important computational problem. This is the problem of taking a string $w \in \Sigma^*$ (a *pattern*) and a string u (a *text*), and determining if w is a substring of u. Any Internet search engine implements some solution to this problem. Given key words supplied by a user (the pattern), the engine searches for texts that contain this pattern. The key issue here is *how fast* the engine can test if the pattern is a substring of a text — to be efficient, it must handle this task really fast. Fortunately, a desired algorithm can be specified by a finite automaton, and, consequently, implemented as a very efficient computer program.

Let us take a closer look at a finite automaton as vehicles to solve the pattern-matching problem. Given a pattern, say, *abbab*, it is very easy to design a nondeterministic finite automaton that accepts the language $L = \{u | u \in \Sigma^*, abbab$ is a substring of $u\}$ of the texts that contain *abbab* (see Figure 2.22). However, a nondeterministic automaton cannot be directly implemented as a computer program. One must first convert it into a determinisitic one. As mentioned previously, the

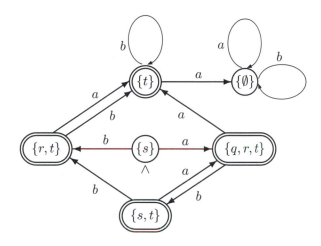

Figure 2.21 Transformed Automaton

number of states of the resulting determinisitc finite automaton may increase exponentially. Fortunately, it is not the case with nondeterministic finite automata solving pattern-matching problems. The resulting deterministic finite automaton has the same number of states as the nondeterministic one (see Figure 2.23). Moreover, it has the *minimum* possible number of states among deterministic finite automata solving this problem! In practical implementations of the algorithm implicit in Theorem 2.3.1, there is yet an obstacle. The number of characters in the input alphabet Σ may be large (tens or even hundreds of characters), which results in too many *arrows* in the diagram, and, consequently, in testing too many cases in the resulting computer program. This problem can be resolved by a more clever design of the underlying nondeterministic finite automaton. Every state in the nondeterministic finite automata (except the initial and the favorable ones) has exactly two arrows coming out of it, one labeled by e. It turns out that the conversion algorithm applied to such an nondeterministic finite automata produces a deterministic finite automata, resulting in an efficient computer program.

2.4   Regular Expressions

In the previous sections we observed automata accepting some languages. Although it was never explicitly stated, we actually implemented the methodology familiar to every programmer: deriving a program from a specification. The specifications that we have used so far were written in plain English. It worked well for our simple

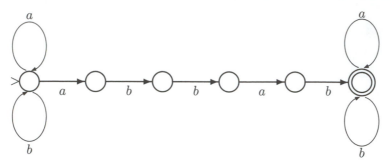

Figure 2.22 Recognizing Strings Containing *abbab*

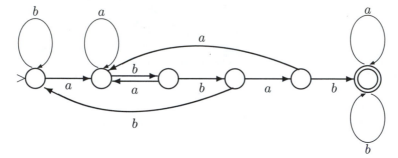

Figure 2.23 Deterministic Version of Figure 2.22

examples. However, as it usually happens in programming, verbal specifications have a tendency to get more vague and ambiguous as the complexity of the object that they specify increases. Our goal in this section is very ambitious. We intend to design a language for precise mathematical specifications of the languages acceptable by finite automata. Furthermore, we are going to show that a finite automaton can be derived from its specification by a general algorithmic procedure. Moreover, we will show that a finite automaton can be converted into its specification, and the conversion can again be carried out by an algorithmic procedure.

In order to design an algorithm that derives a finite automaton from its specification, we shall develop some technical tools that will allow us to build complex automata from simple ones. These technical ideas, in various forms, implement a very important programming idea: **simulation**. Roughly speaking, simulation means mimicking the actions of some process by a collection of subprograms.

The more complex automata accept languages that can be obtained from simpler languages by certain set-theoretical operations. Some of these operations, in particular, union, intersection, and complementation are familiar to the reader. Now we introduce two new operations: concatenation and the Kleene star.

We start by fixing an alphabet Σ. Define the **concatenation** of two strings u and v over the alphabet Σ as the string uv, that is, the string u followed by *v.* Given two languages L_1 and L_2, their **concatenation** $L_1 L_2$ is the language $\{uv | u \in L_1, v \in L_2\}$. For example, if $L_1 = \{a^n | n = 0, 1, 2, \ldots\}$ and $L_2 = \{b^m | m = 0, 1, 2, \ldots\}$ then

$$L_1 L_2 = \{a^n b^m | n = 0, 1, 2, \ldots, m = 0, 1, 2, \ldots\}$$

that is, all strings of a's followed by all strings of b's. The definition of concatenation can be extended naturally to any finite number of languages. For example, if $L_3 = \{c^k | k = 0, 1, 2, \ldots\}$, then

$$L_1 L_2 L_3 = \{a^n b^m c^k | n, m, k = 0, 1, 2, \ldots\}$$

Any language can obviously be concatenated with itself. Moreover, it can be concatenated with itself any finite number of times. Let L^n denote a language L concatenated with itself $n - 1$ times. For instance, $L^3 = LLL$.

The **Kleene star** L^* of a language L is the infinite union

$$\{e\} \cup L \cup L^2 \cup L^3 \ldots$$

Note that L^* contains the empty word. Actually, $L^0 = \{e\}$ by convention and L^1 becomes a synonym for L.

An equivalent definition of L^*: all strings

$$w_1 w_2 \ldots w_k$$

where $w_1, w_2, \ldots, w_k \in L$.

Here are some examples of forming the Kleene star of languages:

(1) $L = \{a\}$. Then $L^* = \{e, a, aa, aaa, aaaa, \ldots\}$ (in other words, L^* is the set of all a-strings, including the empty string).

(2) $L = \{a, bb\}$. Then $L^* = \{e, a, bb, aa, bbbb, abb, bba, aaa, bbbbbb, aabb, abbbb, bbabb, bbaa, bbbba, \ldots\}$ (in other words, L^* is the set of all finite concatenations of the strings a and bb, including the empty string).

We intend to show now that if any two languages L and M are acceptable by finite automata, so are their unions, complements, differences, intersections, concatenations, and Kleene stars. In other words, languages acceptable by finite automata are **closed** under the above set-theoretical operations.

Theorem 2.4.1 *If the languages L and M are acceptable by finite automata, so are the languages*

- $L \cup M$,

- $\Sigma^* - L$ *(the complement of L),*

- $L \cap M$,

- $L - M$,

- LM, and

- L^*.

Moreover, there exists an algorithm that, given the diagrams of the automata accepting L and M, constructs the automata accepting the languages obtained by the above set-theoretical operations.

Suppose the languages L and M are accepted by the automata A and B, respectively. The diagrams of A and B are schematically represented in Figures 2.24 and 2.25

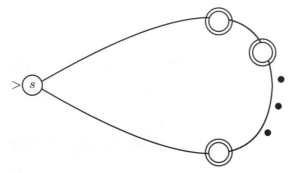

Figure 2.24 Automaton A

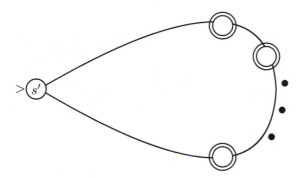

Figure 2.25 Automaton B

(1) **Union.** The required algorithm creates a new initial state q and connects it to the initial states of A and B by arrows labeled by e (Figure 2.26). The new diagram clearly accepts the language $L \cup M$.

(2) **Complement.** For the complement of L, the algorithm first converts the automaton for L to a deterministic automaton for L, and then just "flips" the favorable and nonfavorable states in the diagram of A; that is, favorable states become nonfavorable ones and vice versa.

(3) **Intersection.** First, note that $L \cap M$ can be expressed as the complement of the set $(\Sigma^* - L) \cup (\Sigma^* - M)$. Thus, the algorithm builds diagrams for the complements of L and M, then forms their union, and, finally, forms the complement of the union.

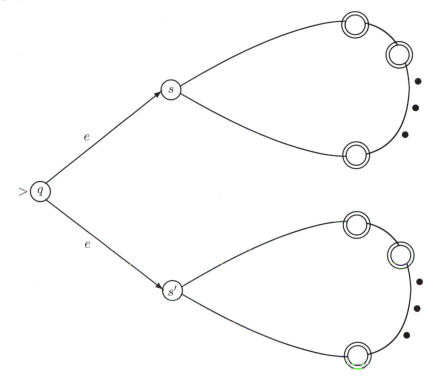

Figure 2.26 The Union of A and B

(4) **Difference**. The difference $L - M$ can be expressed as the intersection of the languages L and $\Sigma^* - M$. The algorithm finds a diagram accepting the complement of M and then builds the diagram accepting the required intersection.

(5) *Concatenation*. In this case, the algorithm connects every favorable state of L to the initial state of M by an arrow labeled by e (Figure 2.27). The favorable states of B become favorable states of the new automaton.

If the string xy is in the concatenation LM, the new automaton reads x, "jumps" to the former initial state of B, reads part y, and reaches a favorable state. If the string w is not in LM, then either A, reading the initial fragment x, cannot reach a favorable state of A, or, if for some x such that $w = xy$ for some y, A reaches a favorable state on x, but B cannot reach a favorable state reading the remainder y of the string.

(6) *Kleene star*. In this case, the algorithm utilizes an idea similar to that used for concatenation. All the favorable states of A are connected to the initial state by arrows e, making looping possible. However, as the empty word must be a part of L^*, we create a new initial state s, make it the only favorable state, and connect it to the old initial state by an arrow labeled e (see Figure 2.28).

Our next step is to define the language of formal specifications from which finite

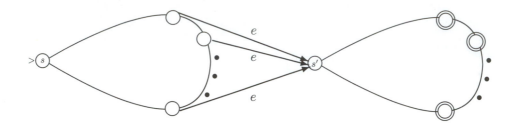

Figure 2.27 Concatenation of L and M

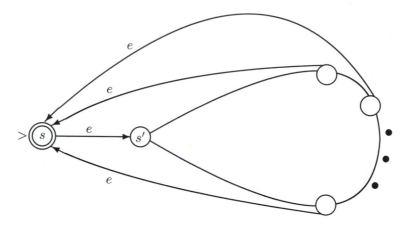

Figure 2.28 Kleene Star of A

automata can be derived by application of a formal procedure. Note that specifications, being finite statements, must be able to describe infinite languages. The
specifications we are going to define are known by the name **regular expressions**.
A **regular langauge** is any language that is described by a regular expression.

Now, every regular expression is a string over the alphabet $\Sigma \cup \{(,), e, \emptyset, \cup, *\}$.
The set of regular expressions can be obtained, via an inductive definition, as follows:

- $\emptyset$, e, and each $a \in \Sigma$ are regular expressions (ground elements).

- If α and β are regular expressions, then so are $(\alpha \cup \beta)$, $(\alpha\beta)$, and α^* (inductive
  step).

- No other string over the above alphabet is a regular expression.

Some examples of regular expressions are: (a^*b^*) and $(a^* \cup ((ab)^* \cup b^*)^*)^*$.
Regular expressions are supposed to specify languages. Therefore, we are going

to map every regular expression α to a language $L(\alpha)$ represented by the regular expression α. The mapping can be defined as follows:

- $L(\emptyset) = \emptyset$, $L(e) = \{e\}$, and $L(a) = \{a\}$ for any $a \in \Sigma$.

- If α and β are regular expressions, then

  - $L((\alpha \cup \beta)) = L(\alpha) \cup L(\beta)$,
  - $L((\alpha\beta)) = L(\alpha)L(\beta)$, and
  - $L(\alpha^*) = (L(\alpha))^*$.

Example 2.4.1 Find the language $L((ab^*)a)$.
According to our definition,

$$
\begin{aligned}
L((ab^*)a) &= L((ab^*))L(a) \\
&= L((ab^*))\{a\} \\
&= L(a)L(b^*)\{a\} \\
&= \{a\}(L(b))^*\{a\} \\
&= \{a\}\{b\}^*\{a\} \\
&= \{w|w \text{ is of the form } ab^na, n = 0, 1, 2, \ldots\}
\end{aligned}
$$

End Example

Example 2.4.2 Find the language for the expression $L((a(a \cup b)^*))$. We have

$$
\begin{aligned}
L((a(a \cup b)^*)) &= L(a)L((a \cup b)^*) \\
&= \{a\}\{w|w \text{ is any word in } \Sigma^*\} \\
&= \{aw|w \in \Sigma^*\}
\end{aligned}
$$

End Example

Example 2.4.3 What is the language represented by the expression $(b^*a)^*$?
Any substring of b's in any word w in this language must be followed by a **nonempty** string of a's. That is, no w in the language can end by b.

End Example

Example 2.4.4 Now we will describe the language L represented by the expression $(b \cup (aa)a^*)^*$.

This language obviously does not contain the word a, no word $w \in L$ can begin with ab, end with ba, or have a subword bab.

$$\boxed{\text{End Example}}$$

Example 2.4.5 The regular expression we are going to define specifies all identifiers in a C-like programming language. Any such identifier begins with a letter, which may be followed by a string consisting of letters and numeric digits. Let expression $[a - z]$ stand for the regular expression $(a \cup b \cup c \cup \ldots \cup z)$, $[A - Z]$ stand for the regular expression $(A \cup B \cup C \ldots \cup Z)$, and $[0 - 9]$ stand for the regular expression $(0 \cup 1 \cup 2 \cup \ldots \cup 9)$ (dots stand for missing letters and numbers). Then the regular expression

$$([a - z] \cup [A - Z])([a - z] \cup [A - Z] \cup [0 - 9])^*$$

represents all identifiers.

Some programming languages permit the use of the underscore character "_" between letters and numeric digits. For example; Ab_55_c, ab_b_5. Every character _ must be followed by a letter or a numeric digit. The regular expression generating all such identifiers is

$$([a - z] \cup [A - Z])((\_([a - z] \cup [A - Z] \cup [0 - 9]))^*([a - z] \cup [A - Z] \cup [0 - 9])^*)^*$$

A part of every compiler is a *lexical analyzer*, which, in particular, finds all identifiers in the text of the source program. More specifically, the lexical analyzer uses a list of regular expressions that are used to determine if strings of characters are identifiers, that is, if they match at least one of the given expressions. This is one of multiple applications of regular expressions in programming.

$$\boxed{\text{End Example}}$$

Note that concatenation and union are associative operations. In other words, $(L_1 L_2)L_3 = L_1(L_2 L_3)$ and $(L_1 \cup L_2) \cup L_3 = L_1 \cup (L_2 \cup L_3)$. This means that we can omit parentheses in subexpressions of the type $(\alpha\beta)\gamma$, or, say, $\alpha \cup (\beta \cup \gamma)$. For example, we can write $(abb \cup ab \cup a)^*$ instead of $(((ab)b) \cup (ab)) \cup a)^*$.

Now we are in a position to design an algorithm $\mathcal{A}$ that converts any regular expression α into a diagram of a finite automaton A such that $L(\alpha) = L(A)$. Note that any regular expression is built up from *ground components*, for example, the singletons e, $a \in \Sigma$ and $\emptyset$, to which operations $\cup$, concatenation, and the Kleene star are being applied. The required algorithm operates as follows.

1. It converts every ground singleton a or e or $\emptyset$ (if any) to an automaton accepting just this singleton; (see Figure 2.29).

2. Then it applies the algorithm designed in Theorem 2.4.1 to every concatenation, union, and Kleene star present in the expression.

Let us apply algorithm $\mathcal{A}$ to the regular expression $((a \cup ab)^*ba)^*$. As the first
step, the algorithm creates automata for the "ground" singletons of Figure 2.29.
Then it carries out the five steps of Figures 2.30—2.34.

Figure 2.29 Singleton Automata

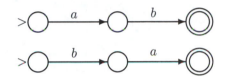

Figure 2.30 Transformation Step 1 of 5

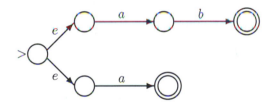

Figure 2.31 Transformation Step 2 of 5

Now we will design an algorithm $\mathcal{B}$ that converts any finite automaton A into a
regular expression α such that $L(A) = L(\alpha)$.

Our algorithm will carry out conversion step by step, replacing "chunks" of
diagram A by regular expressions. Moreover, it uses the results of intermediate
steps of conversion to build more complex expressions. In order to "visualize" every
step of conversion, we need a way to represent every intermediate result in the form
of a diagram with arrows labeled by the subexpressions obtained so far. A natural
idea is to extend the notion of a state diagram using arbitrary regular expressions
as labels.

Thus, an **expression diagram** is a labeled directed graph in which the arrows
are labeled by regular expressions. Like a finite state diagram, it has an initial state
and a number of favorable states. An example of such a diagram is presented in
Figure 2.35.

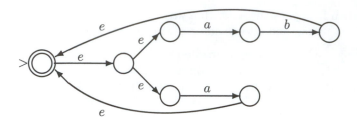

Figure 2.32 Transformation Step 3 of 5

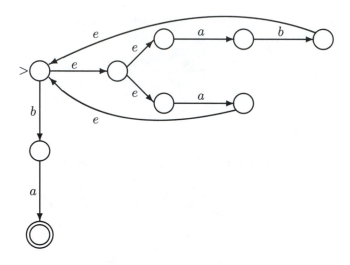

Figure 2.33 Transformation Step 4 of 5

We can naturally associate a language with any expression diagram (this is done in Exercise 2.21). However, in our construction we use an expression diagram merely as a tool to aid in the conversion of a finite automaton into a regular expression.

Our goal is, given any finite automaton A, to convert it into an expression diagram that has a single arrow connecting the initial state and the final state and labeled by the expression representing $L(A)$. For example, we would like to convert the diagram of a finite automaton of Figure 2.36 into the diagram of Figure 2.37.

However, there is still one obstacle. Finite state diagrams may have more than one favorable state, while the algorithm we are going to define can be applied only to finite state diagrams with a single accepting state. The problem can easily be resolved in two different ways: We can transform the input finite state diagram into the equivalent one (that is, one accepting the same language) that has a single favorable state, adding arrows from the favorable states in the original diagram labeled by the empty string (see Figure 2.38).

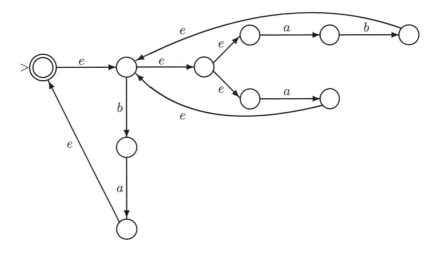

Figure 2.34 Transformation Step 5 of 5

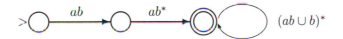

Figure 2.35 An Expression Diagram

Or we can apply the algorithm to the copies of the original diagram, each time choosing a single, different favorable state and then taking the union of the obtained expressions.

An additional useful assumption we are going to make is that the input state diagram has no arrows directed to the initial state and no arrows coming out of the favorable state. If the diagram does not satisfy this condition, it can easily be transformed into a diagram with this requirement satisfied. For instance, we can add a "dummy" initial state and connect it with the state in the original diagram by an arrow labeled by the empty word. A "dummy" favorable state can be added in the same way.

Now, let us number all nodes in the input finite state diagram, say, from 1 to n. Without loss of generality, we can assume that the starting state has number 1 and the favorable state has number n. Let $l_{i,j}$ denote the label of an arrow from the node i to the node j (if there are many arrows from i to j, we will use a superscript to distinguish corresponding labels: $l_{i,j}^1, l_{i,j}^2, \ldots, l_{i,j}^m$). Algorithm $\mathcal{B}$ is defined in Algorithm 2.4.1.

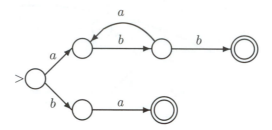

Figure 2.36 Initial Automaton

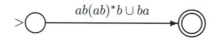

Figure 2.37 Converted Automaton

Algorithm 2.4.1

For every pair of nodes j and k (j may be equal k),
if there are arrows from j to k with labels
$$l^1_{j,k}, l^2_{j,k}, \ldots, l^m_{j,k}$$
then replace them by a single arrow from j to k labeled by
$$l^1_{j,k} \cup l^2_{j,k} \cup \ldots \cup l^m_{j,k},$$
for $i = 2, 3, \ldots n - 1$ **do**

for every pair of nodes j and k (j may equal k)
in the diagram such that there is an arrow from
j to i and there is an arrow from i to k.

(1) If there is no arrow from i to i then
add an arrow from j to k labeled by
$l_{j,i} l_{i,k}$.

(2) If there is an arrow from i to i then
add an arrow from j to k labeled by
$l_{j,i} (l_{i,i})^* l_{i,k}$.

(3) If there are arrows from j to k with
labels $l^1_{j,k}, l^2_{j,k}, \ldots, l^m_{j,k}$,
then replace them by a single arrow
labeled by $l^1_{j,k} \cup l^2_{j,k} \cup \ldots \cup l^m_{j,k}$.

(4) Remove node i and all the arrows
coming in and out of i from the
diagram.

End Algorithm

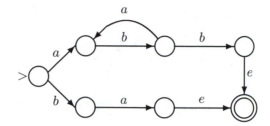

Figure 2.38 Automaton with One Accepting State

The transfomations of the steps 1, 2 and 3 are illustrated in Figure 2.39.

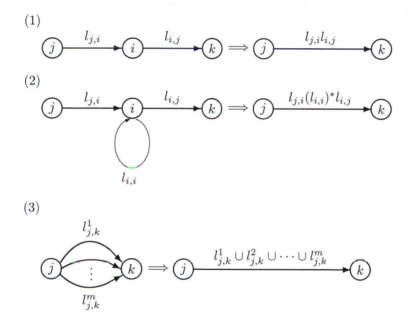

Figure 2.39 Steps 1, 2 and 3

At first glance, step 3 seems to be somewhat irrelevant to the "activity" resulting in deletion of node i. However, when a node i is deleted, it may result in creating new "parallel" arrows from j to k; step 3 takes care of this situation by combining them into one arrow (see Figure 2.42).

We illustrate algorithm $\mathcal{B}$ by applying it to the automaton in Figure 2.40. First, the algorithm deletes node 2. Note that $l_{3,2} = a$ and $l_{2,4} = b$. Similarly, $l_{1,2} = a$ and $l_{2,4} = b$. Finally, notice that $l_{4,2} = b$ and $l_{2,4} = b$. Hence, according to Algorithm $\mathcal{B}$, we get three new arrows when we eliminate node 2. Two of these arrows, from node 3 to node 4 and from node 1 to node 4, are labeled ab. The last of these new arrows

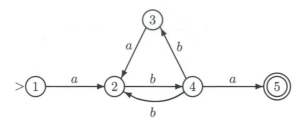

Figure 2.40 Example Input for Algorithm $\mathcal{B}$

goes from node 4 to node 4 and is labeled bb. The resulting diagram is presented in Figure 2.41. Then, after node 3 is deleted, we get the diagram of Figure 2.42.

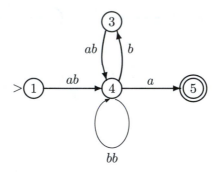

Figure 2.41 Node 2 Deleted

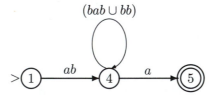

Figure 2.42 Node 3 deleted

Note that step 3 has been applied to replace two arrows labeled abb and bb by a single loop labeled $abb \cup bb$. Now, after node 4 is removed, the algorithm terminates with the resulting diagram given in Figure 2.43.

Thus the desired regular expression is $ab(abb \cup bb)^*a$. The results obtained above can be summarized in the following theorem.

Theorem 2.4.2 (Kleene) *There exists an algorithm that converts any regular expression α into an NFA A such that $L(\alpha) = L(A)$. There exists an algorithm that*

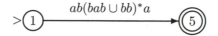

Figure 2.43 Final Expression Diagram

converts any NFA A into a regular expression α such that $L(A) = L(\alpha)$. That is, a language is accepted by an NFA if and only if it is regular.

Formal proof of the correctness of algorithm $\mathcal{B}$ can be carried out using mathematical induction. This is suggested in Exercise 2.21.

Notice the similarity between regular expressions and the syntax of the query languages used by search engines on the World Wide Web. This is no accident as the heart of the pattern-matching algorithm that checks for occurrences of your pattern on a particular Web page is precisely a finite automaton. Comparing the operations of building regular expressions and the operations for building search queries, we see that regular expressions are much more expressive. Search queries do not generally include anything like the Kleene star. Search queries often include "wild cards." These are also easy in the language of regular expressions. For example, an arbitrary lowercase letter is captured by the regular expression $\alpha = (a \cup b \cup \ldots \cup z)$. So to find, for example, all Web pages that contain an occurrence of "peace" following an instance of "world," one constructs a finite automaton to recognize the language $world\alpha^*peace$. Any page that is accepted by this automaton will match the search query. Furthermore, every page matching the query will be accepted by the automaton and any page that doesn't match the query will not be accepted.

One of the more useful programs in the UNIX operating system is called **grep**. This program takes two arguments; the first, a pattern, and the second, a file. The program returns all lines of the file that match the pattern. In fact, "grep" is a mnemonic that stands for "**g**et **r**egular **ex**pression."

2.5 Nonregular Languages

In the previous sections we have developed a variety of techniques for demonstrating that languages are regular (or, accepted by finite automata). As we pointed out in the beginning of this chapter, finite automata are programs that use fixed amounts of memory (represented by states) regardless of the input. One ought to expect that the power of such programs should be quite limited. Consider, for example, the language $L = \{a^n b^n | n \in N\}$. Suppose that a finite automaton A tries to recognize strings in this language. Then A must attempt to store the entire prefix a^n (or, at least, a string of comparable length) before the first b shows up in the input; otherwise A will not be able to compare the length of the coming string of b's with the length of the prefix. This argument shows that probably no such an automaton A exists. We use the word ***probably***, because our argument is not a mathematical proof of nonexistence of a desired automaton A. In order to be able to prove nonregularity of certain languages, we have to develop a mathematically sound technique.

Note first that any nonregular language must be infinite. Many infinite languages are still regular; we observed numerous examples of infinite regular languages in previous sections of this chapter. What makes a regular language infinite? It is obvious that an underlying automaton must contain a loop. If such a language is represented by a regular expression, this expression must contain a Kleene star. When we run through the loop few times, it results in a number of repetitions of some substring in a string belonging to the language. Potentially, we can run the loop any finite number of times. This way we can generate infinite subsets of strings in the language based on the same underlying repetitive structure specified by the loop (or a Kleene star in a regular expression).

The above intuitive argument can be mathematically formalized to prove the following.

Lemma 2.5.1 (Pumping Lemma) *Let L be a regular language. There exists an integer $n > 0$ such that any string $w \in L$, with length $|w| \geq n$, can be represented as the concatenation xyz such that,*

- *The substring y is nonempty,*

- *$|xy| \leq n$, and*

- *$xy^i z \in L$ for each $i \geq 0$.*

Proof: If L is finite, then choose any n longer than the longest word in L and the theorem follows since there are no words of length at least n. Suppose, then, that L is infinite. Let A be a finite automaton that accepts the language L. Let n be the number of states of A. Consider any string $w = w_1 w_2 \ldots w_m \in L$ that has the length $m \geq n$. Consider a computation of A on the initial segment $w_1 w_2 \ldots w_n$ of the string w. For any k, $0 \leq k \leq n$, let $(q_k, w_{k+1} w_{k+2} \ldots w_n)$ be the configuration of A after k steps of computation. Since A has only n states, and there are more than n configurations in the above fragment of computation, by the pigeon hole principle there exist r and j, $0 \leq r < j \leq n$, such that $q_r = q_j$. This means that the string $y = w_{r+1} w_{r+2} \ldots w_j$ brings the automaton A from state q_r back to the same state. Note that this string is nonempty, since $r < j$. Now, if we remove string y from the original string w, or insert y^i instead of y for any i, we get a string that will be still accepted by A. Thus, any string $xy^i z$, where $x = w_1 w_2 \ldots w_r$, $y = w_{r+1} w_{r+2} \ldots w_j$, and $z = w_{j+1} w_{j+2} \ldots w_m$, is accepted. Moreover, the total length of the prefix x and the substring y does not exceed n.

$$\boxed{\text{End Proof}}$$

The word ***Pumping*** reflects the fact that some nonempty string can repeatedly be inserted (pumped) into the word w without violating acceptability. How can we apply the pumping lemma to show that a language L is **not** regular? A possible application can work as follows.

1. The language L is likely to be nonregular. Thus, we cannot hope to have a description of L as concise as a regular expression. Still, we usually have some description (verbal, set-theoretical, graphical, etc.) that fully specifies the language in question. What we need from this description is the opportunity, given any string w, to determine if w is in L. For example, $L = \{a^n b^n | n \in N\}$ definitely provides such an opportunity since $abbb$ is clearly not in this language.

2. Now we get to the key idea. Assume that the language L **is** regular. Using the pumping lemma (Lemma 2.5.1), we may try to generate a string that must be in the language L; however, it does not satisfy specifications in the description of L. That is, our assumption that the language L is regular has led us to contradiction. We now give a specific example of this technique.

Example 2.5.1 Consider the language $L = \{a^k b^k | k \in N\}$. Assume that the language is regular. Then, according to the pumping lemma, there exists some integer n such that any word in L of length $|w| \geq n$ contains a nonempty subword y that can be pumped in or cut out of the word w. Let us pick the word $a^n b^n$. This word has length $2n \geq n$; thus it can be represented as xyz with $|xy| \leq n$, and y can be pumped in or cut out. Since $|xy| \leq n$, y must be a^k for some $k > 0$. Now, if we cut y out of w, the new word $a^{n-k} b^n$, according to the pumping lemma, must be in L. However, it is obviously not in the language.

> End Example

The technique we just applied reveals a potential problem: **how to pick a word** that can be used to generate a new "faulty" word. In the Example 2.5.1 we could have picked the word $a^{n/2} b^{n/2}$ (assuming that n is even), as it is still not shorter than n. In this case, y could be any subword a^k for any $k > 0$ or $a^k b^m$ for any $k + m > 0$. The pumping lemma, unfortunately, does not tell which case takes place. In this situation, we have to consider **both** possibilities for y. It is not hard, for if, say, y were $a^k b^m$ for $k > 0$ and $m > 0$, pumping in a few copies of y would result in a word with "alternating" a's and b's, but there is no such word in L. However, in our next example, the right choice of a word w plays vital role in the ability to apply the pumping lemma (Lemma 2.5.1).

Example 2.5.2 *Palindromes* are the words that are read the same way from both ends (for example, **atoyota**). We will show that the language of palindromes $L = \{w | w = w^R, w \in \Sigma^*\}$ is not regular. Suppose L is regular. Then, as the pumping lemma states, there exists an n such that every $w \in L$ with length $|w| \geq n$ can be represented as the concatenation xyz satisfying conditions in the lemma. Let us pick the palindrome $a^n b a^n$. Since the total length of x and y should not exceed

n, y is a substring $a^k, k > 0$ in the left subword a^n. According to the pumping lemma, then $a^{n-k}ba^n \in L$. However, it is not a palindrome.

$$\boxed{\text{End Example}}$$

What if in Example 2.5.2 we chose a different word w, say, ab^na? It is a palindrome, and it is long enough. However, if $y = b^k$ for some $k > 0$ (which is very possible), then pumping in or cutting out y brings us nowhere, as every new word of this kind is a palindrome. What this example demonstrates is the fact that every application of the pumping lemma requires an act of creativity from its user: right choice of the word w that can be used to generate words beyond the scope of the language. These words are usually "hard" to recognize by finite automata. a^nba^n is "hard" for a finite automaton, as it must memorize n somehow. On the other hand, ab^na is "easy."

Now we give an example of a nonregular language over a unary (one-character) alphabet.

Example 2.5.3 Consider the language $L = \{a^{k^2}|k = 0, 1, 2, \ldots\}$. We apply the pumping lemma to show that this language is not regular. Assume that it is regular. Then, using the number n, as provided by the lemma, we choose the string $w = a^{(n+1)^2} \in L$ of length $(n+1)^2 \geq n$. If it is represented as xyz with $|xy| \leq n$, then $y = a^i$ for some $0 < i \leq n$. Thus $a^{(n+1)^2-i}$ must be in L. Now note that n^2, the square closest to $(n+1)^2$, is smaller than $(n+1)^2 - i : (n+1)^2 = n^2 + 2n + 1$ and $i \leq n$; therefore $(n+1)^2 - i \geq n^2 + n + 1 > n^2$. Thus, we get a contradiction.

$$\boxed{\text{End Example}}$$

Our next example shows that sometimes closure properties of regular languages and previously obtained results can be used to establish nonregularity of new languages.

Example 2.5.4 We are going to show that the language

$$M = \{w \in \Sigma^*|w \text{ has equal number of } a\text{'s and } b\text{'s}\}$$

is not regular. The intersection of this language with the regular language a^*b^* is the language L from Example 2.5.1. If M is regular, so the intersection L should be. However, we just showed that L is not regular.

$$\boxed{\text{End Example}}$$

More examples of nonregular languages can found in the exercises for this section.

2.6 Algorithms for Finite Automata

In the previous section we found that there is an algorithm that converts finite automata to regular expressions. This algorithm uses the diagram of a finite automaton as its input. What else can algorithms do, given the finite state diagram as the input? In this section we provide few examples of such algorithms.

Algorithm 2.6.1 We are going to design an algorithm that, given a finite state diagram A and a string w, decides if $w \in L(A)$. We will call deciding $w \in L(A)$ the **membership problem**. The algorithm runs the word w using all possible paths in A beginning with the initial state. If, on some path, w drives A to a favorable state, then $w \in L$. Note that the length of every path being observed is $|w|$, that is, only paths of this length should be examined. If no such path drives A to a favorable state, the algorithm terminates and gives the answer $w \notin L$.

> End Algorithm

Algorithm 2.6.2 This algorithm determines if the language $L(A)$ is empty. The language $L(A)$ is empty if there is no path in the diagram A from the initial state to a favorable state. To determine if there is such a path, it is obviously sufficient to observe only the paths in the diagram that do not make full loops. Thus, the required algorithm must just follow all the paths that do not have repetitions of states. If no such path contains a favorable state, then $L(A)$ is empty.

> End Algorithm

Algorithm 2.6.3 This algorithm determines if $L(A) \subseteq L(B)$ for any two finite automata A and B. In the previous section we described how, given the diagrams A and B, to find the automaton C accepting the difference $L(A) - L(B)$. Now we can apply Algorithm 2.6.2. If the language $L(C)$ is empty, then $L(A) \subseteq L(B)$.

> End Algorithm

Algorithm 2.6.4 This algorithm, given two automata A and B, determines if they are equivalent, that is, if $L(A) = L(B)$. The languages are equal if and only if $L(A) \subseteq L(B)$ and $L(B) \subseteq L(A)$. Thus, we can apply Algorithm 2.6.3.

> End Algorithm

2.7   The State Minimization Problem

Applications of finite automata can be found in practically any area of computer science. One important field where finite automata are being used is hardware design: Some components of hardware are based on simulation of deterministic finite automata. An important objective here is to utilize finite automata that have a minimum possible number of states. During the initial phase of design, we usually do not care much about the number of states in the automaton solving the problem. Thus, it is important, given any automaton, to be able to transform it into an equivalent automaton that has a minimum number of states; the problem of finding such a minimum deterministic automaton is known as the **state minimization problem**.

An immediate question is if for every automaton A there **exists** an equivalent automaton B with the minimum possible number of states. The answer to this question is obviously positive: If A has n states, then take the minimum $m \leq n$ such that there is an automaton B with m states that is equivalent to A. This argument actually suggests the idea of an algorithm solving our problem. Namely, note that for any positive integer m, there exists only a finite number of different automata with n states. We are assuming for the moment that all the states are drawn from the same set $\{s_1, s_2, \ldots, s_n\}$. Moreover, it is not hard to list all these automata in some order so that all the automata with a fewer number of states precede automata with a greater number of states. Now, given an automaton A with n states, we can apply Algorithm 2.6.4 to find the first automaton in the above list equivalent to A. Obviously, this automaton will have the minimum number of states among all automata equivalent to A.

Unfortunately, the preceding algorithm is completely impractical, as the total number of automata with $m < n$ states is exponentially large (see Chapter 6 for more detailed discussion of the effects of exponential exhaustive search). We intend now to present an efficient algorithm that converts any deterministic finite automaton into the equivalent deterministic finite automaton with the minimal number of states.

Before our algorithm starts to work on a diagram, it makes sense to get rid of the states that cannot be reached from the initial state. Consider, for example, the diagram of Figure 2.44.

State n cannot possibly be reached from the initial state. Therefore, if we remove this state together with all arrows coming out of it, the new diagram (Figure 2.45) will accept the same language.

It is very easy to identify all reachable states: Just follow all possible paths without repeatedly traversing loops. Once all reachable states have been identified, remove all unreachable states and all arrows coming in and out of them. Thus, we can assume that the input diagram does not contain states unreachable from the initial state.

Consider now states t and p in the diagram of Figure 2.45. The only way to enter either state is via an a; both t and p are trap states. It is obvious that these

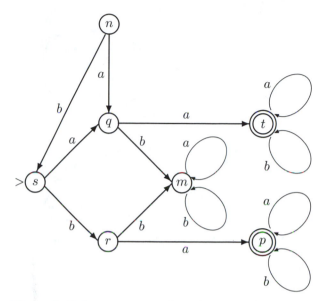

Figure 2.44 Automaton with an Unreachable State

two states can be merged. We say that the states t and p are **equivalent** or, in other words, **indistinguishable**. Take any word w, say, abb, and run A from either state t or p on it. In both cases the word drives A to a favorable state. Now consider states q and r. These states are also indistinguishable. If we take, say, bb, it drives the automaton from either q or r to the nonaccepting trap state, and, therefore, A cannot reach a favorable state on bb from either q or r. That is, any word w drives the automaton A with the diagram of Figure 2.45 from state q to a favorable state if and only if it drives A from r to a favorable state, or, in other words, no word w can distinguish q and r as far as acceptance is concerned. Distinguishability does not depend on how the states q and r can be reached from the initial state. What matters is how the automaton operates **from** the states in question.

The above example suggests the following idea: Given a finite automaton A, *identify the minimal set of distinguishable states, and merge every such state with all the states that cannot be distinguished from it*. Our algorithm below (Algorithm 2.7.1) accomplishes this idea; however, details are subtle. First, we formalize the notion of distinguishability in the following.

Definition 2.7.1 *Any states q and r in the diagram of a finite automaton A are called* **indistinguishable** *(written $q \equiv r$) if the automaton obtained from A by designating q as the initial state is equivalent to the automaton obtained from A by designating r as the initial state.*

We also say that a word w **distinguishes** states q and r of an automaton A if,

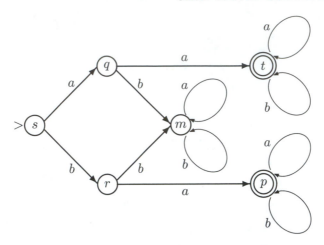

Figure 2.45 Without the Unreachable State

starting from q, w drives A to a favorable state, and, starting from r, w drives A to a nonfavorable state, or vice versa.

It can easily be proved that the relation $\equiv$ is reflexive, transitive, and symmetric. Therefore, it is an equivalence relation. It divides the set of all states into **equivalence classes**: Any two states in the same equivalence class are indistinguishable, any states from different equivalence classes are distinguishable. Now our goal can be reformulated: Given the diagram of an automaton, to find all equivalence classes for the relation $\equiv$, every equivalence class can be represented by a single state in the desired diagram.

The central part of our algorithm is a routine that reduces the problem of distinguishability of any two states r and r' to the same problem for the states q and q' that can be reached from r and, respectively, r' by arrows with identical labels (see Figure 2.46). If distinguishability of q and q' will ever be established, it will

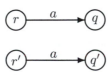

Figure 2.46: Distinguishability of r and r' Related to the Distinguishability of q and q'

result in distinguishability of r and r'. That is, we can first distinguish all favorable states from all nonfavorable states and then move "backwards." To implement this idea, we introduce the sequence of relations $\equiv_0, \equiv_1, \ldots, \equiv_n, \ldots$ defined as follows: For any two states q and r, $q \equiv_i r$ if these states are not distinguishable by any word w with length $|w| \leq i$. One can easily establish that every $\equiv_i$ is an equivalence relation. Any relation $\equiv_i$ is obviously weaker than $\equiv$, because in this case q and r cannot be distinguished if we consider only words of length at most i.

Note that if $q \equiv_0 r$, then q and r are either both favorable, or both nonfavorable. Now we need to link the relation $\equiv_{n+1}$ to the relation $\equiv_n$. Let δ be the transition function of the input automaton A. The desired link is provided by the following simple lemma.

Lemma 2.7.1 *For any two states q and r and any integer $n > 0$, $q \equiv_n r$ if and only if*

1. *$q \equiv_{n-1} r$ and*

2. *for all $a \in \Sigma$, $\delta(q, a) \equiv_{n-1} \delta(r, a)$.*

Proof: Suppose $q \equiv_n r$. By definition of the relation $\equiv_n$, q, and r are indistinguishable by words of length up to n. Therefore, they are indistinguishable by the words of length up to $n-1$. Suppose by way of contradiction that it is *not* the case that $\delta(q, a) \equiv_{n-1} \delta(r, a)$ for some $a \in \Sigma$. Let $q' = \delta(q, a)$ and $r' = \delta(r, a)$. Since not $q' \equiv_{n-1} r'$, q', and r' can be distinguished by some word v of length at most $n - 1$. Hence, av, a word of length n, distinguishes q and r, a contradiction.

Suppose $q \equiv_{n-1} r$ and $\delta(q, a) \equiv_{n-1} \delta(r, a)$ for all $a \in \Sigma$. Let v be a word of length $n - 1$ and a be a member of Σ. Consider the word av. Let $q' = \delta(q, a)$ and $r' = \delta(r, a)$. Since $q' \equiv_{n-1} r'$, q', and r' cannot be distinguished by v. Hence, av cannot distinguish q and r. Since v and a were chosen arbitrarily, $q \equiv_n r$.

End Proof

Now, given equivalence classes for any relation $\equiv_{n-1}$, we can test conditions 1 and 2 of Lemma 2.7.1 for any states q and r to find the equivalence classes for $\equiv_n$. Algorithm 2.7.1 is based on this idea. Let Q be the set of all states of A, and F be the set of the accepting states.

Algorithm 2.7.1
Initialize the equivalence classes for $\equiv_0$ as F and $Q - F$.
    Repeat for $n = 0, 1, 2, \ldots$
        Compute the equivalence classes of $\equiv_n$ from
            those of $\equiv_{n-1}$
    until $\equiv_n$ is identical to $\equiv_{n-1}$.

End Algorithm

Equivalence classes for $\equiv_n$ become states in the resulting automaton. If a class contains a favorable state of the input automaton, it becomes a favorable state.

An arrow labeled by $a \in \Sigma$ connects an equivalence class $\{q_1, q_2, \ldots, q_m\}$ to an equivalence class $\{p_1, p_2, \ldots, p_k\}$ if there is an arrow with the same label connecting a state from the first class to a state from the second class in the input automaton.

To demonstrate the correctness of our algorithm, we have to establish two facts:

- The loop in the definition of the algorithm terminates;

- The final relation $\equiv_n$ is the desired $\equiv$.

As for the first fact, just note that if the states cannot be distinguished by words of length up to n, they are indistinguishable by the words of length up to $n - 1$. That is, the longer the words, the more states they distinguish. Hence, every $\equiv_n$ is a **refinement** of $\equiv_{n-1}$, that is, some equivalence classes in $\equiv_n$ result from dividing classes in $\equiv_{n-1}$. However, the number of equivalence classes cannot grow indefinitely: It cannot be greater than the total number of states $|Q|$. Thus, our algorithm terminates. The second statement easily follows from Lemma 2.7.1. Lemma 2.7.1 implies that if $\equiv_n = \equiv_{n+1}$ for some n, then $\equiv_n = \equiv_{n+1} = \equiv_{n+2} = \cdots$. Now, it remains to be noticed that the relation $\equiv$ is the **limit** of the relations $\equiv_n, n = 0, 1, 2, \ldots$. Hence, no word of any length can distinguish any two states in the same final equivalence class. Consequently, the final set of equivalence classes defines the desired relation.

Now we apply the algorithm to the automaton of Figure 2.45. First, we initialize two equivalence classes for $\equiv_0$ as $\{t, p\}$ and $\{s, q, r, m\}$. After the first iteration of the algorithm, the first class stays the same, but the second class is split into $\{s, m\}$ and $\{q, r\}$. This happened because a drives the automaton from states q and r to a favorable state; while reading the same character from s and m, the automaton reaches a nonfavorable state. The second iteration splits only the class $\{s, m\}$. The character a drives the automaton from s to a state in the class $\{q, r\}$; while reading the same character from state m, the automaton reaches a state in the class $\{s, m\}$. Thus, after the second iteration, we have four different classes: $\{s\}, \{m\}, \{q, r\}, \{t, p\}$. The third iteration gives us the same classes. The resulting deterministic finite automaton with the minimum number of states is given in Figure 2.47.

The automaton obviously accepts the language represented by the regular expression $(aa \cup ba)(a \cup b)^*$.

Note that Algorithm 2.7.1 is quite efficient: The number of iterations in the main loop does not exceed the number of states in the input automaton, and, on every iteration, it is enough to review the set of transitions $\delta(q, a)$.

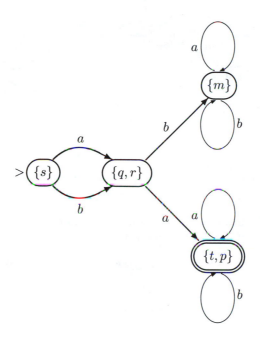

Figure 2.47 A Minimal Deterministic Finite Automaton

Exercises

Section 2.1

Exercise 2.1 Consider the following finite automaton:

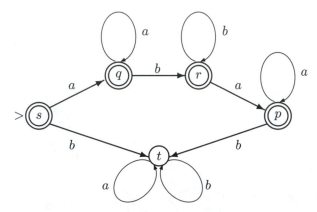

a) Find the sequence of configurations (computation) of the automaton on the string *aaabba* and determine if the string is accepted

b) Find the sequence of configurations of the automaton on the string *aabaab* and determine if it accepts the string *aabbaab*.

c) Describe (informally) the language accepted by the automaton.

Exercise 2.2 Consider the following finite automaton:

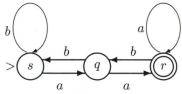

a) Find the sequences of configurations (computations) of the automaton on the strings *aababa* and *bbaababaaa* and determine if the strings are accepted.

b) Find the sequences of configurations of the automaton on the strings *aabaab* and *bbaababb* and determine if they are accepted.

c) Describe (informally) the language accepted by the automaton.

Exercise 2.3 Construct a finite automaton (in form of a diagram) that accepts all strings in the alphabet $\{a, b\}$ of length up to 3.

Exercise 2.4 Construct a finite automaton (in form of a diagram) that accepts all the strings of length $3n, n = 0, 1, 2, \ldots$.

Exercise 2.5 Let $\Sigma = \{a, b\}$. For $m, n, x, y \in N$, let $L(m, n, x, y)$ (for $x < m$ and $y < n$) be the set of all words $w \in \Sigma^*$ such that the number of a's in w is $x \bmod m$ and the nunber of b's in w is $y \bmod n$. How many states are needed for an automaton that accepts the language $L(m, n, x, y)$?

Exercise 2.6 Consider the finite automaton:

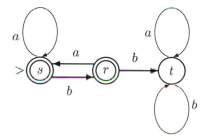

a) Determine if the automaton accepts the strings *abab.* and *aabaab*

b) Determine if the automaton accepts the strings *abbb* and *abbaab.*

c) Describe the language accepted by the automaton.

Exercise 2.7 For each of the following languages over the alphabet $\{a, b\}$, construct a finite automaton accepting it.

a) All strings, where every occurrence of an a is followed by a b.

b) All strings that contain a substring *bbb*.

Exercise 2.8 ◆◆ A deterministic two-tape finite automaton is a computational device that has two input tapes. It operates on pairs $(u\#, v\#)$ of strings, where $u, v \in \Sigma$ for some finite alphabet Σ and $\#$ is the *end marker* not contained in Σ. The set of states is divided into two subsets Q_1 and Q_2. If $q \in Q_1$, the head of the first tape reads a symbol and moves to the right; otherwise the head on the second tape does the same thing. The automaton completes its operation when it reaches the end markers on both tapes. A pair of $(u\#, v\#)$ is accepted if the automaton reaches end markers on both tapes being in a favorable state.

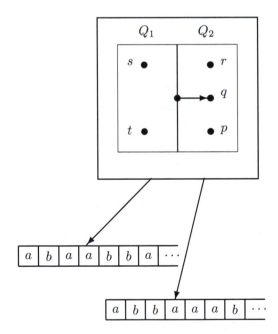

For example, the automaton

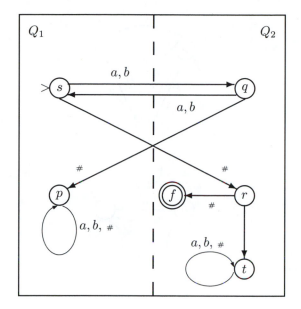

accepts all pairs of strings $(u\#, v\#)$ over the alphabet $\{a, b\}$ of equal length ($|u| = |v|$).

For each of the following languages, construct a two-tape deterministic automaton (in the form of a diagram) that accepts it.

a) $\{(u\#, v\#) | u, v \in \{a, b\}^*, |u| = 2|v|\}$

b) $\{(a^m b^n \#, a^k b^n \#) | n, m, k \geq 0\}$

c) $\{(a^n b^m \#, a^k b^n \#) | n, m, k \geq 0\}$

Section 2.2

Exercise 2.9 Determine if the nondeterministic automaton

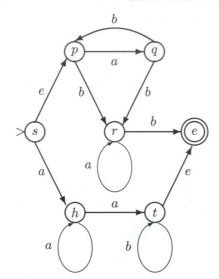

accepts the strings

a) *abb*

b) *abbbb*

c) *aabb*

If the string is accepted, indicate a corresponding sequence of states.

Exercise 2.10 ◆ Consider any nondeterministic automaton A over the unary alphabet $\{a\}$. Describe the language $L(A)$.

Section 2.3

Exercise 2.11 Transform the following nondeterministic finite automata into deterministic finite automata accepting the same languages:

a)

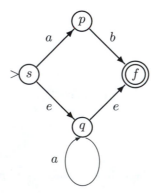

b)

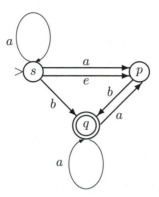

c)

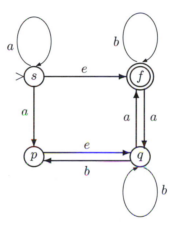

Exercise 2.12 ◆ Show that the language $L = \{e, a\}$ cannot be accepted by a nondeterministic automaton A unless at least one of the following conditions is met:

a) A contains an arrow labeled by e.

b) A has at least two favorable states.

Exercise 2.13 ◆◆ For the construction in Theorem 2.3.1, prove the following:

Claim: For any string $w \in \Sigma^*$, the automaton A reaches some state r, having read w, if and only if, having read w, the automaton A' reaches a state R containing r.

(*Hint*: Use induction on the length of the string w.) The claim easily implies equivalence of the automata A and A'. For any string w, A reaches a favorable state r on w if and only if A' reaches a favorable state R (containing r) on w.

Section 2.4

Exercise 2.14 For each of the following regular expressions, find a shortest string in the corresponding regular language:

a) $a^*(b \cup abb)b^*b$

b) $a^*b^*b(a \cup (ab)^*)^*b^*$

c) $(a \cup ab)(a^* \cup ab)^*b$

Exercise 2.15 For each of the following regular expressions α, find a shortest string $w \notin L(\alpha)$:

a) a^*aabb^*

b) $a^*aa(b \cup a)^*$

c) $(aa)^*(bba)^*(bb)^*$

d) $a^*(bba)^*b^*$

e) $a^*(ab \cup ba)^*b^*$

Exercise 2.16 For each of the following languages $L \subseteq \{a, b\}^*$, find a regular expression representing it:

a) All strings that contain exactly one a.

b) All strings that contain exactly two a's.

c) All strings that contain at least two a's.

d) All strings that begin with aa.

e) All strings that begin with aa and end with bb.

f) All strings that do not begin with aa.

g) All strings that contain the substring aaa or the substring bbb.

h) All strings that contain the substring aa and the substring bb.

i) All strings, where every occurrence of a is followed immediately by a b (in other words, all strings that contain no occurrence of aa).

Exercise 2.17 Let $\Sigma = \{a, b\}$. Show that

$$L = \{w | abba \text{ is a substring of } w\}$$

is regular.

Exercise 2.18 ◆◆ Let L be a regular language over Σ^* and let $w \in \Sigma^*$. Show that $L' = \{x \in L | w \text{ is a substring of } x\}$ is a regular language.

Exercise 2.19 Apply algorithm $\mathcal{A}$ in Section 2.4 to convert each of the following regular expressions to a finite automaton accepting the corresponding language:

a) $(a \cup b)^* ab(abb \cup a^*)^* bb^*$

b) $a(aa \cup b)^* (a^*b \cup b)^* ab$

c) $(ab \cup b)(b \cup aaa)b^* b((a^*b)^* \cup b)^*$

d) $ab((b \cup aa \cup aab)bb^*)^* b$

e) $((b \cup ab)^* b)^* (ba^*)^* b$

Exercise 2.20 ◆ Show that the class of languages accepted by finite automata are closed under intersection by a direct construction. That is, assume L and M are accepted by finite automata and construct an automaton A that accepts precisely $L \cap M$. Show that your automaton is correct.

Exercise 2.21 ◆◆ Consider expression diagrams as defined in Section 2.4. One can naturally associate a language $L(D)$ with any such diagram D. A string w is in $L(D)$ if and only if there exists a sequence of states $s_0, s_1, ..., s_n$ with s_0 being the initial state, s_n being a favorable state and arrows directed from every s_i to s_{i+1}, $i < n$ such that $w \in L(\alpha_1 \alpha_2 ... \alpha_n)$, where $\alpha_i, i = 1, 2, ..., n$ are regular expressions that label arrows connecting s_i with s_{i+1} as in the following:

If the regular expressions α_i are just symbols $a \in \Sigma$, we actually get the definition of acceptance by simple nondeterministic finite automata. Algorithm $\mathcal{B}$, constructed in Section 2.4, can obviously be applied to any finite expression diagram D.

Prove the following statement: For any expression diagram D and any string w, $w \in L(D)$ if and only if $w \in L(\alpha)$, where α is the regular expression produced by $\mathcal{B}$ on the input D.

(*Hint*: Use mathematical induction on the number of states in diagram D.) The assertion of this statement implies correctness of algorithm $\mathcal{B}$.

Exercise 2.22 Apply algorithm $\mathcal{B}$ from Section 2.4 to convert the following non-deterministic finite automata into regular expressions:

a)

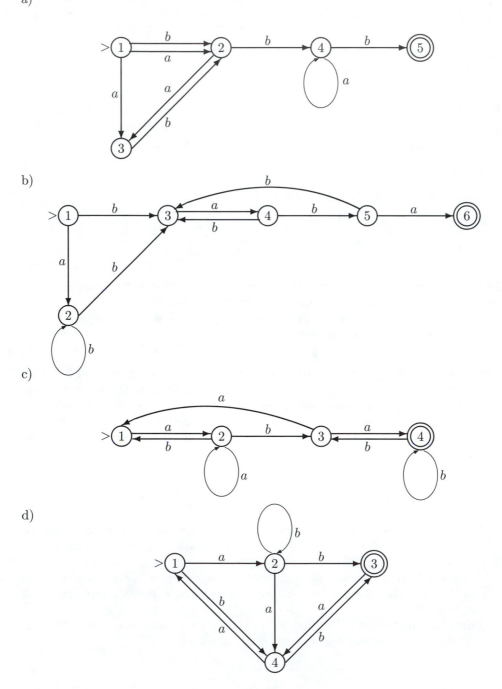

b)

c)

d)

e)

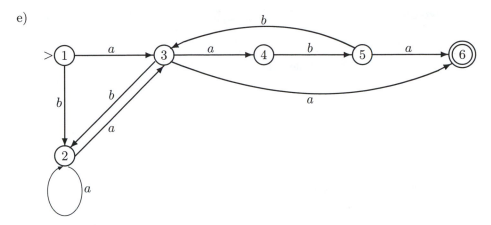

Exercise 2.23 ◆ Consider an arbitrary language L over some finite alphabet Σ. We can define the language of *prefixes* of the strings in L as

$$Pref(L) = \{u | u \in \Sigma^* \text{ and } uv \in L \text{ for some } v \in \Sigma^*\}$$

Similarly, we can define the language of *suffixes* of the strings in L as

$$Suf(L) = \{u | u \in \Sigma^* \text{ and } vu \in L \text{ for some } v \in \Sigma^*\}$$

Prove that if the language L is regular, then

a) $Pref(L)$ is regular,

b) $Suf(L)$ is regular.

(*Hint*: Consider the case when L contains a single string w and try to transform a simple nondeterministic finite automaton accepting just w to finite automata accepting $Pref(\{w\})$ and $Suf(\{w\}))$.

Exercise 2.24 ◆ Let Σ and Γ be two alphabets. A **homomorphism** from Σ^* to Γ^* is a function h from Σ^* to Γ^* that satisfies the following conditions:

a) $h(e) = e$;

b) $h(w) = h(u)h(v)$ for any $w \in \Sigma^*$ and any strings $u, v \in \Sigma^*$ such that $w = uv$.

For example, if $\Sigma = \Gamma = \{a, b\}$, $h(a) = ab$, and $h(b) = bba$, then

$$h(aabb) = h(aa)h(bb) = h(a)h(a)h(bb) = h(a)h(a)h(b)h(b) = ababbbabba.$$

Given any language $L \subseteq \Sigma^*$, let the *image* $h(L)$ be the language $\{w \in \Gamma^* | w = h(u)$ for some $u \in L\}$. Show that if a language $L \subseteq \Sigma^*$ is regular, so is the language $h(L)$.

---   **Section 2.5**   ---

Exercise 2.25 Prove that the following languages over the alphabet $\{a, b\}$ are not regular:

a) $L = \{a^n b a^{3n} | n \neq 0\}$

b) $L = \{a^n b^n a^n | n \neq 0\}$

c) $L = \{a^i b^n | i, n \neq 0, i = n \text{ or } i = 2n\}$

d) $L = \{ww | w \text{ is any string}\}$

Exercise 2.26 Consider languages over a fixed alphabet Σ with $|\Sigma| = 2$. Answer true or false to the following questions. Justify your answers, giving examples of the languages L_1 and L_2 where appropriate.

a) If L_1 is nonregular and $L_1 \subseteq L_2$ then L_2 is nonregular,

b) If $L_1 \subseteq L_2$ and L_2 is nonregular, then L_1 is nonregular,

c) If L_1 is nonregular, then its complement $\overline{L_1}$ is nonregular,

d) If L_1 is regular, then $L_1 \bigcup L_2$ is regular for any language L_2,

e) If L_1 and L_2 are nonregular, then $L_1 \bigcap L_2$ is nonregular.

Exercise 2.27 ◆ For each of the following languages over the alphabet $\{a, b\}$, determine if it is regular. If the language is regular, find a corresponding regular expression. If the language is not regular, prove it using the pumping lemma (Lemma 2.5.1).

a) All strings that contain a substring ww,

b) All strings that contain the substring aa exactly in the middle,

c) All strings that contain the substring aa or the substring bb exactly in the middle,

d) All strings that end with a palindrome of length 3.

Exercise 2.28 ◆ Suppose L is a regular language. Show that $L^R = \{w^R | w \in L\}$ is also a regular language.

Section 2.6

Exercise 2.29 Describe an algorithm that, given finite automata accepting languages L_1 and L_2, determines if $L_1 \cap L_2 = \emptyset$.

Exercise 2.30 Describe an algorithm that, given any finite automaton A and any of its states q, determines if there exists a string w such that starting at the state q and having read w, A reaches a favorable state.

Exercise 2.31 Describe an algorithm that, given a finite automaton A and a string w, determines if any substring of w is accepted by A.

Exercise 2.32 Describe an algorithm that, given a finite automaton A and states q and p, determines if the states are distinguishable. (The definition of distinguishability is given in Section 2.7.)

Exercise 2.33 Describe an algorithm that, given a finite automaton A and a string u, determines if u is a prefix of some string $w \in L(A)$ (that is, $w = uv$ for some string v).

Section 2.7

Exercise 2.34 Given the following finite automata, find the equivalence classes of states:

a)

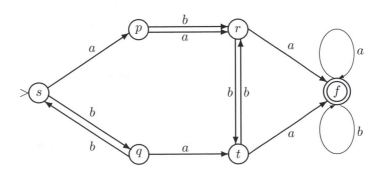

b)

c)

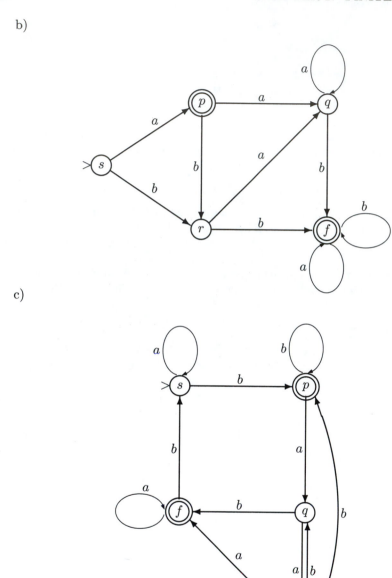

Exercise 2.35 Find the minimal finite automata for the automata in Exercise 2.34.

Chapter 3

Context-Free Languages

Chapter 3

Context-Free Languages

3.1 Context-Free Grammars

Finite automata recognize languages. The limits of what they can recognize have been described in the previous chapter. We have found out that even such a simple language as $\{a^n b^n | n = 0, 1, 2, \ldots\}$ cannot be recognized by a finite automaton. What about legal sentences of a human language, say English? Can a finite automaton make distinction between a legal English statement "The cat sat on the mat" and a senseless sequence of words "Mat the sat the cat on"? Considering the complexity of the rules defining legal English statements, one can hardly expect a positive answer to this question. Another important practical problem is checking syntactical correctness of statements in programs — the first job of any compiler. Rules of programming languages are much simpler than those of human languages; however, even this problem turns out to be too hard for a finite automaton.

Let us take a closer look on how human and/or computer languages are specified. Here are examples of some rules specifying legal English sentences (a very small subset, actually):

1. A **sentence** is a **noun phrase** followed by a **verb phrase**,

2. A **noun phrase** is a **proper noun** or a **determiner** followed by a **common noun**,

3. A **verb phrase** is a **verb** or a **verb** followed by an **adverb**.

Noun phrase is not defined in the first rule; however, this term is clarified in the second rule. We can obviously continue to extend the set or rules to cover all possible situations.

How do these rules work? We apply them to *generate* or *derive* syntactically correct English sentences. For example, if our set of rules contained in addition

4. **Proper noun** is **John**,

5. **Verb** is **sings**,

we could start with rule 1., substitute **noun phrase** by **proper noun** using rule 2., **verb phrase** by **verb** using rule 3., and then substitute **proper noun** by **John** and **verb** by **sings** using rules 4. and 5., respectively.

Thus, such a set of rules together with a derivation mechanism can be viewed as a program *generating* strings rather than *recognizing* them. That is, we expect that our program can potentially generate all strings in the language but will never generate any invalid string (say, **sings John** in the above example). In this sense information that we get from such programs about the language in question is somewhat incomplete: Given an invalid string (that is not in the language), a program of this type can never positively confirm this fact.

On the other hand, as the above example shows, program generators may provide an adequate model for describing human languages. However, the class of context-free languages that we will study is not rich enough to express common human languages. Many constructs in natural languages are context dependent. For example, gender-specific constructs in English are hard to model using context-free production rules.

More importantly, such generating programs are widely being used to specify and provide the means of syntactical analysis for computer programming languages. Beyond this practical aspect, a theory has been developed that establishes the computational power of such programs and relates them to finite automata whose computational capacity is extended by important data structures.

One can note that regular expressions provide an example of language generators. Consider, for instance, the expression ba^*. It can be interpreted as follows: "Output b and generate a string of $a's$." How can we represent this description in form of a rule (or a set of rules)? Suppose we have some character initiator, say, S to start with (like **sentence** in our first example). Then we can use the rule

$$S \rightarrow bA$$

to indicate that an output string is going to be a b followed by *something* (interpret $\rightarrow$ as *is* or *can be*). Now the second rule

$$A \rightarrow aA$$

being applied a number of times, can generate any number of a's after the first b. The character A, similar to noun phrase and verb in our first example, is actually an intermediate descriptor of substrings that can potentially be generated and become parts of output strings. Suppose our goal is to generate the string $baaa$. We can apply the first rule and the second rule three times to generate the string $baaaA$. Now, to get rid of A, we may introduce the rule

$$A \rightarrow e$$

Applying this rule gives us the desired string $baaa$. (In fact, we also need the latter rule to cover the case when the output string should be just b.)

The set of **rules** $\{S \rightarrow bA, \ A \rightarrow aA, \ A \rightarrow e\}$ together with the **derivation mechanism** is an example of a **context-free grammar**. To clarify the meaning of the word **context-free** consider strings $aaAbb, abAba$ and the rule $A \rightarrow c$. The substrings aa, bb in $aaAbb$ and ab, ba in $abAba$ are called the **context** of A in the strings $aaAbb$ and $abAba$, respectively. For a grammar, being **context-free** means that the rule $A \rightarrow c$ can be applied to the occurrences of A in any of the strings $aaAbb, abAba$, *regardless* of the context surrounding A in those words. For, if the rule were, say, $aAb \rightarrow acb$, (depending on the context of the descriptor A), it could be applied to the first string only. Thus, in context-free rules the strings to the left of $\rightarrow$ contain *exactly one* character.

In the above example we used uppercase and lowercase to distinguish between intermediate descriptors (uppercase) and output characters (lowercase). Characters of the latter type are called **terminals**, which reflects the fact that they make up output strings of the derivation process. Uppercase characters are called, accordingly, **nonterminals**, as they are never present in the output strings.

Now we are ready to give a formal definition of a context-free grammar.

Definition 3.1.1 *A **context-free grammar** G is a quadruple $(\Sigma, \ NT, \ R, \ S)$, where*

- *Σ is an alphabet (of **terminals**).*

- *NT is a set (of **nonterminals**).*

- *R (the set of **rules**) is a subset of $NT \times (\Sigma \cup NT)^{*}$.*

- *$S \in NT$ is the **starting symbol**.*

Formally, according to our definition, any rule is a pair (A, v), where $A \in NT$ and v is a string over the alphabet $\Sigma \cup NT$. However, from now on we will use a more convenient notation $A \rightarrow_{G} v$ for rules (we will often omit G when it is clear which grammar is being considered).

Thus, on the left from an arrow, we always have a nonterminal. For the strings v to the right of the arrow, we will use the term **sentential forms** . This term reflects the role of these strings: They are intermediate *forms* for possible legal *sentences* (output strings).

Grammars are useless unless there exists an appropriate **derivation mechanism**. To specify such a mechanism, we will say that a sentential form v is **one-step derivable** from a sentential form u in grammar G (written $u \Rightarrow_{G} v$, or, sometimes just $u \Rightarrow v$) if $u = xAy$ and $v = xzy$ for some $x, y, z \in (\Sigma \cup NT)^{*}$ and $A \in NT$, and there is a rule $A \rightarrow z$ in the set R. Then, we say that v is **derivable** from u in G (written $u \Rightarrow_{G}^{*} v$, or sometimes just $u \Rightarrow^{*} v$), if there exists a sequence of sentential forms $u_0, u_1, \ldots, u_n$ such that $u_0 = u, u_n = v$ and

$$u_0 \Rightarrow_{G} u_1, u_1 \Rightarrow u_2, \ldots, u_{n-1} \Rightarrow u_n$$

Any sequence of the above form is called a **derivation** in G.

Note that a grammar G can contain rules with the same left part and different right parts (cf. our examples above). Moreover, a sentential form can contain many different nonterminals and many occurrences of the same nonterminal. The definition of derivation does not specify *which* rule must be applied to *which* occurrence of a nonterminal at any step. That is, derivation is a *nondeterministic* process (familiar to the reader from Chapter 2). One must look for the "right" derivation. Sometimes there can be a choice of rules to be applied and a choice of places where the chosen rule may be applied.

Now we can define the language $L(G)$ **generated** or **derivable** in the grammar G as the set $\{w | w \in \Sigma^*, S \Rightarrow^*_G w\}$ of all terminal strings derivable from the starting nonterminal. If the grammar G is context-free, the language $L(G)$ is called a **context-free language**. Here are some examples of context-free grammars, derivations, and context-free languages.

Example 3.1.1 Let G be the grammar (Σ, NT, R, S), where $NT = \{S\}$, $\Sigma = \{a, b\}$, and $R = \{S \rightarrow aSb, S \rightarrow e\}$. An example of a derivation in this grammar is

$$S \Rightarrow aSb \Rightarrow aaSbb \Rightarrow aaaSbbb \Rightarrow aaabbb$$

We applied the rule $S \Rightarrow aSb$ three times and then the rule $S \rightarrow e$. It is quite obvious that the language $L(G)$ is $\{a^n b^n | n = 0, 1, 2, \ldots\}$.

$$\boxed{\text{End Example}}$$

Thus, we have an example of a context-free language that is not regular.

Example 3.1.2 Now consider the grammar G with the same terminal and nonterminal alphabets and starting symbol as in Example 3.1.1, but with the different set of rules:

$$R = \{S \rightarrow aS, S \rightarrow Sb, S \rightarrow e\}$$

An example of a derivation in this grammar is

$$S \Rightarrow aS \Rightarrow aaS \Rightarrow aaSb \Rightarrow aaSbb \Rightarrow aaaSbb \Rightarrow aaabb$$

The grammar obviously generates the regular language represented by the regular expression a^*b^* (note how the nonterminal separates "left" a's from "right" b's in the derivation). We shall show later that every regular language is context-free.

$$\boxed{\text{End Example}}$$

Now here is yet another example of a nonregular context-free language.

Example 3.1.3 Let G be a grammar with the same terminal and nonterminal alphabets as in Example 3.1.1 and with the set of rules $\{S \to aSa, S \to bSb, S \to e\}$. An example of a derivation in this grammar is

$$
\begin{aligned}
S &\Rightarrow aSa \\
&\Rightarrow aaSaa \\
&\Rightarrow aabSbaa \\
&\Rightarrow aabaSabaa \\
&\Rightarrow aababSbabaa \\
&\Rightarrow aababbabaa
\end{aligned}
$$

The reader has probably already figured out that the left half of the word is the "mirror image" of the right half. That is, the grammar generates the language $L(G) = \{ww^R | w \in \{a, b\}^*\}$. Note that some palindromes (of odd length) are not generated by the given grammar, for example, *abbba*. Exercise 3.4 suggests how to alter the grammar to generate all palindromes.

$$\boxed{\text{End Example}}$$

Our next example generates a small part of English. It is a slight extension of the example in the beginning of this section.

Example 3.1.4 Let G be the grammar with the nonterminal alphabet $NT = \{S, N_p, V_p, A_p, N, V, A\}$, $\Sigma = \{$ *big, stout, John, bought, white, car*$\}$ and the set of rules

$$
\begin{aligned}
R = \{S &\to N_p V_p \\
N_p &\to N \\
N_p &\to A_p N \\
A_p &\to A_p A \\
V_p &\to V N_p \\
N_p &\to e \\
A_p &\to e \\
A &\to big \\
A &\to stout \\
A &\to white \\
N &\to John \\
N &\to car \\
V &\to bought\}
\end{aligned}
$$

In this grammar, S stands for *sentence*, N_p stands for *noun phrase*, V_p stands for *verb phrase*, A_p stands for *adjectives*, N stands for *noun*, V stands for *verb*, and A stands for *adjective*. The grammar generates, in particular, the following strings:

John bought car.

John bought big car.

big stout John bought big white car.

Unfortunately, it generates also sentences like

big stout car bought big white car.

$$\boxed{\text{End Example}}$$

Example 3.1.5 The first job of every compiler is to check syntactical correctness of a program. Context-free grammars provide compilers with the opportunity to *parse* programs (parsing will be discussed in Section 3.2) in order to check syntactical validity. Many programs, in one or another form, contain algebraic expressions. Thus, every grammar specifying a programming language must contain a fragment generating such expressions. Our example represents such a fragment (in a simplified form). The alphabet Σ of terminals of our grammar G is the set $\{+, -, /, *, (,), v\}$, where v stands for a *variable*. The set NT contains the single nonterminal E (which is obviously the starting nonterminal; the letter E stands for *expression*). The set of rules R contains

$$
\begin{aligned}
E &\rightarrow (E) \\
E &\rightarrow -(E) \\
E &\rightarrow (E + E) \\
E &\rightarrow (E * E) \\
E &\rightarrow (E/E) \\
E &\rightarrow (E - E) \\
E &\rightarrow v
\end{aligned}
$$

The grammar obviously generates algebraic expressions over the generic variable v using addition, subtraction, multiplication, and division. For example, it generates the expression $((v + (v * v)) * (v - v))$ using the following derivation:

$$
\begin{aligned}
E &\Rightarrow (E * E) \\
&\Rightarrow ((E + E) * E) \\
&\Rightarrow ((E + E) * (E - E)) \\
&\Rightarrow ((E + (E * E)) * (E - E))
\end{aligned}
$$

$$\Rightarrow \quad ((v + (E * E)) * (E - E))$$
$$\Rightarrow \quad ((v + (v * E)) * (E - E))$$
$$\Rightarrow \quad ((v + (v * v)) * (E - E))$$
$$\Rightarrow \quad ((v + (v * v)) * (v - E))$$
$$\Rightarrow \quad ((v + (v * v)) * (v - v))$$

The generic identifier v in real grammars specifying programming languages is then replaced by identifiers or numbers, which, in turn, can be specified by fragments of a context-free grammar. (See Exercise 3.12.)

$$\boxed{\text{End Example}}$$

Example 3.1.6 Adding the following set of rules to those of Example 3.1.5 we can derive some assignment statements in C or C++. Let I stand for *Identifier*:

$$S \quad \rightarrow \quad I = E;$$
$$I \quad \rightarrow \quad u$$

For example, one can derive the statement

$$u = (v + v) * v$$

Now let C stand for *Condition* and add the rules

$$S \quad \rightarrow \quad S\textbf{while}(C)\{S\}S;$$
$$S \quad \rightarrow \quad e$$
$$C \quad \rightarrow \quad E > E$$
$$E \quad \rightarrow \quad a$$
$$E \quad \rightarrow \quad b$$

Using these rules, one can derive whole programs in C/C++ that use assignment and **while** statements. In particular, we can derive the following statement in C/C++:

$$
\begin{aligned}
S \quad &\Rightarrow \quad S\textbf{while}(C)\{S\}; S \\
&\Rightarrow \quad \textbf{while}(C)\{S\}; S \\
&\Rightarrow \quad \textbf{while}(E > E)\{S\}; S \\
&\Rightarrow \quad \textbf{while}(a > E)\{S\}; S \\
&\Rightarrow \quad \textbf{while}(a > b)\{S\}; S \\
&\Rightarrow \quad \textbf{while}(a > b)\{I = E; \}; S
\end{aligned}
$$

$\Rightarrow$ **while**$(a > b)\{u = E; \}; S$

$\Rightarrow$ **while**$(a > b)\{u = (E + E); \}; S$

$\Rightarrow$ **while**$(a > b)\{u = (v + E); \}; S$

$\Rightarrow$ **while**$(a > b)\{u = (v + u); \}; S$

$\Rightarrow$ **while**$(a > b)\{u = (v + u); \};$

$\boxed{\text{End Example}}$

3.2   Parsing

As we noted in Section 3.1, any derivation is a nondeterministic process. There are many factors that contribute to inherent nondeterminism of a derivation process:

(a) An intermediate sentential form can contain many different nonterminals A, B, C, ...;

(b) It can have many occurrences of the same nonterminal; and

(c) For any nonterminal A, there exist many rules in the grammar that can be applied to A.

Thus, a string $w \in L(G)$ can potentially have many different derivations. Let us examine how the above factors influence the derivation process. Recall Example 3.1.4. The sentence *John bought car* has many different derivations, for example,

$$S \Rightarrow N_p V_p \quad \Rightarrow \quad N V_p \Rightarrow \text{John} V_p \Rightarrow \text{John} V N_p \Rightarrow \text{John bought} N_p$$
$$\Rightarrow \quad \text{John bought} N \Rightarrow \text{John bought car}$$

and

$$S \Rightarrow N_p V_p \Rightarrow N_p V N_p \quad \Rightarrow \quad N V N_p \Rightarrow N V N \Rightarrow N V \text{car}$$
$$\Rightarrow \quad N \text{bought car} \Rightarrow \text{John bought car}$$

At every step, we choose a nonterminal and apply a rule to it. However, the occurrence of a nonterminal in an intermediate sentential form determines *which* rule is to be applied. That is, every application of a rule that occurs in one derivation occurs in another one. In other words, the only difference between derivations in our example is in the relative order in which the rules are applied; otherwise both derivations are identical. We can picture both derivations as in Figure 3.1.

Such a picture is called a **parse tree**. Each internal node in a parse tree is labeled by a nonterminal, say, A. A is connected to its children that are labeled $A_1, A_2, \ldots, A_n$, where $A \rightarrow A_1 A_2 \ldots A_n$ is a rule in the grammar. All leaves are

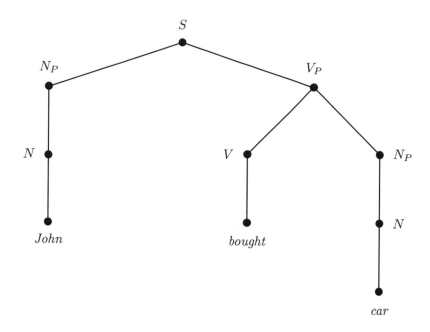

Figure 3.1 Parse Trees for *John bought car*

labeled with terminals or *e*. The concatenation of *all* the labels forms the string obtained by any derivation represented by the given parse tree. Every derivation tree represents a set of derivations that are identical unless two occurrences of the *same* nonterminal are replaced by the *same* rule on two consecutive steps (that is, nonterminals are replaced by the *same* strings), but in *opposite* order.

Parse trees reflect the choice that one may have at any phase of a derivation. There are a few occurrences of nonterminals, say, A_1, A_2, ..., A_n in a sentential form. The rules to replace all of them are *preselected*, and it is only a matter of choice in which order to replace them. In particular, we can choose to always replace the **leftmost** nonterminal in a sentential form. Such derivations are called **leftmost derivations**. Our first derivation of the statement *John bought car* is an example of a leftmost derivation. Or, we can always replace the **rightmost** nonterminal, getting what is called the **rightmost derivation**. All derivations that have the same parse tree are called **equivalent** (one can show that this defines an equivalence relation—cf. Exercise 3.16). Leftmost (or rightmost) derivations can be considered *canonical* derivations of some sort, as we remove one source of nondeterminism from our derivation process. Still, one can choose *which* rule to apply to any given nonterminal. As for the statement *John bought car*, the reader can see that no other choice of rules can result in the same statement. However, changing rules, we can generate different parsing trees for the same string, as the following example shows.

Example 3.2.1 Consider the following grammar G:

$$
\begin{aligned}
S &\rightarrow A \\
S &\rightarrow B \\
S &\rightarrow AB \\
A &\rightarrow aA \\
B &\rightarrow bB \\
A &\rightarrow e \\
B &\rightarrow e
\end{aligned}
$$

that obviously generates the language represented by the regular expression a^*b^*. We can generate the string aa using derivation

$$S \Rightarrow A \Rightarrow aA \Rightarrow aaA \Rightarrow aa$$

or

$$S \Rightarrow AB \Rightarrow aAB \Rightarrow aaAB \Rightarrow aaB \Rightarrow aa$$

Note that both derivations are leftmost. The corresponding parse trees are presented in Figures 3.2 and 3.3.

$$\boxed{\text{End Example}}$$

Grammars with strings having two or more distinct parse trees are called **ambiguous**. Thus, if a grammar G is ambiguous, a string $w \in L(G)$ can have two or more distinct leftmost derivations.

How does ambiguity relate to the compilation process of programming languages? When a compiler scans a statement in a program, it tries to form a parse tree for this statement. In a sense, a parse tree describes the structure of the statement, or rather, its "meaning." From this point of view, it is clear that ambiguity may result in different "meanings" of the same statement, which is obviously undesirable. A good example of ambiguity is the "dangling else" problem familiar to every programmer. Consider the expression

$$\text{if A if B then C; else D;}$$

In an ambiguous grammar, this statement would have two different parsing trees, one relating *else* to the first *if*, the other relating it to the second *if* (an example of such a grammar is given in Exercise 3.17). Thus, for programming languages, we would rather use **unambiguous** grammars, that is, a grammar, where every string has at most one parse tree. Can an ambiguous grammar be replaced by an equivalent (generating the same language) unambiguous grammar? Sometimes it is

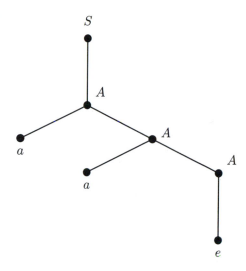

Figure 3.2 Parse Tree for the First Derivation of aa

possible. For instance, the rules $S \rightarrow A$ and $S \rightarrow B$ in Example 3.2.1 are obviously redundant. Removing them, we get the grammar that generates the same languages and is unambiguous. In this case, the transformation to an unambiguous grammar was very easy. In other cases, such transformation may be more complex (it may involve introduction of new nonterminals and transformation of rules). However, there exist context-free languages that have no unambiguous generating context-free grammars. Such context-free languages are called **inherently ambiguous**. Fortunately, no programming language is inherently ambiguous.

3.3 Pushdown Automata

So far, our approach to computing in this chapter has seemed quite different from that of Chapter 2. We adopted a *grammar* as a computing vehicle and a *derivation* as the computational process. However, a closer look at finite automata reveals obvious similarities between computations carried out by these simple computational devices and derivations using rules. In fact, any transition $\delta(a, s) = s'$ can be viewed as a rule $s \rightarrow as'$ (with s and s' as nonterminals), which makes computation by a finite automaton a sort of derivation. We will formalize this argument later to show that every finite state diagram A can easily be transformed into a context-free grammar generating the language $L(A)$. However, as we have seen already, there exist nonregular context-free languages, and, therefore, some derivation processes cannot be carried out by finite automata. One "ideological" reason for this seems to be obvious: If a string w is not in the language generated by a context-free grammar G, no derivation of w will ever terminate, while every computation carried out

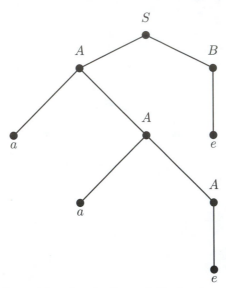

Figure 3.3 Parse Tree for the Second Derivation of aa

by a finite automaton A terminates and gives a definite answer about the status of w in $L(A)$. Still, is there a more powerful type of computational device that will terminate on any input w and determine its status? And if yes, what extra computational resources could one add to finite automata to make them recognize context-free languages?

Suppose one is to design a program recognizing strings in the context-free language $L = \{a^n b^n | n \in N\}$. What such a program needs is a "stack," where it can store the first half of an input string. Then, when the program starts to read the second half of the input, it can *pop* the content of the stack to compare its length with the length of the suffix b^n. The input can obviously be scanned only once, from left to right. The reading of the input can be carried out by a finite automaton. Thus, the desired program can be implemented as a combination of a finite automaton and an auxiliary "data structure," a stack, where data are pushed onto and popped from the top.

The role of a stack in dealing with arbitrary context-free languages becomes transparent if we consider the problem of simulating any rule $A \rightarrow aBb$ by an automaton like computational device. As we have already observed, any transition of a finite automaton can be interpreted as a rule of the type $A \rightarrow aB$; obviously, one can also easily interpret any such rule as a transition of an automaton. However, the extra b in the rule poses a problem: The device must remember it to preserve integrity of the computation. A stack turns out to be an appropriate storage for b. Later, b can be used to match some symbol (or a group of symbols) from the input, as every b from the stack matched an input symbol a in the above example. Of course, our informal argument is just a hint. However, we will formalize it later to show that any derivation can be carried out by a finite automaton using a stack.

As we have observed, a derivation in a context-free grammar may be a nondeterministic process. Thus, one should expect nondeterminism to show up in computational devices that recognize context-free languages. Consider, for instance, the context-free language $L = \{ww^R | w \in \{a, b\}^*\}$ of palindromes of even length (Example 3.1.3). L can be recognized by a simple computer program that stores the input string u and then scans it, comparing corresponding characters starting simultaneously from both ends. However, such a program cannot be implemented as a finite automaton, even if one used a stack to store the input u. When the program has completed copying u onto the stack, it cannot "jump" back to the first character on the input tape to start matching u with its "reversed" counterpart on the stack. Still, we can design a nondeterministic finite automaton with a stack. This automaton first "pushes" the first half w onto the stack. The end of the first half is found by nondeterministically "guessing" its end. Then, the automaton matches the content of the stack against the rest of the input. Formally, an automaton using a stack as an auxiliary storage can be defined as follows.

Definition 3.3.1 *A **pushdown automaton** A is given by a sextuple $(Q, \Sigma, \Gamma, s_0, \Delta, F)$, where*

> *Q is a finite set of **states**;*
> *Σ is the **input** alphabet;*
> *Γ is the set of stack symbols;*
> *$s_0 \in Q$ is the **initial state**;*
> *Δ, the **transition relation**, is a subset of*
> *$(Q \times (\Sigma \cup \{e\}) \times \Gamma^*) \times (Q \times \Gamma^*)$;*
> *$F \subseteq Q$ is the set of **favorable** states.*

Similar to a finite automaton, any pushdown automaton A can be visualized as a device with finite control, one-way reading-only tape, one reading head observing one input character at a time. In addition, this automaton has a stack with another head always observing the top of the stack (Figure 3.4).

Now, consider any *transition* $((s, a, \beta), (q, \gamma)) \in \Delta$. If a pushdown automaton is in state s, its reading head observes the character a on the input tape and the word β is on the top of the stack, it can then use this transition to move to the state q, its reading head moves one step to the right, and the word β on the stack is replaced by γ. Note that a may be e, in which case the reading head does not move as no input is being used. We say that A *can use* the transition, because there may be a few transitions in Δ with the same triple (s, a, β). Since our automaton is nondeterministic, it can "choose" any of them for its next move. In fact, the automaton can choose any transition that starts with (s, a', β'), for a', a prefix of a, and either β, a prefix of β', or β', a prefix of β.

When A places a character onto the top of the stack, we say that it **pushes** a. If it removes a from the stack, we say that A **pops** it.

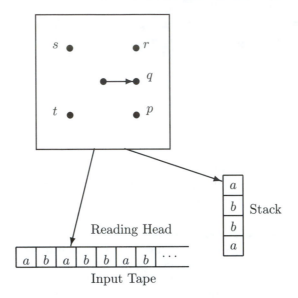

Figure 3.4 Pushdown Automaton

Now we can formally define computation by a pushdown automaton A. Roughly, starting with the reading head observing the first character on the input tape, A moves from configuration to configuration. Any configuration is a "snapshot" of the automaton's state, internal "memory" (stack), and the portion of the input yet to be read. Since the reading head always moves to the right, the input read so far cannot affect the automaton's operation starting from the given configuration. An example of a configuration is a triple $(s, abb, abab)$, where the reading head observes the character a in abb, the top of the stack is a and the bottom is b. For any two configurations $C_1 = (s, u, \alpha)$ and $C_2 = (q, v, \beta)$, we say that C_1 **yields** C_2 **in one step** (denote it $C_1 \vdash C_2$) if there is a transition $((s, a, \eta), (q, \gamma)) \in \Delta$ such that $u = av$, $\alpha = \eta\theta$, and $\beta = \gamma\theta$ for some $\theta \in \Gamma^*$. That is, applying this transition, the automaton reads a on the input tape, moves the reading head to the right, and replaces the "tail" η on the top of the stack by the string γ with the first character of γ on the top of the stack (if $a = e$, the reading head stays intact). Furthermore, we say that A **accepts** a string w if there exists a finite sequence of configurations (a **computation**)

$$(s_0, w, e) = C_0 \vdash C_1 \vdash \ldots \vdash C_n = (p, e, e)$$

where p is a favorable state. That is, the string w is accepted if A, having read the input, has the stack empty and is in a favorable state. All the strings w accepted by A form the language $L(A)$ accepted by A.

Here are some examples of pushdown automata.

Example 3.3.1 The following pushdown automaton A accepts the language $L = \{a^n b^n | n \in N\}$. $Q = \{s_0, s, f\}$, $\Sigma = \{a, b\}$, $\Gamma = \{a\}$, $F = \{s_0, f\}$, and Δ is the set

$$
\begin{aligned}
&(1) \quad ((s_0, a, e), (s, a)) \\
&(2) \quad ((s, a, e)(s, a)) \\
&(3) \quad ((s, b, a), (f, e)) \\
&(4) \quad ((f, b, a), (f, e))
\end{aligned}
$$

Note that the state s_0 is favorable, which causes the automaton to accept the empty string e. If the input string is nonempty, the automaton first applies transition 1 to enter the nonaccepting state s. Then, reading a's, the automaton pushes them onto the stack, applying transition 2. When the first b shows up in the input, A applies transition 3 to make the "turn" and then continues popping from the stack, one character from the stack per one b in the input, using transition 4. If the number of b's equals the number of a's, then, after the input has been read, the automaton arrives to the favorable state with an empty stack.

What happens if the input string w is not in the language? If, for example, $w = aaabb$, then, when the input has been read, A is in the favorable state. However, the stack is not empty yet, and, furthermore it never empties, as there is no transition with (f, e, a) as the left triple. If $w = aabbbb$, or, say, $w = aabbab$, then A enters state f with the empty stack; however, it is then unable to complete reading the rest of the input, as there are no transitions with the left triples (f, a, e) or (f, b, e). Intuitively, in both cases, A gets "stuck," being unable either to clear the stack, or to complete reading the input.

> End Example

Example 3.3.2 Now we design a pushdown automaton A that accepts the language $L = \{ww^R | w \in \{a, b\}^*\}$ of even-length palindromes. For the sake of simplicity, we will define only the set of transitions and assume that f is the only favorable state and s is the starting state. The rest of the definition will be clear from the context.

$$
\begin{aligned}
&(1) \quad ((s, a, e), (s, a)) \\
&(2) \quad ((s, b, e), (s, b)) \\
&(3) \quad ((s, e, e), (f, e)) \\
&(4) \quad ((f, a, a), (f, e)) \\
&(5) \quad ((f, b, b), (f, e))
\end{aligned}
$$

The automaton pushes the prefix w onto the stack, then nondeterministically "guesses" the middle of the input string (chooses transition 3) and starts to compare the content of the stack, that is, w in the reverse order, with the rest of the input. If, when all the input has been read the stack happens to be empty, A accepts the input string. If more input characters remain to be input, A gets "stuck" as there is no transition that can be applied to read the rest of the input.

$$\boxed{\text{End Example}}$$

Example 3.3.3 Now we consider the language $L = \{w|w \in \{a, b\}^*, w \text{ has the same}$ number of a's and b's$\}$. The pushdown automaton A that recognizes this language is an "extension" of the automaton in Example 3.3.1. If the number of a's and b's in the input read so far is equal, the stack is empty. If there are more a's than b's, the excess is pushed onto the stack where reading a b from the input results then in popping one a from the stack. Analogously, if there are more b's than a's, it is the b's that go on the stack to be popped off against a's from the input. To implement this idea, the automaton must be able to recognize *when the stack becomes empty* so it can "change its mind" and start to fill the stack by either a's or b's all over again. The empty stack test can be achieved by adding a special marker $c \in \Gamma$ that is placed on the bottom of the stack at the very beginning of the automaton's operation. The marker c is used only in this situation. Now the automaton is able to recognize if it has reached the bottom of the stack. As in the previous example, we assume that $s = s_0$ and $F = \{f\}$; the set of transitions is

$$
\begin{array}{ll}
(1) & ((s, e, e), (q, c)) \\
(2) & ((q, a, c), (q, ac)) \\
(3) & ((q, a, a), (q, aa)) \\
(4) & ((q, a, b), (q, e)) \\
(5) & ((q, b, c), (q, bc)) \\
(6) & ((q, b, b), (q, bb)) \\
(7) & ((q, b, a), (q, e)) \\
(8) & ((q, e, c), (f, e))
\end{array}
$$

Being fed the input *abbbaaaabb*, the automaton first applies transition 1 to place the marker on the bottom of the stack. Then it uses transition 2 to push the first a onto the stack. Then transition 7 is applied to pop the stack. Now the stack is empty, and the automaton applies transition 5 to push the first b and transition 6 to push the next b onto the stack. Then it applies transition 4 two times to clear the b's from the stack. Now A starts to push the rest of the a's onto the stack, applying transitions 2 and 3. Then two applications of transition 7 clear the stack of a's, and the automaton uses transition 8 to enter the favorable state. This operation is illustrated in Figure 3.5.

$$\boxed{\text{End Example}}$$

state	input left	stack	transition
s	*abbbaaaabb*	e	—
q	*abbbaaaabb*	c	1
q	*bbbaaaabb*	ac	2
q	*bbaaaabb*	c	7
q	*baaaabb*	bc	5
q	*aaaabb*	bbc	6
q	*aaabb*	bc	4
q	*aabb*	c	4
q	*abb*	ac	2
q	*bb*	aac	3
q	*b*	ac	7
q	e	c	7
f	e	e	8

Figure 3.5 Operation of the Automaton Accepting *abbbaaaabb*

The last example suggests a different way of accepting the strings in $L(A)$: just **by empty stack**. Suppose there is no distinction between favorable and unfavorable states in some automaton A. Then the fact that the stack is empty when the entire input string has been read can be used as the criterion for acceptance. An automaton of this type is a quintuple (rather than a sextuple in the original Definition 3.3.1) $(S, \Sigma, \Gamma, s_0, \Delta)$ as the set of favorable states is gone. We say that such a pushdown automaton accepts an input string w **by empty stack** if, starting from the configuration (s_0, w, e), it reaches the configuration (s, e, e) for some state $s \in S$.

It is sometimes useful to accept strings by empty stack as opposed to by favorable states and empty stack. As the following theorem states, any language accepted by a pushdown automaton with favorable states can be accepted by a pushdown automaton using empty stack acceptance.

Theorem 3.3.1 *There exists an algorithm that, given any pushdown automaton* $A = (Q, \Sigma, \Gamma, s_0, \Delta, F)$, *constructs the pushdown automaton* $A' = (Q', \Sigma', \Gamma', s_0', \Delta')$ *accepting the language* $L(A)$ *by empty stack.*

Proof: The desired automaton A' has the same input alphabet $\Sigma' = \Sigma$ and the set of states $Q' = Q \cup \{s_0'\}$, where s_0' is a new starting state. The stack alphabet Γ' contains all symbols from Γ and a special bottom marker $c \notin \Gamma$. The automaton A' basically simulates A [that is, uses $\Delta \subset \Delta'$]. However, before starting the simulation of A, A' pushes the marker c onto the stack and enters the state s_0, the initial state of the original automaton A. This is accomplished by using the new transition $((s_0', e, e), (s_0, c)) \in \Delta'$. If A reaches a configuration (f, e, c) with $f \in F$, the automaton A' pops the "marker" c from the stack and enters the accepting configuration (f, e, e) (that is, uses the transition $((f, e, c), (f, e)) \in \Delta'$). If the stack never reaches the "bottom marker" c, or A enters the configuration (s, e, c) for $s \notin F$, then the bottom marker c is not removed and the input is not accepted. The automaton A' clearly accepts the same language as A.

$$\boxed{\text{End Proof}}$$

3.4   Languages and Automata

As we hinted in the beginning of this chapter, pushdown automata are the devices that recognize context-free languages. In this section we are going to construct algorithms that translate any context-free grammar into a pushdown automaton accepting the same language, and vice versa.

Theorem 3.4.1 *There exists an algorithm that, given any context-free grammar G, constructs a pushdown automaton A such that $L(A) = L(G)$.*

Proof: (Sketch) Let G be a context-free grammar. The required pushdown automaton A has two states, the starting state s and the *permanent* favorable state f, at which it carries out its entire operation except its first move. It begins with pushing the starting nonterminal S onto the stack and enters the state f. On every subsequent step

1. If the topmost symbol on the stack is a nonterminal, say, C, then A picks some rule $C \to w$ in G and replaces C on the top of the stack by w.

2. If the topmost symbol on the stack is a terminal, say, a, then A advances the head on the input tape to the next symbol, and if it matches a, A pops the top of the stack.

Here are the transitions of the automaton A with f being the only favorable state:

1. $((s, e, e), (f, S))$

2. $((f, e, C), (f, w))$ for each rule $C \to w$ in the grammar G

3. $((f, a, a), (f, e))$ for each terminal a

The computation of our pushdown automaton A simulates a leftmost derivation of the input string. Every step of the derivation is implemented by pushing the right side of the rule $C \to w$ onto the stack. Between derivation steps, the automaton strips the terminals from the stack, matching them with the input. When the leftmost nonterminal on the stack is observed by the pushdown head, the automaton carries out the next derivation step.

Example 3.4.1 Consider the grammar G with the rules $\{S \rightarrow aSa,\ S \rightarrow bSb,$ $S \rightarrow e\}$ that generates the language $L = \{ww^R | w \in \{a,b\}^*\}$ of palindromes of even length. The pushdown automaton A accepting L has the following set Δ of transitions:

$$(1) \quad ((s,e,e),(f,S))$$
$$(2) \quad ((f,e,S),(f,aSa))$$
$$(3) \quad ((f,e,S),(f,bSb))$$
$$(4) \quad ((f,e,S),(f,e))$$
$$(5) \quad ((f,a,a),(f,e))$$
$$(6) \quad ((f,b,b),(f,e))$$

> End Example

The computation of A on the string *ababbaba* is presented in Figure 3.6. When the automaton reaches the middle of the input word, it "guesses" that transition 4 should be applied. Otherwise, its operation is deterministic.

state	input left	stack	transition
s_0	ababbaba	e	—
f	ababbaba	S	1
f	ababbaba	aSa	2
f	babbaba	Sa	5
f	babbaba	$bSba$	3
f	abbaba	Sba	6
f	abbaba	Sba	6
f	abbaba	$aSaba$	2
f	bbaba	$Saba$	5
f	bbaba	$bSbaba$	3
f	baba	$Sbaba$	6
f	baba	$baba$	4
f	aba	aba	6
f	ba	ba	5
f	a	a	6
f	e	e	5

Figure 3.6 Computation of Automaton A on *ababbaba*

To formally prove the theorem, one must show that

(a) If $w \in L(G)$, then $w \in L(A)$ and

(b) If $w \in L(A)$, then $w \in L(G)$.

The first statement can be proved by induction on the length of the leftmost derivation of w. The second statement can be proved by induction on the number of
transitions of the type $((s, e, C)(s, w))$ in the computation by automaton A. Detailed proofs are suggested in Exercise 3.33.

$$\boxed{\text{End Proof}}$$

Now we will show that every pushdown automaton can be simulated by a
context-free grammar.

Theorem 3.4.2 *There exists an algorithm that, given any pushdown automaton
A, constructs a context-free grammar G such that $L(G) = L(A)$.*

Proof: (Sketch) We will begin by imposing some constraints on pushdown automata. As we will see, these constraints do not restrict the class of acceptable
languages. However, pushdown automata satisfying those constraints have a sort
of "standard form" helpful for transforming them into context-free grammars.

First, we will consider pushdown automata that accept by empty stack. As we
showed in Theorem 3.3.1, this condition does not restrict the class of acceptable
languages. Any pushdown automaton accepting by empty stack is called **simple**
if, for every transition $((s, a, \alpha), (q, \beta))$ it turns out that $\alpha \in \Gamma$ (that is, every
transition replaces the top symbol from the stack). We are going to convert any
pushdown automaton $M = (Q, \Sigma, \Gamma, s_0, \Delta)$ accepting by empty stack into a simple
automaton accepting the same language. However, there is one obstacle in the
original definition of the pushdown automaton that prevents such a conversion. In
the beginning of any computation, the stack is assumed to be empty, and, therefore,
the first transition $((s_0, a, \alpha), (q, \beta))$ must have $\alpha = e$. The problem can easily be
resolved if we change the definition of the pushdown automaton slightly. Namely,
we add to the alphabet Γ a new special "bottom marker" $\lhd \notin \Gamma$ and assume that
this symbol is placed on the bottom of the stack before the computation begins.
Now, every transition $((s_0, a, e), (q, \beta)) \in \Delta$ is converted to $((s_0, a, \lhd), (q, \beta\lhd))$, and,
for every state $q \in Q$, the transition $((q, e, \lhd), (q, e))$ is added to Δ [that is, if the
automaton M has accepted the input string by entering a configuration (q, e, e),
then the new automaton enters the configuration $(q, e, \lhd)$, erases the marker $\lhd$
from the bottom of the stack, and enters the same accepting configuration (q, e, e)].
The modified automaton clearly accepts the same language $L(A)$, and, for every
transition $((s, a, \alpha), (q, \beta))$, $|\alpha| \geq 1$.

Thus, we can assume that our pushdown automaton M is a sextuple $(S, \Sigma, \Gamma, s_0,$
$\lhd, \Delta)$, where $\lhd \in \Gamma$ is the special bottom marker and every transition "consults"
at least one symbol on the top of the stack. Now we can convert it to a simple
automaton accepting the same language. Consider any transition $((s, a, \alpha), (q, \beta))$.
Let α be $A_1 A_2 \ldots A_n$ for some $n > 1$. We can replace this transition by the set of
new transitions that sequentially pop symbols A_i, $i < n$ and replace the last symbol
A_n by β:

$$((s, e, A_1), (s_{A_1}, e))$$
$$((s_{A_1}, e, A_2), (s_{A_1 A_2}, e))$$
$$\vdots$$
$$((s_{A_1 A_2 \ldots A_{n-2}}, e, A_{n-1}), (s_{A_1 A_2 \ldots A_{n-1}}, e))$$
$$((s_{A_1 A_2 \ldots A_{n-1}}, a, A_n), (q, \beta))$$

where every $s_{A_1 A_2 \ldots A_i}$ for $i = 1, 2, \ldots, n - 1$ is a new state encoding the fact that the symbols A_1, A_2, ..., A_i have been popped. It is clear that, replacing each such transition with the above set, we get a simple pushdown automaton equivalent to the original automaton M. Thus, we can assume that M is simple.

Now consider any transition $((s, a, A), (q, B_1 B_2 \ldots B_n))$ (we have assumed that $A \in \Gamma$). We would like to replace it by a rule $\alpha \to \beta$ that will perform one step in a leftmost derivation of a string accepted by the automaton M. First, we will make a, a terminal symbol, a prefix of β. Then the input symbol a will appear as the leftmost symbol in the substring resulting from the application of this rule. Stack symbols A and $B_1, \ldots, B_n$ should probably represent nonterminals.

However, in implementing this approach directly, we will ignore states whose role is to "witness" which replacements $A \to B_1 B_2 \ldots B_n$ are valid. For instance, if, for (s, a, A) and $B_1 B_2 \ldots B_n$, there is no transition $((s, a, A), (q, B_1 B_2 \ldots B_n)) \in \Delta$, then the replacement $A \to B_1 B_2 \ldots B_n$ cannot be legitimate. Moreover, even if there were such a transition, the fact that M, performing the replacement $A \to B_1 B_2 \ldots B_n$, moves to state q, must be reflected in the rule. A solution to the problem is to introduce nonterminals $[s, A, p]$ for every $A \in \Gamma$ and all states $s, p \in Q$. Now, an application of the rule $\alpha \to \beta$ with α being $[s, A, p]$ and β being $a\gamma$ for some γ will correspond to the execution of the above transition.

Recall that for the transition we are considering, the automaton M from state s, reads the input symbol a, pops A from the stack, replaces it with $B_1 B_2 \ldots B_n$, and moves to state q. Where does q appear in the rule? From state q, the automaton M replaces B_1 on the stack and enters another state. At some point in the computation M will be in some state q' and have B_2 as the leftmost symbol on the stack. M will then replace it and enter some state, and so on. At some point, M replaces the last symbol B_n on the stack and enters state p. Hence, the p in $[s, A, p]$ represents the ultimate result of removing A from the stack. When A is ultimately removed from the stack, it will be replaced by a substring w of terminals that M has read from the input while moving from state s to p. In the derivation, accordingly, $[s, A, p]$ gets replaced at this point by w in the string being derived (Figure 3.7).

The rule $\alpha \to \beta$ formalizes the above reasoning. We agreed that our nonterminals are triples $[p, C, r]$ for states p, r, and stack symbols C. Thus, we define the rule $\alpha \to \beta$ as

$$[s, A, q_k] \to a[q, B_1, q_1][q_1, B_2, q_2] \ldots [q_{k-1}, B_k, q_k]$$

where $q_1, q_2, \ldots, q_k$ are arbitrary states in of M. Why can we take all possible sequences $q_1, q_2, \ldots, q_k$? What if M does not actually go through these states removing (ultimately) $B_1, B_2, \ldots, B_n$ from the stack? For example, there may be

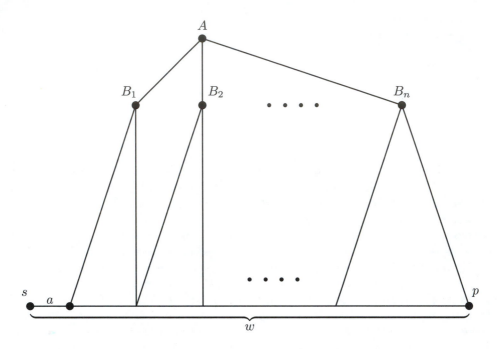

Figure 3.7 Schematic Parse Tree for w

no transition with the left triple (q, B_1, q_1) in Δ. Then the rule will never be applied. That is, some rules we have defined will never be used, but it does not enhance the set of derivable strings.

Now we can formally define the the grammar G. Let G be the quadruple (Σ, NT, R, S), where Σ is the input alphabet of M, $NT = \{S\} \cup \{[s, A, q] | A \in \Gamma, s, q \in Q\}$, and S is the special starting nonterminal. The set R contains the following rules:

1. For every $s \in Q$, the rule $S \to [s_0, \triangleleft, s]$, for every $s \in Q$,

2. The rule $[s, A, q] \to a$, for every $s, q \in Q$, every $a \in \Sigma \cup \{e\}$, and $A \in \Gamma$, if $((s, a, A)(q, e)) \in \Delta$,

3. The rule
$$[s, A, q_k] \to a[q, B_1, q_1][q_1, B_2, q_2] \ldots [q_{k-1}, B_k, q_k]$$
for every $s, q \in Q$, for every $a \in \Sigma \cup \{e\}$, if
$$((s, a, A)(q, B_1 B_2 \ldots B_k)) \in \Delta$$
for some $B_1, B_2, \ldots, B_k \in \Gamma$, for every sequence $q_1, q_2, \ldots, q_k$ of elements in Q.

The proof of the equality $L(M) = L(G)$ is based on the following characterization of all strings derivable from any nonterminal $[s, A, p]$.

Lemma 3.4.3 *For any $s, p \in Q$, any $A \in \Gamma$, and any string $w \in \Sigma^*$, the automaton M, starting in configuration (s, w, A), enters the configuration (p, e, e) if and only if w is derivable from the nonterminal $[s, A, p]$ in the grammar G.*

The lemma easily implies the equality $L(M) = L(A)$. If $w \in L(M)$ then, according to Lemma 3.4.3, if, starting at configuration $(s_0, w, \lhd)$, the automaton M arrives at (s, e, e) for some $s \in Q$, then w is derivable from the nonterminal $[s_0, \lhd, s]$ in the grammar G. To get a derivation of w from the starting nonterminal S, it is enough to apply the rule $S \to [s_0, \lhd, s]$ as the first step of derivation. If $w \in L(G)$, then we can drop the first step of derivation, assume that w is derivable from $[s_0, \lhd, s]$, and apply Lemma 3.4.3.

Both parts of the Lemma 3.4.3 can be proved using mathematical induction. One can show that, for any $w \in \Sigma^*, n > 0, s \in Q$, and for any $A \in \Gamma$

(a) If M, starting from configuration (s, A, q) for some $q \in Q$ arrives at the configuration (q, e, e) in n steps, then $[s, A, q] \Rightarrow^* w$ in G,

(b) If w is derivable in n steps from the nonterminal $[s, A, q]$ in the grammar G for some $q \in Q$, then M accepts w, starting from the configuration (s, A, q).

The detailed proofs of parts a and b are suggested in Exercises 3.34 and 3.35.

End Proof

Using the established equivalence of context-free grammars and pushdown automata, we can easily prove the following

Theorem 3.4.4 *Every regular language is context-free.*

Proof: Let A be a finite automaton accepting a language L. A can be viewed as a pushdown automaton that never uses its stack. Thus, L is accepted by a pushdown automaton, and, therefore, is context-free.

End Proof

3.5 Closure Properties

In Chapter 2 we found out that regular languages are closed under many set-theoretical operations. Which of these properties hold for context-free languages? We will show that context-free languages are closed under union, concatenation, and the Kleene star. However, the class of context-free languages is not closed under intersection; this will be shown in Section 3.6.

Theorem 3.5.1 *Let L and M be any two context-free languages. Then*

1. *the union $L \cup M$ is a context-free language;*

2. *the concatenation LM is a context-free language;*

3. *L^* is a context-free language.*

Proof: Let $G_1 = (\Sigma_1, NT_1, R_1, S_1)$ be a context-free grammar that generates L and $G_2 = (\Sigma_2, NT_2, R_2, S_2)$ be context-free grammar that generates M. Without loss of generality, we can assume that the sets of nonterminals NT_1 and NT_2 are disjoint, that is, do not intersect. Let $S \notin (NT_1 \cup NT_2)$ be a new nonterminal.

Part 1: The grammar G that generates the union $L \cup M$ is defined as

$$(\Sigma_1 \cup \Sigma_2, NT_1 \cup NT_2 \cup \{S\}, R_1 \cup R_2 \cup \{S \to S_1, S \to S_2\}, S)$$

It easily follows from the definition of G that $L \cup M \subseteq L(G)$. We also have to show that G does not generate strings $w \notin L \cup M$. Potentially, this could have happened, if NT_1, NT_2 had common nonterminals. However, we assumed that this is not the case. Thus, G generates the union of L and M.

Part 2: For concatenation LM, we will take the grammar

$$G = (\Sigma_1 \cup \Sigma_2, NT_1 \cup NT_2 \cup \{S\}, R_1 \cup R_2 \cup \{S \to S_1 S_2\}, S)$$

Part 3: For the Kleene star we will consider the grammar

$$G = (\Sigma_1, NT_1, R_1 \cup \{S_1 \to e, S_1 \to S_1 S_1\}, S_1)$$

$$\boxed{\text{End Proof}}$$

As already mentioned, the class of all context-free languages will be shown to be not closed under intersection. However, the intersection is context-free if one of the languages is *regular*.

Theorem 3.5.2 *The intersection of a context-free language L with a regular language M is a context-free language.*

Proof: Let $A = (Q_1, \Sigma, \Gamma, \Delta_1, s_1, F_1)$ be a pushdown automaton accepting L, and $B = (Q_2, \Sigma, \delta, s_2, F_2)$ is a deterministic finite automaton recognizing M. We "combine" A and B into a new pushdown automaton C whose states are elements of the *Cartesian product* of the sets Q_1 and Q_2. C simulates computations of A and B on any input string w *in parallel*. Only strings accepted by both A and B will be accepted by C. Since B does not employ a stack, we still can use one stack to handle the part of computation performed by A.

Formally, we define the pushdown automaton $C = (Q, \Sigma, \Gamma, \Delta, s_0, F)$ as follows:

1. Q is the Cartesian product $Q_1 \times Q_2$;

2. Σ and Γ are the same as in A;

3. $s_0 = (s_1, s_2)$;

4. $F = F_1 \times F_2$;

5. Δ is defined as follows.

   (a) For each transition $((q_1, a, \alpha), (p, \beta)) \in \Delta_1$ with $a \in \Sigma$, and for every state $q_2 \in Q_2$ of automaton B, the transition $(((q_1, q_2), a, \alpha), ((p, \delta(q_2, a)), \beta))$ is added to Δ.

   (b) For each transition $((q_1, e, \alpha), (p, \beta)) \in \Delta_1$ and any state $q_2 \in Q_2$, the transition $(((q_1, q_2), e, \alpha), ((p, q_2), \beta))$ is added to Δ (that is, A makes a move, but B does not, as it does not read any input).

Suppose w is accepted by both A and B. We will show that w is also accepted by C. Since w is accepted by A, there is a sequence of configurations, with transitions between them in A: $(s_1, w, e), \ldots, (f_1, e, e)$ for $f_1 \in F_1$. Since w is accepted by B, there is a sequence of configurations, with transitions between them in B: $(s_2, w), \ldots, (f_2, e)$ for $f_2 \in F_2$. Hence, by the construction of C above, there is a sequence of configurations, with transitions between them in C: $((s_1, s_2), w, e), \ldots, ((f_1, f_2), e, e)$. Since $(f_1, f_2) \in F_1 \times F_2 = F$, C accepts w.

Now suppose that C accepts w. We will show that both A and B accept w. There is a sequence of configurations, with transitions between them in C: $((s_1, s_2), w, e), \ldots, ((f_1, f_2), e, e)$, for $(f_1, f_2) \in F$. By the construction above, there is a computation in A: $(s_1, w, e), \ldots, (f_1, e, e)$ for $f_1 \in F_1$. Hence, A accepts w. Also by the construction, there is a computation in B: $(s_2, w), \ldots, (f_2, e)$ for $f_2 \in F_2$. Hence, B accepts w.

$\boxed{\text{End Proof}}$

Example 3.5.1 Consider the language L that contains all strings in the context-free language $\{a^n b^n | n = 0, 1, 2, \ldots\}$ except the string $aaabbb$. This language is context-free as it is the intersection of the language from Example 3.3.1 and the regular language

$$\{a, b\}^* - \{a, b\}^* aaabbb \{a, b\}^*$$

$\boxed{\text{End Example}}$

3.6   Languages That Are Not Context-Free

In Chapter 2 we proved the pumping lemma (Lemma 2.5.1) for regular languages that enabled us to show nonregularity of several languages. This result is based on the fact that a sufficiently long input string forces a finite automaton to enter some state more than once. That is, the automaton follows a loop in its diagram, which corresponds to a number of identical substrings in the input string forming a contiguous group $vv \ldots v$. Now, if we consider a sufficiently long derivation $S \Rightarrow^* w$ in a context-free grammar G, it must involve some nonterminal A more than once. That is, the derivation can be divided into the following phases:

$$S \Rightarrow^* uAz \Rightarrow^* uvAyz \Rightarrow^* uvxyz$$

This means that $A \Rightarrow^* x$ and $A \Rightarrow^* vAy$. The latter part of derivation can obviously be iterated as many times as we wish:

$$S \Rightarrow^* uAz \Rightarrow^* uvAyz \Rightarrow^* uv^2Ay^2z \Rightarrow^* uv^3Ay^3z \Rightarrow^* \ldots \Rightarrow^* uv^nxy^nz$$

We will generalize the above argument to show that this kind of "pumping" occurs in a sufficiently long derivation of any string $w \in L(G)$. We will also see that the strings u, v, x, y, z satisfy conditions similar to those in the pumping lemma for regular languages (Lemma 2.5.1).

First, we are going to define a number of notions that will give us an opportunity to obtain a helpful quantitative characteristics of parse trees. Let G be any context-free grammar. A **path** in a parse tree of G is either an empty sequence of nodes, or consists of a node, one of its descendants, and all the nodes between them. The **length** of a path is 0 if the path is empty, or the number of all nodes it contains minus one (which is the number of edges connecting all consecutive nodes in the path, using standard graphic representation of trees). The **height** of a parse tree is the length of its longest path. The **fanout** of G, denoted $f(G)$, is the greatest number of symbols on the right side of any rule in G. Note that the string of leaf nodes of any parse tree is the string derived in G using this parse tree. The following useful lemma shows that, for any string $w \in L(G)$, the parse tree for w contains a sufficiently long path.

Lemma 3.6.1 *If the string of the leaf nodes in a parse tree of G has length greater than $f(G)^h$, then the height of this tree is greater than h.*

Proof: To prove the statement of the lemma, we can prove its contraposition: The number of leaf nodes of a parse tree of G of height h is at most $f(G)^h$. We proceed by induction on h.

If $h = 1$, then the parse tree corresponds to just one rule of the grammar G. Therefore, the number of its leaf nodes cannot exceed $f(G) = f(G)^h$.

Now, suppose the statement is true for parse trees of height up to $h \geq 1$. Any parse tree of height $h+1$ consists of a root connected to at most $f(G)$ parse subtrees of height at most h. By the induction hypothesis, these subtrees have numbers of leaf nodes at most $f(G)^h$ each. Thus, the total number of leaf nodes in the given tree is at most $f(G)f(G)^h = f(G)^{h+1}$.

$$\boxed{\text{End Proof}}$$

Now we can prove the pumping lemma for context-free languages.

Lemma 3.6.2 *Let $G = (\Sigma, NT, R, S)$ be a context-free grammar. Then there exists a number n such that any string $w \in L(G)$ with length $|w| \geq n$ can be written as $w = uvxyz$ for some strings $u, v, x, y, z \in \Sigma^*$ such that*

1. $|v| > 0$, or $|y| > 0$

2. $|vxy| \leq n$

3. for any $k \geq 0, uv^k xy^k z \in L(G)$.

Proof: Let $n = f(G)^{|NT|+1}$. Consider any $w \in L(G)$ with length $|w| \geq n$. Let T be a parse tree with the root node S whose leaf nodes form w, and which has the *smallest* number of leaves among all parse trees for w (note that some leaves may be empty symbols e, which means that a parse tree can have any number of leaves $r \geq |w|$). Consider a path P of maximum length in T. Since $|w| > f(G)^{|NT|}$, it follows from Lemma 3.6.1 that path P has length at least $|NT| + 1$. The number of nodes on this path is, accordingly, at least $|NT| + 2$. Consider the end portion P' of P that has exactly $|NT| + 2$ nodes. Only one of these nodes (the leaf) is labeled as a terminal. Thus, there are at least two nodes in the portion P' labeled by the same nonterminal A. The paths P, P', and their results within the tree T are represented in Figure 3.8.

T' in Figure 3.8 represents the subtree corresponding to the portion P' of P. It is clear that the shaded part can be repeated any number of times, even 0 number of times. Repeating it k times for any $k \geq 0$, we obtain a string $uv^k xy^k z \in L(G)$. The length of P' is not greater than $|NT| + 1$, and as we began with the path P of maximum length in T, the height of T' is not greater than $|NT| + 1$ (otherwise, we would find a path consisting of the initial fragment of P and the end portion in T' that would be longer than P). Then, according to Lemma 3.6.1, $|vxy| \leq n$.

Now we have to show that $|v| > 0$ or $|y| > 0$. Suppose $|vy| = 0$. This means that $v = e$ and $u = e$. In this case, excluding the shaded part from the parse tree of Figure 3.8, we still get a parse tree for w. However, this parse tree would have fewer leaves than T, which contradicts our assumption that T has the smallest number of leaves among all parse trees for w.

$$\boxed{\text{End Proof}}$$

Now we can show that a number of languages are not context-free.

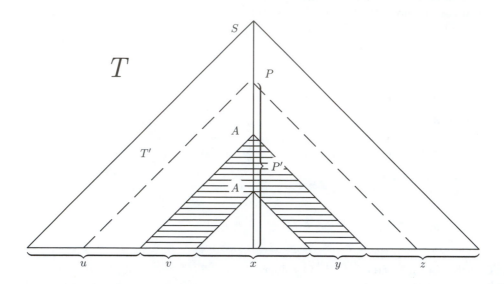

Figure 3.8 Schematic Parse Tree for $w = uvxyz$

Example 3.6.1 We apply Theorem 3.6.2 to show that the language

$$L = \{a^k b^k c^k | k = 0, 1, 2, \ldots\}$$

is not context-free.

Suppose L is a context-free language. Then we can apply Lemma 3.6.2. Let n be a large enough number mentioned in Lemma 3.6.2. Let us pick the string $w = a^n b^n c^n$ with the length $|w| = 3n > n$. Let u, v, x, y, z be the substrings of w satisfying the conditions of Lemma 3.6.2. As $|vxy| \leq n$, the string vxy contains at most two different symbols — a's and b's, or b's and c's. Lemma 3.6.2 does not tell which case takes place, so we have to consider both possibilities. We will assume that vxy contains just a's and b's (maybe, even only a's or only b's). As $|vy| > 0$, either v or y contains at least one symbol. Consider the string uv^2xy^2z. For at least one of the symbols a and b, the total number of occurrences of this symbol in the given string is greater than n. However, the number of c's has not increased. Thus, we got a string not in L, a contradiction. The second case (vxy contains only b's and c's) is treated similarly.

> End Example

Example 3.6.2 Sometimes direct applications of Lemma 3.6.2 can be difficult, however, we can get the desired result applying set-theoretical operations involving noncontext-free languages. Consider the language

$$L' = \{w | w \in \{a, b, c\}^*, w \text{ contains an equal number of } a\text{'s, } b\text{'s and } c\text{'s } \}$$

The language L from Example 3.6.1 is obviously the intersection of L' and the regular language represented by the expression $a^*b^*c^*$. If L' were context-free, then, according to Theorem 3.5.2, the language L from Example 3.6.1 would be context-free. Thus, we can conclude that L' is not context-free.

$$\boxed{\text{End Example}}$$

Example 3.6.3 Now consider the language $L = \{tt | t \in \{a, b\}^*\}$. This language seems to be similar to the context-free language of palindromes (of even length). However, a pushdown automaton is not appropriate for recognition of strings in this language. Having completed reading the prefix t, the machine must match the first symbol of the coming suffix t with the *first* symbol of the prefix, but it would be located on the *bottom* of the stack. Still, this reasoning is not proof that L is noncontext-free. To formally establish this fact, we will apply the Pumping Lemma 3.6.2.

Thus, suppose L is context-free. Let n be a large enough number from Lemma 3.6.2. We must now carefully choose a string w to apply Lemma 3.6.2. Our objective is to "pump in" or "cut out" substrings v and y to get a new string not in L. An easy way would be to choose $w = a^{2n}$. However, pumping in or cutting out any even number of a's would result in a string still in L. What if we considered another extreme, an arbitrary $w = tt$ for some t? Then we would not have any means to "control" how pumping or cutting out v and y affected w. It still could be a string in the language L.

Our choice for w is the string $w = a^n b^n a^n b^n$. Its length is $4n > n$, and it is in L. Let us apply Lemma 3.6.2 to this string and consider the string vxy. As its length does not exceed n, it may be a substring of either the prefix $a^n b^n$, or the "middle" $b^n a^n$, or the "tail" $a^n b^n$. As Lemma 3.6.2 does not tell which case takes place, we must consider all three of them. We will pick the tail case and leave other two cases to the reader. Consider the string uxy obtained from w. As at least one of v or y is nonempty, uxz can be represented as $a^n b^n a^m b^k$, where m or k (or both of them) is smaller than n. Now assume that uxz is ss for some s with $|s| < 2n$. Then two cases are possible: (1) First, s begins with an a and ends with a b; (2) s is the prefix a^n (this is the case when both m and k are zeros). In both cases the second s begins with b, a contradiction.

$$\boxed{\text{End Example}}$$

Using Example 3.6.1, we can establish the following.

Theorem 3.6.3 *The class of context-free languages is not closed under intersection or complementation.*

Proof: The noncontext-free language L in the Example 3.6.1 is the intersection of context-free languages $L_1 = \{a^n b^n c^k | n, k = 0, 1, 2, \ldots\}$ and $L_2 = \{a^k b^n c^n | k, n = 0, 1, 2, \ldots\}$ (see Exercise 3.5). Thus, context-free languages are not closed under intersection. As the intersection $L_1 \cap L_2$ of any two languages L_1 and L_2 can be represented as

$$\left(\overline{\overline{L_1} \cup \overline{L_2}}\right)$$

context-free languages are not closed under complementation either.

End Proof

More examples of applications of the pumping lemma for context-free languages are suggested in the exercises.

3.7   Chomsky Normal Form

In the previous chapter we found a number of algorithms solving important algorithmic problems about finite automata: emptiness (Algorithm 2.6.2), equivalence (Algorithm 2.6.4), and so on. In this section we will show that some of these problems can be solved by algorithms for context-free languages.

The Membership Problem "$w \in L(G)$" for any w and any context-free grammar G?

The Emptiness Problem "$L(G) = \emptyset$" for any context-free grammar G?

The Finiteness Problem "Is the language $L(G)$ finite" for any context-free grammar G?.

We will see that the membership problem is the key for solving the two other problems. Thus, we first concentrate on an algorithm solving the membership problem: Given a context-free grammar G and a string w, decide if $w \in L(G)$. How can we attack the problem? We could use a pushdown automaton A accepting $L(G)$. Just run A on w to find out if it accepts. However, A may be nondeterministic. Thus, the fact that one computation results in nonacceptance does not mean that all computations are nonaccepting. Given the rules of G, we may try to generate all possible derivations. If $w \in L(G)$, it will show up eventually among the derived strings, but what if it is not in L? If, given w, we could bound the length of possible derivations of w by some number, say, $g(w)$, the problem would be solved by trying all derivations of the length up to $g(w)$. If w is not found, then it is not in $L(G)$. Can we come up with such a bound on the length of the derivations of w? It would be possible, if every rule in the grammar G *increased* the length of the sentential form it was applied to. Then no derivation longer than $|w|$ could possibly generate w. Accordingly, we could just generate all derivations of length up to $|w|$ and check if w is among generated strings. However, this idea cannot be applied directly as a context-free grammar may contain rules such as $A \to e$ or $A \to B$ or $A \to a$, which do not increase the length of a string being derived. The rules of the type $A \to a$ cannot increase the length of derivation for w indefinitely. Each application of such a rule eliminates one nonterminal, replacing it by a symbol in w, so no more that $|w|$ applications of such rules are possible in any derivation of w. Rules $A \to e$ and $A \to B$ are more problematic. A rule $A \to e$ decreases the length of a string being derived, and a rule $A \to B$ may be a part of a "loop" $A \to B \ldots B \to A$. In both these cases there is no way to bound the length of derivation in advance. Fortunately, as we will show below, these specific types of rules can be eliminated, while preserving the power of context-free grammars. Moreover, the length of the right-hand side of any rule can be limited by 2.

Definition 3.7.1 *A context-free grammar is said to be in* **Chomsky normal form** *if every rule in the grammar is of one of the following two types:*

$$A \to BC$$

$$A \to a$$

where A, B, C are nonterminals and a is a terminal.

It is easy to see that a language $L(G)$ for a grammar G in Chomsky normal form cannot contain the empty string. Thus, not every grammar can have an equivalent Chomsky normal form. However, if we forget about the empty string, transformation to Chomsky normal form is possible.

Theorem 3.7.1 *There exists an algorithm that transforms any context-free grammar G into a context-free grammar G' in Chomsky normal form such that $L(G') = L(G) - \{e\}$*

Proof: Let $G = (\Sigma, NT, R, S)$ be a context-free grammar. Our algorithm will consist of three "subprograms." The first one, Algorithm 3.7.1, given any context-free grammar G, eliminates all rules of the form $A \to e$. The second, Algorithm 3.7.2 eliminates the rules of the form $A \to B$. The third, Algorithm 3.7.3, converts any rule $A \to \alpha$ with $|\alpha| \geq 2$ to an equivalent group of rules of the form $B \to CD$.

Algorithm 3.7.1 Let us call a nonterminal A **erasable** if $A \Rightarrow^* e$. It is easy to see that a nonterminal A is erasable if and only

1. There is a rule $A \to e$ in G, or

2. There is a rule $A \to B_1 B_2 \ldots B_n$ in G, where all nonterminals $B_1, B_2, \ldots, B_n$ are erasable.

Using the above characterization of the erasable nonterminals, apply the following procedure to find the set E of all erasable nonterminals:

1. Set $E := \emptyset$.

2. Add to E all nonterminals in the left-hand sides of rules satisfying 1.

3. While there is a rule $A \to B_1 B_2 \ldots B_n \in R$ with $B_1, B_2, \ldots, B_n \in E$ and $A \notin E$, add A to E.

Now, for every rule $A \to \alpha$ in G, Algorithm 3.7.1 adds to R all rules obtained by eliminating one or more erasable nonterminals in α. For example, if G contains the rule $A \to BCD$ and C and D are erasable, add the rules

$$
\begin{aligned}
A &\to B \\
A &\to BC \\
A &\to BD.
\end{aligned}
$$

Finally, eliminate from R all rules of the type $A \to e$ and terminate.

> End Algorithm

The result of applying Algorithm 3.7.1 to G is a grammar G_1 that does not generate e. Other than that, any derivation in G can obviously be simulated by a derivation in G_1. Thus, $L(G) - \{e\} = L(G_1)$.

Algorithm 3.7.2 operates similarly to Algorithm 3.7.1, using nonterminals instead of e.

Algorithm 3.7.2 For any nonterminal A in G, let $NT(A)$ be the set $\{B | B \in NT, A \Rightarrow^* B\}$ of all nonterminals derivable from A. Find the set $NT(A)$ using a procedure similar to the one used by Algorithm 3.7.1 to find E:

1. Set $NT(A) := \{A\}$.

2. While there is a rule $B \to C$ with $B \in NT(A)$ and $C \notin NT(A)$, add C to $NT(A)$.

For every pair (A, B) such that $B \in NT(A)$ and every rule $B \to \alpha$ with $\alpha \notin NT$, add the rule $A \to \alpha$ to R. For example, if G contains the rule $B \to CD$ and $NT(A) = \{A, B\}$, then the rule $A \to CD$ is added to R. Finally, eliminate all rules of the type $A \to B$ from R and terminate.

> End Algorithm

It is clear that any derivation in G can be simulated by a derivation in the grammar obtained by application of Algorithm 3.7.2. If G contains the rules $A \to B$ and $B \to \alpha$, then replacing them by $A \to \alpha$ creates the same opportunities as their combination.

Algorithm 3.7.3 This algorithm converts any rule $A \to \alpha$ with $|\alpha| > 1$ to a group of rules $B \to C_1 C_2$, where C_1 and C_2 are nonterminals. Given any rule $A \to B_0 B_1 \ldots B_k$, where $B_i \in (\Sigma \bigcup NT), 1 \le i \le k$, the algorithm converts it to the rules

$$
\begin{aligned}
A &\to X_{B_0} X_{B_1 B_2 \ldots B_k} \\
X_{B_1 B_2 \ldots B_k} &\to X_{B_1} X_{B_2 B_3 \ldots B_k} \\
X_{B_2 B_3 \ldots B_k} &\to X_{B_2} X_{B_3 B_4 \ldots B_k} \\
&\vdots \\
X_{B_{k-1} B_k} &\to X_{B_{k-1} B_k}
\end{aligned}
$$

where X_{B_0}, X_{B_1}, ..., X_{B_k}, $X_{B_1 B_2 \ldots B_k}$, $X_{B_2 B_3 \ldots B_k}$, ..., $X_{B_{k-1} B_k}$ are *new* nonterminals. Now, if B_i is a nonterminal, then the algorithm uses just B_i instead of X_{B_i}. If B_i is a terminal, the algorithm adds the rule $X_{B_i} \to B_i$ to the set of rules.

This step is described by the following example. The rule $A \to BabDBE$ is replaced by

$$
\begin{aligned}
A &\to B X_{abDBE} \\
X_{abDBE} &\to X_a X_{bDBE} \\
X_{bDBE} &\to X_b X_{DBE} \\
X_{DBE} &\to D X_{BE} \\
X_{BE} &\to BE \\
X_a &\to a \\
X_b &\to b.
\end{aligned}
$$

The new nonterminals are used in the above set of rules for $A \to BabDBE$ only. Thus, the new set of rules is equivalent to the given rule. A string w can be derived from $A \to BabDBE$ if and only if it can be derived from the set of rules replacing it. The obtained set of rules satisfies the required condition, so terminate.

> End Algorithm

To complete the proof of the theorem, we consecutively apply Algorithms 3.7.1, 3.7.2, and 3.7.3 to the grammar G. The grammar G_1 obtained by application of

Algorithm 3.7.1 satisfies the condition $L(G) - \{e\} = L(G_1)$. The application of Algorithm 3.7.2 to G_1 and Algorithm 3.7.3 to the result preserves equivalence. Thus, the resulting context-grammar G' satisfies the required conditions.

$$\boxed{\text{End Proof}}$$

Example 3.7.1 We convert the following grammar G to Chomsky normal form:

$$
\begin{aligned}
S &\rightarrow ABCa \\
A &\rightarrow aAbb \\
A &\rightarrow e \\
B &\rightarrow bB \\
B &\rightarrow b \\
B &\rightarrow AC \\
C &\rightarrow aCa \\
C &\rightarrow e.
\end{aligned}
$$

First we apply Algorithm 3.7.1 to eliminate the rules $A \rightarrow e$ and $C \rightarrow e$. Algorithm 3.7.1 determines that A, B, and C are the erasable nonterminals and adds the following rules to the grammar:

$$
\begin{aligned}
S &\rightarrow BCa \\
S &\rightarrow ACa \\
S &\rightarrow ABa \\
S &\rightarrow Aa \\
S &\rightarrow Ba \\
S &\rightarrow Ca \\
S &\rightarrow a \\
A &\rightarrow abb \\
B &\rightarrow A \\
B &\rightarrow C \\
C &\rightarrow aa
\end{aligned}
$$

Algorithm 3.7.2 determines that $NT(S) = \{S\}$, $NT(A) = \{A\}$, $NT(B) = \{B, A, C\}$, $NT(C) = \{C\}$, eliminates the rules $B \rightarrow A, B \rightarrow C$ and adds the rules

$$
\begin{aligned}
B &\rightarrow aAbb \\
B &\rightarrow abb \\
B &\rightarrow ab
\end{aligned}
$$

$$B \rightarrow aCa$$
$$B \rightarrow aa$$

Algorithm 3.7.3 completes the transformation, replacing 17 rules that do not have exactly two nonterminals on the right-hand side by the following set:

$$S \rightarrow AX_{BCa}$$
$$X_{BCa} \rightarrow BX_{Ca}$$
$$X_{Ca} \rightarrow CX_a$$
$$X_a \rightarrow a$$
$$A \rightarrow X_a X_{Abb}$$
$$X_{Abb} \rightarrow AX_{bb}$$
$$X_{bb} \rightarrow X_b X_b$$
$$X_b \rightarrow b$$
$$B \rightarrow X_b B$$
$$C \rightarrow X_a X_{Ca}$$
$$X_{Ca} \rightarrow CX_a$$
$$S \rightarrow BX_{Ca}$$
$$S \rightarrow AX_{Ba}$$
$$X_{Ba} \rightarrow BX_a$$
$$S \rightarrow AX_a$$
$$S \rightarrow BX_a$$
$$S \rightarrow CX_a$$
$$A \rightarrow X_a X_{bb}$$
$$C \rightarrow X_a X_a$$
$$B \rightarrow X_a X_{Abb}$$
$$B \rightarrow X_a X_{bb}$$
$$B \rightarrow X_a X_a$$
$$B \rightarrow X_a X_{Ca}$$

End Example

Now we can design an algorithm that solves the membership problem.

Theorem 3.7.2 *There exists an algorithm that, given any context-free grammar G and any string w, decides if $w \in L(G)$.*

Proof: We consider two cases: $(1)w = e$ and $(2)w \neq e$. In the first case we have $S \Rightarrow^* e$. That is, S is an erasable terminal, as defined in the proof of Theorem 3.7.1. Therefore, to decide if $e \in L(G)$, we can apply Algorithm 3.7.1 to determine if S is an erasable nonterminal.

Now consider the second case. We can apply Theorem 3.7.1 to convert G into a grammar G' in Chomsky normal form. As $w \neq e$, obviously $w \in L(G)$ if and only if $w \in L(G')$. Therefore, it remains to determine if $w \in L(G')$. Any derivation of w in G' can use at most $|w|$ rules of the type $A \to BC$, as every application of such a rule increases the length of a string being derived. Then, any derivation of w can use at most $|w|$ rules of the type $A \to a$; otherwise the derived string would be longer than w. Thus, to determine if $w \in L(G')$, we can generate all derivations of the length up to $2|w|$ and check if w shows up among the derived strings.

End Proof

Now we can design algorithms solving the emptiness and finiteness problems. First, we prove a useful lemma.

Lemma 3.7.3 *For any context-free grammar G, there exists a number n such that*

1. If $L(G) \neq \emptyset$, then there exists $w \in L(G)$ with the length $|w| < n$;

2. If $L(G)$, is infinite then there exists $w \in L(G)$ with the length $n \leq |w| < 2n$.

Proof: We can assume that G is in Chomsky normal form. A simple application of the pumping lemma (Lemma 3.6.2) proves part 1: If a string w of minimal length has length $|w| \geq n$, then applying the pumping lemma ($k = 0$ case) we a get a string w' of a shorter length. If w' is still too long, we can repeat the pumping as needed to get a string in $L(G)$ with length less than n.

To prove part 2 we can again apply the pumping lemma (Lemma 3.6.2), though this time its application is more subtle. Assume that $L(G)$ is infinite, n is the constant provided by Lemma 3.6.2, and there are no strings w in the language with the length $n \leq |w| < 2n$. Since the language $L(G)$ is infinite, there exist strings $w \in L(G)$ with length at least $2n$ (otherwise, the language $L(G)$ would be finite). Let us choose the string $w \in L(G)$ of minimal length among them. As $|w| \geq 2n$, $w = uvxyz$ for some u, v, x, y, z satisfying the conditions of the pumping lemma (Lemma 3.6.2), then $uxz \in L(G)$. Since the total length of v and y does not exceed n, the length of uxz must be greater than or equal to n. As, according to our assumption there are no strings in $L(G)$ with the length between n and $2n$, we must conclude that $|uxz| \geq 2n$. However, this contradicts our assumption that w has the minimal length among all strings in $L(G)$ with the length greater or equal $2n$.

End Proof

Theorem 3.7.4 *There exist algorithms that, given any context-free grammar* G, *decide if* $L(G) = \emptyset$ *and if* $L(G)$ *is finite.*

Proof: First, we can apply the algorithm guaranteed by Theorem 3.7.2 to determine if $e \in L(G)$. If not, then we can find the grammar G' in Chomsky normal form generating the language $L(G) - \{e\}$. Let n be the number in Lemma 3.7.3 for G'. For every string w with the length $|w| < n$, we can test the membership $w \in L(G')$. If no such w is in $L(G')$, then, according to Lemma 3.7.3, the language $L(G')$ is empty.

For finiteness, one must test membership for all strings w with the length between n and $2n$. If there is no such string in $L(G')$, then according to Lemma 3.7.3, the language $L(G')$ must be finite.

$$\boxed{\text{End Proof}}$$

3.8 Determinism

Solving the membership problem discussed in Section 3.7 is an important part of every compiler. So-called *parsers* determine if statements in your programs are syntactically correct, that is, if they belong to the programming language generated by an appropriate context-free grammar. As we have shown, there exists an algorithm that solves the problem of parsing for any context-free language. However, computer implementations of our algorithm turn out to be impractical as they are too slow for handling programs containing, sometimes, thousands of instructions. Many other, much more efficient, parsing algorithms have been developed over the years, making compilers more and more feasible. Most of these algorithms, in one way or another, simulate computations by pushdown automata, whose computational power, as the reader has learned, is equivalent to the computational power of context-free grammars. The major reason why pushdown automata are simulated by syntactical analyzers is that they provide a natural data structure for their computer implementation: the stack. However, some pushdown automata cannot be simulated efficiently by computer programs since they are nondeterministic. For example, a pushdown automaton recognizing the language of palindromes $\{w | w = w^R\}$ nondeterministically "guesses" the middle of the input string w to begin matching the "tail" of the string with the reversed half stored in the stack. Can we eliminate nondeterminism preserving computational power of pushdown automata? For finite automata, we found a positive solution. Every nondeterministic automaton can be transformed to an equivalent deterministic one (Theorem 2.3.1). Unfortunately, as we will show below, some nondeterministic pushdown automata do not have deterministic counterparts.

First we are going to formally define what a deterministic pushdown automaton is. What we want is to eliminate the possibility of making a choice. If a pushdown automaton A were in any configuration C, it should be able to apply *at most one* transition to carry out the next step of computation. First we have to eliminate transitions $((s, e, e), (q, e))$ that give pushdown automata an opportunity to just "jump" from one state to another, without reading anything from input tape or stack or even changing the content of stack. Now suppose we eliminated such transitions. Let us call two transitions $((s, a, \alpha), (q, \beta))$ and $((s', a', \alpha'), (q', \beta'))$ *compatible* if

- $s = s'$,

- $a = a'$ or $a = e$ or $a' = e$, and

- either α is a prefix of α', or α' is a prefix of α.

It is easy to see that, if no two transitions are compatible, then there will never be a choice of applicable transitions. Thus, we get the following.

Definition 3.8.1 *A pushdown automaton A is called* **deterministic** *if it has no distinct compatible transitions and no transitions*

$$((s, e, e), (q, e))$$

Note that we have not eliminated transitions $((s, e, \alpha), (q, \beta))$ with β nonempty. Unlike similar transitions in finite automata, these transitions do not make pushdown automata nondeterministic. Their application depends on the content of the stack and will change only the stack contents.

Consider the language $L = \{a^n b^n | n = 0, 1, 2, \ldots\}$ and the pushdown automaton accepting this language in Example 3.3.1. The pushdown automaton satisfies Definition 3.8.1. Thus it is deterministic, which is consistent with our intuition about the language L in that one does not have to make any "guesses" to identify strings in the language. On the other hand, the automaton in Example 3.3.2 is not deterministic. The conditions of Definition 3.8.1 are violated on two counts:

- Transition 3 is compatible with both transitions 1 and 2.

- Transition 3 is a "jump" of the type $((s, e, e), (q, e))$.

Transition 3 implements the "guess" of the middle of the input string, which is essentially a nondeterministic step.

We are about to define the class of deterministic context-free languages. However, there is one problem. Consider Example 3.3.3. Intuitively, the language of all strings having equal numbers of a's and b's is deterministic. However, the machine in Example 3.3.3 is nondeterministic, since transition 8 is compatible with transition 5. Moreover, there does not seem to exist any obvious way to make the automaton deterministic. The automaton has to "guess" the end of the string to remove the bottom marker from the stack. One faces a similar problem trying to design a deterministic pushdown automaton for the language $a^* \cup \{a^n b^n | n = 0, 1, 2, \ldots\}$. Any such automaton should have a transition $((s, a, e), (s, a))$ pushing a's onto the stack. However, if no b's follow a group of a's, the automaton must apply a transition of the type $((s, e, a), (f, e))$ to begin "cleaning" the stack. Intuitively, this step is not nondeterministic, since there is nothing depending on the input, and the transition $((s, a, e), (s, a))$ cannot be applied. However, formally the two transitions are compatible, making the machine nondeterministic. Our examples show that the problem lies with "sensing" the end of the input string. If transitions of the type $((s, e, \alpha), (q, \beta))$ were applied just at the end of the program, when all the input had been read, the problem would be solved. To force the machine to follow this rule, we must make it "sense" the empty symbol e after the input string. A more convenient way that does not require a different "interpretation" of transitions depending on what portion of the input has been read is to assume that every input string is appended by the special "end marker" $, where $ \notin \Sigma$ is a new symbol being used just for the purpose of marking the end of the input. Thus, with every language $L \subseteq \Sigma^*$, we associate the language $L\$ = \{w\$ | w \in L\}$.

Definition 3.8.2 *A language L is called* **deterministic context-free** *if the language $L\$ is accepted by some deterministic pushdown automaton.*

An obvious observation shows that any deterministic context-free language L is context-free. A deterministic pushdown automaton A accepting $L\$ can easily be transformed into a (nondeterministic) automaton A' that "guesses" the end of the string and then simulates the part of A that operates after reading $ (see Example 3.3.3).

We are going to show that the class of deterministic context-free languages is closed under complement. We will use this fact to show that some context-free languages are not deterministic.

Theorem 3.8.1 *The class of deterministic context-free languages is closed under complement.*

Proof: Consider a language $L\$ accepted by a deterministic pushdown automaton A. We can assume that A is *simple* and accepting by empty store, as defined in Section 3.4. Then, as in the proof of Theorem 3.4.2, we assume that the initial configuration contains the bottom marker $\lhd$ on the stack, every transition pops one symbol from the stack, and the marker $\lhd$ is removed at the end of every computation. We defined simple pushdown automata assuming nondeterminism and acceptance by empty stack, but it is clear that any deterministic finite automaton accepting by empty stack can easily be transformed into a simple deterministic pushdown automaton satisfying the above conditions and accepting by empty stack.

The obvious idea seems to reverse accepting by empty stack to accepting by nonempty stack, similar to flipping the favorable and nonfavorable states in deterministic finite automata (the idea used in the proof of Theorem 2.4.1). That is, the automaton A' for the complement $\Sigma^* - L$ would have accepted any string w by empty stack if A had a nonempty stack in the final configuration on w. However, this idea does not work, at least, directly. A' must complete reading the input, and a string w may be rejected (not accepted) by A, because A *never completed reading the input*. This situation can occur because of two reasons. First, A may reach a configuration C, at which no transition can be applied. Secondly, A may enter a configuration C from which it can apply an infinite sequence of transitions $((s, e, \alpha), (q, \beta))$ that do not read any input. Such configurations C can be called **dead ends**. Being in such a configuration C, a deterministic pushdown automaton A can neither complete reading the input, nor even reduce the length of data in the stack.

We are going to show that every simple deterministic pushdown automaton can be transformed into an equivalent deterministic pushdown automaton without dead ends. Note that our automaton A is simple: Every move is determined by (1) current state s, (2) the input symbol to be read a, and (3) the top stack symbol A. Thus, only this part of any configuration C determines if the configuration is dead or not. We can say that the triple (s, a, A) is a **dead end** if, from any configuration C, A must apply a transition with left-hand triple (s, a, A) and then it never reaches either configuration (q, e, α) (that is, it never reaches the end of the input), or a configuration (q, a, e) (empty stack with some input to be read). Thus, we can replace whole dead-end configuration $C = (s, u, \alpha)$ by dead-end triples (s, a, A). Such triples form a subset $DeadEnds$ of all triples that are left-hand sides of the transitions in Δ. Determining which triples are dead ends is a different problem. We can assume that the set $DeadEnds$ is given to us. This step of construction is sort of "existential" in that we claim that the finite set $DeadEnds$ *exists*, but we do not describe how to find it. The goal of construction is now clear. We have to transform A so that when A' reaches a dead end, it just completes reading the input and empties the stack (thus, accepting the input string).

Thus suppose $(s, a, A) \in DeadEnds$. First we remove all transitions in Δ that are compatible with (s, a, A). This will guarantee that A' will not get stuck or enter an indefinite loop when it reaches (s, a, A). Then, we add to Δ the transition $((s, a, A), (q, e))$ that reads a and pops A from the stack. Here, q is a new state. We add also the transitions $((q, b, e), (q, e))$ for all $b \in \Sigma$ and $((q, \$, e), (p, e))$ (where p is a new state) that A' can apply to complete reading the input. This last step renders A' not simple, but this is not a problem. Finally, we add to Δ the transitions $((p, e, B), (p, e))$ for all $B \in \Gamma$ to complete "cleaning" the stack. To complete the construction of A', we must make sure that when A completes reading the input and empties its stack (removing $\lhd$ on its last step), A' does not "clean" the stack, and if A completes reading the input, but does not accept it, A' completes reading the input and empties the stack (thus, accepting it). Obviously, this can be done, preserving determinism.

The automaton A' with the new set of transitions Δ is clearly deterministic. If A does not accept a string $w\$$, since it never completes reading the input, A' obviously accepts $w\$$ as it does not have dead-end configurations, and, therefore, always completes reading the input. For all other cases, acceptance of $w\$ \notin L\$$ and nonacceptance of $w\$ \in L\$$ follows from the rest of our construction.

End Proof

Theorem 3.8.2 *There exist context-free languages that are not deterministic.*

Proof: Consider the language $L = \{a^n b^m c^k | n \neq m \text{ or } m \neq k\}$. This language is obviously context-free. We are going to show that it is not deterministic context-free. For, if it were, then its complement $\overline{L}$ would be deterministic context-free, and, therefore, context-free. The intersection of $\overline{L}$ with the regular language $a^*b^*c^*$ is the language $\{a^n b^n c^n | n = 0, 1, 2, \ldots\}$ that is not context-free. However, according to Theorem 3.5.2, it must be context-free. Thus, the language L cannot be deterministic context-free.

End Proof

In many applications context-free grammars specifying programming languages are converted into deterministic pushdown automata to implement parsers that check the syntactical correctness of programs.

Exercises

---------   **Section 3.1**   ---------

In all grammars below, capital letters are nonterminals, lowercase letters are terminals, and S is the initial nonterminal. Grammars are determined only by giving the set of rules.

Exercise 3.1 Consider the grammar

$$G = S \rightarrow SS, S \rightarrow aS, S \rightarrow b$$

a) Give a derivation for the string $aabaaab$.

b) Describe the language $L(G)$.

Exercise 3.2 Consider the grammar

$$G = S \rightarrow aS, S \rightarrow aSbS, S \rightarrow e$$

a) Give a derivation for the string $aaabaab$.

b) ◆Describe the language $L(G)$.

Exercise 3.3 Consider the grammar

$$G = S \rightarrow AB, A \rightarrow aAa, B \rightarrow bBb, A \rightarrow e, B \rightarrow e$$

a) Give a derivation for the string $aaaabbbbbb$.

b) ◆Describe the language $L(G)$.

Exercise 3.4 Alter the grammar in Example 3.1.3 to generate the language $L = \{w | w = w^R\}$ of all palindromes.

Exercise 3.5 Construct context free-grammars that generate the following languages:

a) $L_1 = \{a^n b^n c^k | n, k = 0, 1, 2, ...\}$

b) $L_2 = \{a^n b^k c^k | n, k = 0, 1, 2, ...\}$

Exercise 3.6 Consider the grammar $G = \{S \rightarrow aSbS, S \rightarrow bSaS, S \rightarrow e\}$.

a) Give a derivation for the strings *aaabbabb* and *baaaabbabb*.

b) ◆ Describe the language $L(G)$.

Exercise 3.7 Using the grammars from Examples 3.1.5 and 3.1.6, derive the following segment of a program in C/C++:

$u = v - b;$
while$(a > v)\{u = a + a; \};$

Exercise 3.8 Construct a grammar that generates the language $L = \{a^n u | u \in \{a, b\}^*, |u| = n, n = 0, 1, 2, \ldots\}$.

Exercise 3.9 Construct grammars that generate the following languages:

a) ◆ $L_1 = \{a^n b^n a^m b^m | n, m = 0, 1, 2, \ldots\}$

b) ◆ $L_2 = \{a^n b^{n+m} a^m | n, m = 0, 1, 2, \ldots\}$

c) ◆◆ $L_3 = \{a^n b^m a^p b^r | n, m = 0, 1, 2, \ldots, n + m = p + r\}$

d) ◆ $L_4 = \{a^n b^m | n, m = 0, 1, 2, \ldots, n \leq 2m\}$

Exercise 3.10 ◆ Construct a grammar that generates the language of all identifiers represented by the regular expression $[A - Z]([A - Z] \cup [a - z] \cup [0 - 9])^*$ (cf. Example 2.4.5).

Exercise 3.11 ◆ Construct a grammar that generates all regular expressions over the alphabet $\{a, b\}$.

Exercise 3.12 Consider the grammar in Example 3.1.5. Suppose parentheses $(,)$ have been dropped from all rules. Give two different parse trees for the string $v + v * v$.

Section 3.2

Exercise 3.13 Consider the grammar $\{S \to aSb, S \to abS, S \to e\}$.

a) Show that the grammar is ambiguous.

b) ◆ Find an equivalent unambiguous grammar.

Exercise 3.14 Consider the grammar $\{S \to aSb, S \to aaSb, S \to e\}$.

a) Show that the grammar is ambiguous.

b) ◆◆ Find an equivalent unambiguous grammar.

Exercise 3.15 Consider the grammar $\{S \to ABAB, A \to aA, B \to bB, A \to e, B \to e\}$.

a) Show that the grammar is ambiguous.

b) ◆◆ Find an equivalent unambiguous grammar.

Exercise 3.16 Let G be a context-free grammar. Show that the relation $R(x, y)$ = "*x and y have the same parse tree*" defined for all derivations $x = (S \Rightarrow^* u), y = (S \Rightarrow^* w)$ for any $u, w \in L(G)$ is an equivalence relation.

Exercise 3.17 Give an ambiguous grammar to generate "if ... then ... else" statements, in which the statement

$$\text{if } a \text{ then if } b \text{ then } c \text{ else } d$$

would have two different parse trees.

Section 3.3

Exercise 3.18 Give three different computations of the pushdown automaton from Example 3.3.2 on the string *aabaab*.

Exercise 3.19 Trace the pushdown automaton of Example 3.3.3 on the following strings:

a) *aabbb*

b) *aabababb*

Exercise 3.20 Consider the following pushdown automaton

1. $((s, a, e), (s, a))$

2. $((s, b, a), (f, e))$

3. $((f, b, a), (f, e))$

4. $((f, a, a), (f, e))$

where s is the initial state and f is the favorable state.

a) Give computations of the pushdown automaton on the strings *aaabba*, *abbaaa*, *aabba*, and *aaaababa*. Determine which of the strings are accepted by the pushdown automaton.

b) Describe the language accepted by the pushdown automaton.

Exercise 3.21 Consider the following pushdown automaton

1. $((s, a, e), (s, c))$

2. $((s, b, e), (s, c))$

3. $((s, b, e), (f, e))$

4. $((f, a, c), (f, e))$

5. $((f, b, c), (f, e))$

where s is the initial state and f is the favorable state.

a) Show that the strings *aababaaab* and *baaabbaab* are accepted by the pushdown automaton. Show that the strings *aabbabbaa* and *abbbabbbb* are not accepted. Show accepting computations for accepted strings and nonaccepting computations for the strings that are not accepted (you may show one to two nonaccepting computations and describe how other computations are similar to those shown).

b) Describe the language accepted by the pushdown automaton.

Exercise 3.22 Consider the language $\{a^m b^{2m} | m = 0, 1, 2, \ldots\}$. Construct a pushdown automaton that accepts it.

Exercise 3.23 As defined in Section 3.3, given any string w, let $n_a(w)$ denote the number of occurrences of the symbol a in the string w. Construct a pushdown automaton that accepts the language $\{w | w \in \{a, b\}^*, n_a(w) = 2n_b(w)\}$.

Exercise 3.24 Construct pushdown automata accepting the following languages:

a) $L_1 = \{a^k b^k c^i | k, i \geq 0\}$

b) $L_2 = \{a^k b^i c^i | k, i \geq 0\}$

Exercise 3.25 ◆ Construct a pushdown automaton that accepts the language $\{a^i b^j c^k | i = j \text{ or } i = k \text{ for } i > 0\}$.

Exercise 3.26 ◆ Construct a pushdown automaton that accepts the language $\{a^i b^j c^k | i = j \text{ or } j = k \text{ for } j > 0\}$.

Exercise 3.27 ◆◆ Suppose, for some pushdown automaton A, there exists a constant k such that A never stores more than k elements on the stack. Show that the language $L(A)$ is regular. (Hint: Show that the pushdown automaton A can be transformed to a finite automaton accepting the same language.)

Exercise 3.28 ◆◆ Show that if a language L over an alphabet Σ is accepted by a pushdown automaton, then the language $\{u \# v | u \in L \text{ and } uv \in L\}$ for some symbol $\# \notin \Sigma$ is accepted by a pushdown automaton.

━━━━━━   **Section 3.4**   ━━━━━━

Exercise 3.29 For the grammar G in Example 3.4.1, trace the corresponding pushdown automaton accepting $L(G)$ on the string $aaabbb$. (Create a table similar to Figure 3.6 without the last column; that is, do not indicate the numbers of the used transitions.)

Exercise 3.30 For the grammar G in Example 3.1.5, trace the corresponding push-down automaton accepting $L(G)$ on the string $((v + v) * (v - v))$. (Create a table similar to Figure 3.6 without the last column.)

Exercise 3.31 ◆ A grammar $G = (\Sigma, NT, R, S)$ is **r**ight-linear if every rule in R is of the form $A \rightarrow \alpha$ where $A \in NT$ and either $\alpha \in \Sigma \times NT$, $\alpha \in \Sigma$, or $\alpha = e$. Prove that if G is a right-linear grammar, then $L(G)$ is regular.

Exercise 3.32 ◆ Prove that if L is a regular language then there is a right-linear grammar G such that $L = L(G)$.

Exercise 3.33 ◆◆ For the construction in Theorem 3.4.1, prove that for any string $\alpha \in NT(NT \bigcup \Sigma)^* \cup \{e\}$ and for any string $w \in \Sigma^*$,

a) If $w\alpha$ is derivable from S, then starting at configuration (f, w, S), the automaton A arrives at the configuration (f, e, α) [If $\alpha = e$, we get that if $w \in L(G)$, then $w \in L(A)$.] (Hint: use induction on the length of the leftmost derivation of $w\alpha$ from S.)

b) If, starting at configuration (f, w, S), the automaton A arrives at the configuration (f, e, α), then $w\alpha$ is derivable from S. (If $\alpha = e$, we get that if $w \in L(A)$ then $w \in L(G)$. This statement together with the one in part a completes the proof of Theorem 3.4.1.) (Hint: Use induction on the number of transitions of the type 2 in the computation.)

Exercise 3.34 ◆◆ Prove statement a in the sketch of the proof of Lemma 3.4.3.

Exercise 3.35 ◆◆ Prove statement b in the sketch of the proof of Lemma 3.4.3.

Exercise 3.36 ◆ Transform the pushdown automaton in Example 3.3.2 to an equivalent simple pushdown automaton.

Section 3.5

Exercise 3.37 Use the construction of Theorem 3.5.1 to find context-free grammars for the following languages:

a) $\{a^n b^n a^m b^m | n, m = 0, 1, 2, \ldots\}$

b) $\{a^n b^m c^k | n = m \text{ or } m = k, n, m, k = 0, 1, 2, \ldots\}$

c) $\{w | w = uu^R \text{ or } w = ua^n, n = |u|, u \in \{a, b\}^*\}$

Section 3.6

Exercise 3.38 ◆ Prove that the following languages are not context-free:

a) $L_1 = \{a^{3k} b^{2k} c^k | k = 0, 1, 2, \ldots\}$

b) $L_2 = \{10^k 10^k 10^k | k = 0, 1, 2, \ldots\}$ (Notice that L_2 is over the alphabet $\{0, 1\}$.)

c) $L_3 = \{a^{k+m} b^k a^m b^k | k, m = 0, 1, 2, \ldots\}$

d) $L_4 = \{www | w \in \{a, b\}^*\}$ (where the function n_a is defined in Exercise 3.23)

Section 3.7

Exercise 3.39 Apply Algorithm 3.7.1 to eliminate all rules of the type $H \to e$ from the following grammars:

a) $\{S \to ABC, A \to aA, A \to e, B \to bB, B \to b, C \to cC, C \to A\}$

b) $\{S \to AB, A \to aAa, A \to a, B \to BC, B \to bB, B \to e, C \to DD, D \to dDd, D \to e\}$

c) $\{S \to ABC, S \to e, A \to aA, A \to e, B \to bBS, B \to SD, B \to b, C \to CD, C \to cC, C \to D, D \to dD, D \to e\}$

Exercise 3.40 For each of the following grammars, apply Algorithm 3.7.2 to eliminate all rules of the type $E \to H$:

a) $\{S \to AB, A \to aAb, A \to B, B \to BC, B \to D, C \to cC, D \to dDd, D \to d\}$

b) $\{S \to ABC, A \to aA, A \to B, A \to a, B \to C, C \to cC, C \to c\}$

c) $\{S \to SA, S \to a, A \to aA, A \to B, B \to cS, B \to S, B \to b\}$

Exercise 3.41 Find the Chomsky normal forms for the following grammars:

a) $\{S \to SS, S \to (S), S \to e\}$ (with the set of terminals $\Sigma = \{(,)\}$)

b) $\{S \to ABC, S \to a, A \to aAaa, A \to e, B \to bBbb, B \to e, C \to cCa, C \to c\}$

c) $\{S \to aSa, S \to AB, S \to a, A \to CC, A \to aaA, A \to e, B \to bBb, B \to e,$
$C \to cCc, C \to e\}$

d) $\{S \to ABC, A \to Aaa, A \to e, B \to DD, B \to bDD, D \to ddB, D \to e,$
$C \to cCc, C \to c\}$

━━━━━ **Section 3.8** ━━━━━

Exercise 3.42 Show that the following languages are deterministic context-free:

a) $L_1 = \{a^m b^k c^m | m, k = 0, 1, 2, \ldots\}$

b) $L_2 = \{wcw^R | w \in \{a, b\}^*\}$

c) $L_3 = \{a^m b^n | m \neq n, m, n = 0, 1, 2, \ldots\}$

d) $L_4 = \{a^m ba^m | m = 0, 1, 2, \ldots\} \cup \{a^k ca^{2k} | k = 0, 1, 2, \ldots\}$

Exercise 3.43 ◆ Show that the class of deterministic context-free languages is not closed under union.

Exercise 3.44 ◆ Show that the class of deterministic context-free languages is not closed under intersection.

Exercise 3.45 ◆ Show that the class of deterministic context-free languages is not closed under difference.

Chapter 4

Turing Machines

Chapter 4

Turing Machines

4.1 Definition of a Turing Machine

We have observed in the last two chapters that neither finite automata nor pushdown automata are powerful enough to serve as real models of arbitrary algorithms, let alone modern computers that can run any algorithm. For example, an algorithm recognizing the language $L = \{ww|w \in \{a,b\}^*\}$ would need a *queue* to memorize the first half of the input. However, none of the computational devices we have observed so far, provides this kind of storage. Even for the language of palindromes $L = \{w|w = w^R\}$ there does not seem to exist any obvious way to implement a deterministic pushdown automaton recognizing this language. Any such solution would probably require *memorizing the entire input* before the algorithm would start to carry out the necessary comparisons. Any computer program can easily store the input, while a pushdown stack does it in a way that makes any reasonable operation after the input has been read in impossible.

Is it possible to design a formal model of a computational device that would capture capabilities of *any algorithm*? About 60 years ago an English mathematician named Alan Turing made an attempt to formulate an abstract model of a *human computer* that would use a pencil and paper to solve some problem. Turing tried to decompose the operations of such a computer into a number of simple steps. He came to the conclusion that

1. Any such step would consist of erasing a symbol on the paper "observed" by the pencil and writing a new one in its place;

2. The decision as to which symbol should be written and which symbol should be observed next would depend only on the symbol "observed" by the pencil and the "state of mind" of the computer.

Based on these assumptions, Turing suggested a computational device, known now as a **Turing machine**, that was supposed to implement any algorithm carried out by a computer. At the first glance, a Turing machine seems to be a slight generalization of a finite automaton. It has finite control in the form of states, a tape, and a head that can read the tape. The only differences are that a Turing machine can also *write* on the tape and back up to read symbols it read or wrote earlier.

However, this latter capability turns out to be of vital importance. A Turing machine can simulate processing *any data structure* using three major components of any imperative programming language — *sequence, branching, and loop* — at their full strength, including testing conditions that *control* branching and loops. Finite automata are not capable of such testing at all, while pushdown automata can do this only in the very limited form of testing the emptiness of the single stack. This informal observation can be supported by formal arguments. Any attempt to enhance the computational capabilities of a Turing machine — adding tapes, heads, introducing a *random access* mode that practically simulates assembly-level processing by any computer — fail to strengthen computational power. Thus, we can make a very powerful conclusion, known as the **Church-Turing thesis**: *Every computer algorithm can be implemented as a Turing machine.* This itself has very important consequences for computer science.

We begin with the definition of a Turing machine. First we describe such a machine and its operation informally. Like a finite automaton, a Turing machine consists of finite control, a tape divided into cells, and a head positioned on the tape. The head, being in any state s, *reads* the symbol in the cell it observes and either *writes* a new symbol in this cell or *moves one cell* to the *right* or to the *left*. In any case, it enters a new state q.

The tape has a left border and can be extended indefinitely to the right. That is, if the head wants to move to the right and there is no cell to move to, a new cell containing a *blank* symbol ␣ is added . (This is similar to extending random access memory (RAM) of a computer whenever it is needed.) To prevent the machine from moving beyond the left border of the tape, we assume it can "sense" it in the fashion similar to the one used in pushdown automata. That is, the leftmost cell contains the special marker ▷, and when the head observes this symbol, it always moves to the right. This way the machine will never attempt to "fall" from the left frontier of the tape.

Similar to finite and pushdown automata, the tape of a Turing machine is supplied with the input before the machine starts to operate. The input string is located in the leftmost cells of the tape right after the marker ▷ (see Figure 4.1). We can assume there are no cells after the input string, or there are a number of cells containing the empty symbol ␣. What happens if the head reaches the empty portion of the tape? It just continues its operation. Thus we assume that the empty symbol is a (special) tape symbol. An example of a Turing machine is depicted in Figure 4.1.

Now we are going to make our presentation of a Turing machine a bit more formal. Let Σ be a *tape* alphabet containing ▷ and blank ␣. As we just discussed,

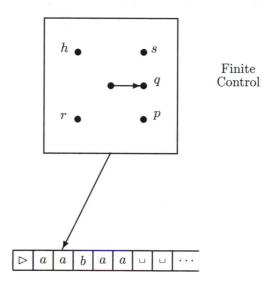

Figure 4.1 A Turing Machine

every transition of a Turing machine is either of the type

$$((s, a), (q, b))$$

or of the types

$$((s, a), (q, \rightarrow)); ((s, a), (q, \leftarrow))$$

where s, q are states, $a, b \in \Sigma$, $\rightarrow$ means that the head must move to the right, and, accordingly, $\leftarrow$ means that the head must move to the left. Unlike finite and pushdown automata, which would terminate operation of the device when reaching the end of the input tape, a Turing machine can move in both directions, and its tape is not bounded. Thus, it must have other means to terminate its operation. Halting is achieved in form of special *halting* states. If a machine enters a halting state, it immediately terminates. Note the difference between halting states and *favorable* or accepting states as used in finite and pushdown automata. Favorable states indicate that an input string is accepted. Thus, they are "external" to the operation of a computational device A. A may enter a favorable state and still continue its operation; changing favorable states does not change the device. Halting states are the "internal" means of terminating operation of a device. Eliminating or even changing halting states changes the device. The question *how* a Turing machine *accepts* the input or *what* it *computes* has not been discussed yet. Such matters are the topic of Section 4.2. In fact, we will relate acceptance to halting, however, the former comes after the latter. As we will see, acceptance can be defined in various ways.

Now we are ready to define a Turing machine formally.

Definition 4.1.1 A Turing machine is a quintuple $(S, \Sigma, \delta, s, H)$, where

- S is the set of **states**;

- Σ is an alphabet containing the **left end marker** $\triangleright$, the **blank** $\sqcup$, but not containing arrows $\rightarrow$ and $\leftarrow$;

- $s \in S$ is the **initial state**;

- $H \subseteq S$ is the set of **halting states**;

- δ, the **transition function**, is a function from $(S-H) \times \Sigma$ to $S \times (\Sigma \bigcup \{\leftarrow, \rightarrow\})$ such that

  1. For any $q \in S - H$, $\delta(q, \triangleright) = (p, \rightarrow)$ for some state p;
  2. If $(p, b) = \delta(q, a)$ for some $q \in S$ and $a \in \Sigma$, then b is not $\triangleright$ (that is, the machine never introduces another marker $\triangleright$).

As we have done before, we will use the notation $((q, a), (p, b))$ rather than $(p, b) = \delta(q, a)$ for the transitions of the machine. As it easily follows from the definition, a Turing machine is a deterministic device (we will define nondeterministic Turing machines later). Note that there is no transition with left-hand pair (h, a), for any $h \in H$. If a Turing machine reaches a halting state, it terminates its operation. Even though we have not yet defined how Turing machines *compute*, it is worthwhile to consider an example.

Example 4.1.1 The Turing machine that just *erases* the input string can be defined as follows: $M = (S, \Sigma, \delta, s, \{h\})$, where $\Sigma = \{a, \triangleright, \sqcup\}$, $S = \{s, q, h\}$, s is the initial state, h is the only halting state, and the set δ of transitions is

1. $((s, \sqcup), (h, \sqcup))$

2. $((s, a), (q, \sqcup))$

3. $((q, \sqcup), (s, \rightarrow)))$

4. $((s, \triangleright), (s, \rightarrow))$

5. $((q, \triangleright), (q, \rightarrow))$

6. $((q, a), (h, a))$

Having started with the tape containing aaa right after the marker $\triangleright$, the machine executes the cycle of using transitions 2 and 3 three times to erase a and move one step to the right. In the end it applies transition 1 to halt. Note that the last three transitions are never applied. They are present just because δ is the function that *must* be defined on the pairs in question.

Next, we consider a modification of the above machine. Replace transition 1 with the transition $((s, \sqcup), (q, \leftarrow))$. Then, when M reaches the $\sqcup$, it starts to move back and forth indefinitely, alternatively applying the modified transition 1 and 3. Thus, it *never terminates* — a phenomenon that is familiar to every reader who ever tried to debug programs containing faulty loops. This type of operation is very different from how finite or pushdown automata work. In the worst case, a pushdown would just get stuck.

$$\boxed{\text{End Example}}$$

Now we can define *computation* by a Turing machine. First, however, we must define a *configuration*. Any configuration obviously must include

(a) The current state;

(b) The symbol on the tape currently observed by the head;

(c) The string on the tape to the left of the head;

(d) The string on the tape to the right of the head (in this case we can assume that it ends with the rightmost nonblank symbol on the tape as otherwise we would get an infinite string).

An example of a configuration is the quadruple

$$(q, a, \triangleright a \sqcup bb, bbb \sqcup \sqcup aa)$$

If q is a halting state, we call a configuration **halting**. To simplify notation, we will combine the last three components of a configuration: Instead of (q, a, u, v) we will write $(q, u\underline{a}v)$ with the underlined symbol being the one observed by the head.

Now consider a configuration $C_1 = (q, u\underline{a}v)$. We say that the configuration C_1 **yields** a configuration $C_2 = (p, u_1\underline{b}v_1)$ in one step of computation (written $C_1 \vdash C_2$) if C_2 is obtained from C_1 by application of the transition in δ with the left-hand side pair (q, a), with the assumption that the underlined symbol a is observed by the head. For example, if $C_1 = (q, \triangleright ab \sqcup \underline{a} \sqcup aa)$ and the transition $((q, a), (p, \rightarrow)) \in \delta$, then $C_1 \vdash (p, \triangleright ab \sqcup a\underline{\sqcup} aa)$. If the transition was, say, $((q, a), (p, b))$, then C_1 would yield $(p, \triangleright ab \sqcup \underline{b} \sqcup aa)$.

We say that a configuration C **yields** a configuration C' (written $C \vdash^* C'$) if there exists a sequence of configurations

$$C_0 \vdash C_1 \vdash \cdots \vdash C_n$$

such that $C = C_0$ and $C' = C_n$. We say that the above sequence is a **computation** by Turing machine M, and n is its **length**.

In Example 4.1.1, starting from the configuration $(s, \triangleright \underline{a}aa)$, machine A carries out the following seven-step computation:

$$
\begin{aligned}
(s, \triangleright \underline{a}aa) \quad &\vdash \quad (q, \triangleright \underline{\sqcup}aa) \\
&\vdash \quad (s, \triangleright \sqcup \underline{a}a) \\
&\vdash \quad (q, \triangleright \sqcup \underline{\sqcup}a) \\
&\vdash \quad (s, \triangleright \sqcup \sqcup \underline{a}) \\
&\vdash \quad (q, \triangleright \sqcup \sqcup \underline{\sqcup}) \\
&\vdash \quad (s, \triangleright \sqcup \sqcup \sqcup \underline{\sqcup}) \\
&\vdash \quad (h, \triangleright \sqcup \sqcup \sqcup \underline{\sqcup})
\end{aligned}
$$

Now we will consider more examples of Turing machines. These machines form a class of *basic* machines that can be used to build more complex machines. Thus, building complex Turing machines, we are going to employ a "modular" approach familiar to every programmer. More complex machines "call" simple machines as "subprograms." It is natural then to use the graphical language of "flowcharts" to represent machines combined from other machines. Any node in such a flowchart will be labeled with the name of a Turing machine. When the flow of control is passed to a node with label A, Turing machine A is started in its initial state with the current configuration. The operation of A will modify the configuration. When A halts, the reading head will be observing a cell containing a symbol. Suppose that symbol is a. If there is an arrow connecting the node with label A to a node labeled B and that arrow itself is labeled a, then Turing machine B is started in its initial state with the configuration left by A, and the process continues. See Figure 4.2.

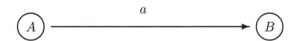

Figure 4.2 A Sequence of Turing Machines

Using this kind of flowchart with labeled arrows, we can design Turing machines that represent conditional branching and loops. For example, the Turing machine depicted in Figure 4.3 represents a Turing machine M that starts in its initial configuration. If M halts and the head observes the symbol a, then A starts to operate from the given configuration. If M halts and the head observes any other symbol, then B takes over. Using the conventional branching construct, one can describe this computation as

$$M;$$
$$\text{if } a \text{ then } A \text{ else } B$$

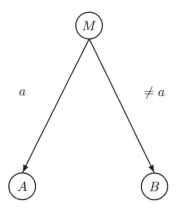

Figure 4.3 Branching Turing Machines

The diagram of the machine in Figure 4.4 represents a machine that starts to

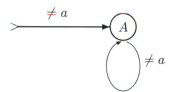

Figure 4.4 A Loop

operate as A every time the symbol observed by the head in the halting state is not a. One can represent this computation by the following conventional programming construct:

$$\text{while } (\text{not}(a)) \text{ do } A;$$

The starting "bricks" for building complex Turing machines using the above constructs could be the machines executing just one basic instruction such as writing a symbol and halting, or moving one step to the left or right and halting. In both cases, the machine "memorizes" the symbol being observed by the state it moves to. We can denote these "atomic" machines as just a (for writing a), R (for moving to the right), and L (for moving left). Then the machine that writes a symbol b if the symbol being observed is a, can be represented as in Figure 4.5.

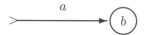

Figure 4.5 Writing b over a

It would also be convenient to denote the "concatenation" of any two machines A and B (B starts to work from the configuration in which A halted regardless of the symbol being observed by the head) as AB. For example, $\sqcup R$ would stand for the machine that erased any symbol being observed by the head and moved one step to the right. In many cases our diagrams will contain parallel arrows (connecting the same nodes), one labeled by each nonblank symbol. All such arrows can be replaced by one arrow labeled $a \neq \sqcup$, which is read "any symbol a different from $\sqcup$." As the actual symbol a on the tape can be memorized by the machine, it can be used in the subsequent "modules." For instance, the machine of Figure 4.6 memorizes a nonblank character a, moves one cell to the right, and writes a over

Figure 4.6 Moving Right and Writing a

whatever happens to be in that cell (it halts instantly if the observed symbol is blank). Sometimes, when we only care that the character being observed is *not* some particular symbol, it is convenient to use the shorthand $\bar{a}$ to mean any symbol different from a.

Now we consider some examples of Turing machines.

Example 4.1.2 The diagram of Figure 4.7 represents the machine that erases the

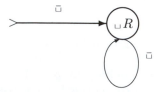

Figure 4.7 Erasing the Input

input string consisting of nonblank characters, starting with the head observing the leftmost character. It halts when it reaches the right end of the string. If the first character is blank, the machine halts instantly. We can represent this machine also as

$$\text{while } (\text{not}(\sqcup)) \text{ do } \sqcup R$$

$$\boxed{\text{End Example}}$$

For our future examples, it is convenient to have Turing machines that find the first blank or nonblank symbol to the right or to the left of the symbol being observed. For example, the machine that finds the first blank to the right can be represented by the diagram of Figure 4.8. Accordingly, it can be represented by the

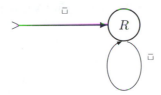

Figure 4.8 Finding the First Blank on the Right

statement

$$\text{while } (\text{not}(\sqcup)) \text{ do } R$$

The shorthand $R_\sqcup$ will be used to denote the machine of Figure 4.8. Similarly the shorthand notation $L_\sqcup$, $R_{\overline{\sqcup}}$, $L_{\overline{\sqcup}}$ will be used for the rest of the above mentioned machines.

Example 4.1.3 Our next example is the machine Cp that copies any string w (possibly empty) containing nonblank symbols. That is, it transforms the input string w, starting with the head observing the leftmost character in w, into the string $w \sqcup w$ and halts. This transformation can be implemented by a loop that, on every iteration

1. Using an internal state, "memorizes" the character a observed by the head in the input w;

2. "Memorizes" the position of the character a observed by the head, temporarily "erasing" it (or, rather, marking this position by $\sqcup$);

3. Moves the head to the right until it reaches the second empty cell and copies the remembered character a; this part can be represented by the concatenation $RR_\sqcup RR_\sqcup a$. The R's are needed to make the next $R_\sqcup$ start from a nonempty symbol;

4. Moves the head to the left until it reaches the second empty cell;

5. Restores the memorized a in the observed cell;

6. Moves ones step to the right and terminates if the observed symbol is blank.

The corresponding machine Cp is presented in Figure 4.9.

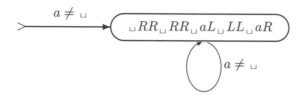

Figure 4.9 The Copying Machine Cp

We could also represent it in the form of the following "program":

while $(a \neq \sqcup)$ do

$$\{ \quad \sqcup;$$
$$R;$$
$$\text{while } (\overline{\sqcup}) \text{ do } R;$$
$$R;$$
$$\text{while } (\overline{\sqcup}) \text{ do } R;$$
$$a;$$
$$\text{while } (\overline{\sqcup}) \text{ do } L;$$
$$L;$$
$$\text{while } (\overline{\sqcup}) \text{ do } L;$$
$$a;$$
$$R$$
$$\}$$

Note that the machine halts to observe the blank between the input w and its copy.

End Example

We recommend that the reader work Exercises 4.3, 4.5, and 4.6 that call for the design of complete sets of transitions for some of the above examples.

4.2 Computations by Turing Machines

So far we have been using Turing machines as simple data processing devices. Now we are going to show that they perform many important computational tasks, in particular, compute functions and recognize languages. In fact, computing functions is enough for language recognition, since every language L can be represented by its *characteristic function*

$$\eta_L(w) = \begin{cases} 1 & \text{if } w \in L \\ 0 & \text{otherwise} \end{cases}$$

First we define how Turing machines compute functions on strings. It will be convenient to introduce the following notation for the case when a machine M never halts on an input w: $M(w) \uparrow$.

Definition 4.2.1 Let $M = (S, \Sigma, \delta, s, H)$ be a Turing machine. Let $\Sigma_0 = \Sigma - \{\triangleright, \sqcup\}$ and let w be a string in the alphabet Σ_0^*. Suppose that M, starting to operate from the *initial configuration* $(s, \triangleright w)$ with the head observing the first character in w, halts, and its final configuration is $(h, \triangleright u)$ for some $h \in H$ and $u \in \Sigma_0^*$ [that is, $(s, \triangleright w) \vdash^* (h, \triangleright u)$]. We denote u by $M(w)$ and call it the **output** of machine M on the input w.

Now let f be any function from Σ_0^* to Σ_0^*. Let $Dom(f)$ be the *domain* of the function f (the set of all $w \in \Sigma_0^*$ on which f is defined). We say that M **computes** the function f if M halts on every $w \in Dom(f)$ with $M(w) = f(w)$, and $M(w) \uparrow$ on every $w \notin Dom(f)$.

Definition 4.2.2 A function f with $Dom(f) \subseteq \Sigma_0^*$ is called **partial Turing computable** if there exists a Turing machine M that computes it.

We use the word *partial* in the definition, since the Turing machine may not halt on some inputs w [those w that are not in $Dom(f)$]. This word is dropped in the following definition that covers the special case when M halts on *all* inputs w.

Definition 4.2.3 A function is called **Turing computable** if it is partial Turing computable and $Dom(f) = \Sigma_0^*$.

Example 4.2.1 Our first example is the Turing computable function $f(w) = wa$ defined on all strings $w \in \{a, b\}^*$. The Turing machine M computing f moves its head to the right until the first blank and replaces the blank by a (see Figure 4.10).

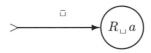

Figure 4.10 Computing the Function $f(w) = wa$

Note the function is Turing computable as M obviously terminates on any input string.

End Example

Example 4.2.2 In Example 4.1.3 we defined a Turing machine that, given the input w, outputs $w \sqcup w$. This machine can be augmented to output ww instead of $w \sqcup w$. To achieve this, after the original machine terminates, the *left-shifting machine Shl* starts to operate. It just shifts the second string one position to the left. More precisely, Shl starts in the configuration $v \sqcup w$ for any v and has one loop. On every iteration of the loop, it moves to the right, memorizes the symbol being observed (say, a) if it is nonblank, erases it, moves to the left, writes a, and moves twice to the right. The diagram of Shl is presented in Figure 4.11.

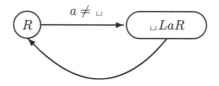

Figure 4.11 The Shifting Machine Shl

Thus, we have defined a Turing machine that computes the Turing computable function $f(w) = ww$.

$$\boxed{\text{End Example}}$$

As every language L can be represented by its characteristic function we can define recognition of languages by Turing machines.

Definition 4.2.4 A language L is called **Turing computable** if its characteristic function is Turing computable.

We will use the term **decidable language** as a synonym term for Turing computable language. A Turing machine recognizing such a language *decides* if a string is in the language or not.

Definition 4.2.5 A language L is called **semidecidable** if there exists a Turing machine M that outputs 1 on any $w \in L$ and does not halt on any $w \notin L$ [in other words, for the f computed by M, $Dom(f) = L$ and f coincides with the characteristic function η_L on its domain].

A Turing machine semidecides a language if it recognizes every string in the language and does not halt on the strings that are not in the language.

We could define the semidecidability of languages using a slightly different approach.

Definition 4.2.6 A language L is **semidecidable** if there exists a Turing machine M that *halts* on every string $w \in L$ and does not halt on any string $w \notin L$.

The reader can easily see that both definitions of semidecidability are equivalent. In some aspects, the latter definition may be regarded as more natural. Outputting 1 after the machine has halted seems to be somewhat "redundant." As we will show later, there are semidecidable languages that are not decidable.

Any deterministic finite automaton can easily be transformed into a Turing machine recognizing the same language (if an automaton completes reading the input and enters a favorable state, the Turing machine simulating it erases the input and writes 1 in the first cell, otherwise it outputs 0). Thus, every regular language is Turing computable. We will show later that all context-free languages are Turing computable as well.

Strings in the alphabet $\{0,1\}$ can be regarded as *binary codes* of nonnegative binary numbers. For example, the string $w = a_1 a_2 \ldots a_n$ represents the number

$$a_1 \cdot 2^{n-1} + a_2 \cdot 2^{n-2} + \ldots + a_n$$

Thus, with the alphabet $\Sigma_0 = \{0,1\}$, we can view a Turing machine as computing a function $f : N \to N$.

Example 4.2.3 In this example we consider a Turing machine that computes the function $f(k) = k + 1$. Starting from the leftmost symbol, the machine first goes to the right until it reaches a blank. Then it turns left and flips all 1's to 0's until it reaches the first 0. Then it flips it to 1 and halts. If it never finds 0 (which means that the input string was all 1's), it writes 1 in the leftmost cell, finds the first blank on the right, writes over 0, and halts. In Exercise 4.9 the reader is asked to draw a chart and give a complete set of transitions for this machine.

$$\boxed{\text{End Example}}$$

Turing machines can be used to compute functions of multiple arguments. Suppose f is a function defined on k-tuples $(n_1, n_2, \ldots, n_k)$ of natural numbers with range N, and n_i is coded by the string w_i, $1 \le i \le k$. A Turing machine computing this function would start with the input $w_1 \sqcup w_2 \sqcup \ldots \sqcup w_k$ on the tape and halt with the output $f(n_1, n_2, \ldots, n_k)$.

Definition 4.2.7 A function f with $Dom(f) \subseteq N^k$ is called a **partial Turing computable** function if it is computable by some Turing machine. Turing computable functions, accordingly, have $Dom(f) = N^k$.

How powerful are Turing machines, or, equivalently, what is the scope of partial Turing computability? As we have shown, Turing machines can copy and add 1. At this moment, the reader probably suspects that Turing machines can do much more than that. We will show later that Turing machines can add and multiply numbers [that is, compute the functions $f(x, y) = x + y$ and $g(x, y) = x \cdot y$]. Based on these two major operations, one can build a Turing machine that computes any conceivable numerical function that involves iterated arithmetical operations. However, details of programming are quickly becoming more and more subtle. Our computational devices spend a lot of effort on relatively easy things. Even to add two numbers, a machine has to move back and forth many times, moving from a bit in one argument to the corresponding bit in the other one. It could be done much easier if the machine could use two more tapes having the second argument written *under* the first one, and the result written under the arguments. As we will show later, additional tapes do not enhance the power of Turing machines. However, they can be used to write more efficient programs for partial Turing computable functions.

4.3   Extensions of Turing Machines

At first glance, Turing machines are clumsy, wasting a lot of operations on steps that can be carried out by a modern computer in just one step. On the other hand, as we have seen, practically any instrument of imperative programming (sequence, conditional branching, and conditional loops) can be implemented by appropriate Turing machines. In this section we are going to show that *no* reasonable attempt to extend the computational power of Turing machines yields a model of computation more powerful than standard one-tape one-head Turing machines. We are using here an informal term *computational power*. By this we understand *what* Turing machines can do, rather than *how fast* they do it. The latter issue will be discussed in the Chapter 6. These results indicate that, as clumsy as they seem to be, Turing machines reach the ultimate computational power of *any* conceivable computer. Moreover, since additional (and quite powerful) features do not enhance the power of our computational devices, we can use them as our programming tools, finding simple solutions to the computational problems that would otherwise require lots of redundant head moving, memorization characters, shifting, and so on used by standard Turing machines (cf. Section 4.2).

4.3.1   Multiple Tapes

Now we consider Turing machines that have several tapes, as in Figure 4.12. Such a machine has one head for every tape. At any step, it scans the symbols observed by all the heads. Depending on this set of symbols, and on the current state, it replaces symbols on some tapes and moves one step to the right or to the left on the others. (A formal definition of such a machine is suggested in Exercise 4.12.)

We are going to show that any k-tape Turing machine can be simulated by a standard Turing machine computing the same function. Suppose, a k-tape Turing machine A computes a function f in the following fashion: Starting to work on any $w \in Dom(f)$ on the first tape, it halts with $f(w)$ on the first tape. The single tape of a one-tape machine B must contain, in one form or another, all information stored on multiple tapes of A. Let us assume that we could divide the tape of B

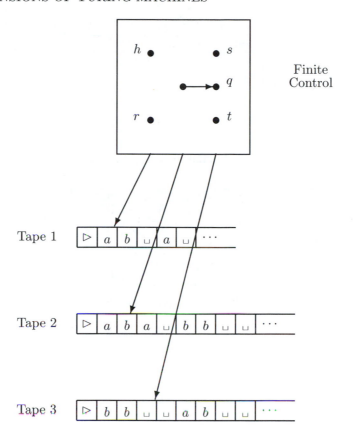

Figure 4.12 Multitape Turing Machine

into k *tracks*, each containing the same information as the corresponding tape of A (Figure 4.13).

This would take care of simulating multiple tapes. The problem of creating multiple "tracks" within one cell will be handled later. However, B can use only one head, while A has k heads positioned in different locations on different tapes. To memorize the positions of k heads, we need additional k tracks, one for every head. Thus, the single tape of B is to be divided into $2k$ tracks. Tracks with odd numbers are identical to the tapes $1, 2, \ldots, k$ of A, tracks with numbers $2, 4, \ldots, 2k$ memorize the positions of the heads. If the head on the tape i is positioned on the cell n, then the track $2i$ has 1 in cell n and 0 in all other cells (see Figure 4.14).

▷	a	b	⊔	⊔	a	⋯
▷	b	b	a	⊔	b	⋯
▷	⊔	b	a	b	a	⋯
▷	a	⊔	a	a	a	⋯

Figure 4.13 A Multitrack Tape

Figure 4.14 Simulating k Tapes by $2k$ Tracks

	▷	a	b	⊔	b	a	a	b			
	0	0	1	0	0	0	0	0			
	▷	b	b	a	⊔	a	⊔	a			
▷	0	0	0	0	0	0	1	0	⊔	⊔	⋯
	▷	a	⊔	a	b	⊔	a	⊔			
	0	1	0	0	0	0	0	0			

Now, how do we divide any cell into $2k$ tracks? Suppose that B could use $2k$-"level" symbols

$$a_1$$

$$b_1$$

$$a_2$$

$$b_2$$

$$\vdots$$

$$a_k$$

$$b_k$$

Then every "level" would represent the corresponding track. What we can do is just extend the alphabet of machine B, providing the code for each such "multilevel" character. To make inputs and outputs of machines A and B compatible, we have to make sure that the alphabet of B contains the alphabet of A. Thereby, B can start with the same input as A, then immediately start using "multilevel" characters, and in the end return the same output as A.

Now we describe how B simulates transitions of machine A. Given the input w and the head position at the first element (say, a), A first "initializes" the tracks in the cells originally containing the marker ▷ and the first character a, reflecting initial positions of all heads on the first cells of the tapes (see Figure 4.15).

To simulate just one transition by the machine A, B must perform many quite complex actions. Let us assume that before simulating any transition of A, the head of B is positioned on the right "end" of the data, that is, on the leftmost cell such that, for any track, all nonblank (for odd track) and 1 (for even track) symbols are located to the left of this cell. Machine B then

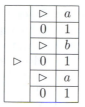

Figure 4.15 Initial Configuration of Tracks

1. Scans all the cells to the left and returns, memorizing by its internal state the symbols observed on each of k tracks simulating the tapes of A by the corresponding heads (represented by 1's on the tracks below).

2. Moves left and updates each combination

$$a$$
$$010$$

in accordance with the instructions of A, either replacing a by some b, or simulating the head move, that is, replacing the whole combination by either

$$a$$
$$100$$

or

$$a$$
$$001$$

3. Returns to the right "end" of the tape.

4. If A halts, B converts the contents of the tapes back to "single-level" format and halts itself.

We omitted many details in this description. However, the "modules" that we described just informally are very similar to those of the previous section, and we hope the reader will believe that they can be implemented as "modules" of standard Turing machines.

Now we can design a simple three-tape Turing machine that computes the function $x + y$, that is, adds two numbers in binary notation.

Example 4.3.1 The machine that computes $x + y$. For the sake of simplicity, we can assume that x and y are written on the first and second tapes, respectively. The result will first be computed on the third tape and then copied to the first tape. The machine executes the following modules in order:

1. Moves the heads on tapes 1 and 2 to the right ends of x and y, respectively, one move on each tape at a time. Simultaneously, moves the head on the third tape, making sure that in the end it will be positioned as far to the right as $\max(|x|, |y|)$;

2. Move the head on tape 3 one more position to the right (giving additional "room" to accomodate the result that may have length up to $max(|x|, |y|)+1$);

3. Bit by bit, adds x and y and writes the result on tape 3 using the following iteration:

   (a) Reads bits on the first and the second tapes and uses the *carry* memorized by the current state from the previous iteration of this loop;

   (b) If the sum of all three bits is 0 or 1, writes 0 or 1, respectively on the third tape;

   (c) If the sum is 2 or 3, writes 0 or 1, respectively, on the third tape and memorizes the *carry* 1 by its internal state;

   (d) Moves all three heads one position to the left.

4. One of the arguments, say, x can be shorter than y; when the machine reaches the marker $\triangleright$ on the first tape, it continues the iteration (formally, it will be a different loop), using 0's for the bits on the first tape and not moving the first head;

5. When the addition is over, it copies the result from the third tape to the first one (erasing x).

All five "modules" can obviously be implemented using the techniques developed in the Section 4.2.

$$\boxed{\text{End Example}}$$

4.3.2   Multiple Heads

Now we consider Turing machines that use one tape and k different heads to view the tape. More specifically, in every state only one head can write or move. Thus, the set of states is partitioned into $Q_1, Q_2, \ldots, Q_k$, where each set Q_i contains the states for head i.

It is easy to show that these machines can be simulated by standard one-head one-tape Turing machines. The simulation can be implemented similarly to the case of multitape tapes. This time one needs only k additional tracks for memorizing positions of the heads on the single tape.

We will use a multihead Turing machine to show that there are noncontext-free languages that can be recognized by Turing machines.

Example 4.3.2 Consider the language $L = \{a^n b^n c^n | n = 0, 1, \ldots\}$. As we have shown (Example 3.6.1), this language is not context-free. A three-head Turing machine that recognizes this language operates as follows. Given an input w, it scans the block of a's with the second head and positions it on the first b (if any). Similarly, the third head scans consecutively the group of a's and then the group of b's until it stops on the first c. Then the machine enters a loop on each iteration, making sure that the symbols observed by heads 1, 2, and 3 are a, b, and c, respectively, and moves all three heads to the right. If the third head reaches the end of the input string w when the first head reaches the first b and the second head reaches the first c, the machine erases the input and writes 1 in the first cell, thus, accepting w. Otherwise, the machine erases the input and writes 0 in the first cell, rejecting w.

Thus we have shown that there exist noncontext-free Turing computable languages.

$\boxed{\text{End Example}}$

4.3.3 Two-Dimensional Tapes

In this section we consider Turing machines that use one head on a two-dimensional "grid" that could potentially expand indefinitely down and to the right. The leftmost column and the uppermost row would be filled by the markers $\triangleright$ and $\triangledown$, indicating the left and the upper frontiers of the tape. The head can move on such a tape in four different directions. Such a machine A can be simulated by a multitape Turing machine as follows. Let us number all the cells of machine A as indicated in Figure 4.16.

Then the first one-dimensional tape of a standard Turing machine B will simulate the cells of the original machine in the consecutive order. Now, if, for example, the head of machine A moves down from cell 8 to cell 13, the head of machine B on the first tape moves to the right until it reaches cell 13 (see Figure 4.17).

To find out how far to move, machine B can use the second tape to find the length of the first half of the path: until the first $\triangleright$. Hence, the second tape is used as a simple counter to find the part beginning from this $\triangleright$ that has the same length. If A had to move its head to the right, then B would perform just one additional right move to cell 14. If A moves left or up, machine B accordingly moves its head on the first tape to the left. An important issue is how machine B would know where the markers $\triangleright$ and $\triangledown$ are located on the first tape. To solve this problem, B can use two tapes simulating counters. When the first counter decreases, the second counter

▽	▽	▽	▽	▽	▽	▽	▽	...
▷	1	2	6	7	15	16		...
▷	3	5	8	14	17			...
▷	4	9	13	18				...
▷	10	12	19					...
▷	11	20	23					...
▷	21	22						...
⋮	⋮	⋮	⋮	⋮	⋮	⋮	⋮	⋱

Figure 4.16 Two-Dimensional Tape with Numbered Cells

Figure 4.17 Simulation of a Two-Dimensional Tape in One Dimension

increases; when the first counter is 0, the second counter indicates the position of ▷ (with its next value indicating the position of the next ▷). Now the counters change their roles (the first counter increases and the second one decreases) with the first counter indicating the locations of the next ▽. We leave details to the reader.

4.3.4　Random Access Turing Machines

As we have seen, Turing machines become more and more versatile with every additional feature even though their ultimate computational power does not change. However, all the models of Turing machines defined so far have one feature that seems to make them much less powerful than modern computers. To access data stored in any location, a Turing machine must move a head to reach this location. That is, it accesses data *sequentially*, as opposed to modern computers which employ *random access memory* where each element of such memory can be accessed in one single step. To implement random access, a computer must be able to access data in memory, using only the *address* of the cell or location holding the data. Then, it must be able to "jump" from one location to another. This capability can be

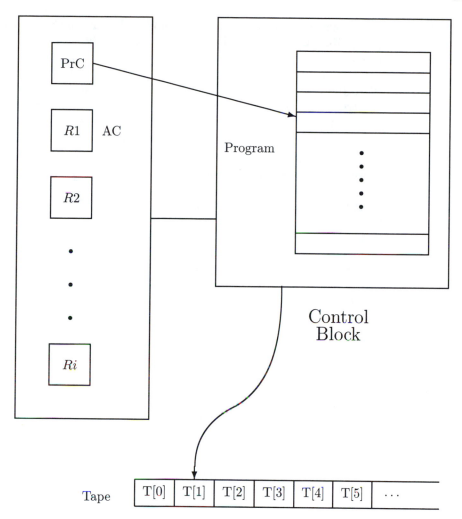

Figure 4.18 Random Access Turing Machine

implemented by adding or subtracting arbitrary numbers from the current address, which, in turn, must be stored in a special *register*. Thus, a **random access Turing machine** or simply RAM machine (see Figure 4.18) has

1. Memory (RAM) in the form of a one-dimensional tape,

2. A finite number of registers, and

3. A program which is a finite sequence of *instructions*.

Instructions are more general than transitions as they implement the commands presented in Figure 4.19. To figure out which instruction must be used next, the machine uses the special register called the *Program Counter* (PrC) that holds the number of the instruction being executed. After the execution of an instruction has been completed, the PrC is automatically incremented by 1, unless otherwise specified by the instruction. For example, a branch instruction would change the PrC, overriding the increment. The register $R1$ is used as an *accumulator* (AC) where the machine carries out its logical and arithmetical operations.

Instruction	Operand	Meaning
read	j	AC:=T$[Rj]$
write	j	T$[Rj]$:=AC
store	j	Rj :=AC
load	j	AC:= Rj
loadC	c	AC:= c
add	j	AC:=AC+Rj
addC	c	AC:=AC+c
sub	j	AC:= $\max\{AC - Rj, 0\}$
subC	c	AC:= $\max\{AC - c, 0\}$
half		AC := $\lfloor AC/2 \rfloor$
jump	s	PrC:= s
jpos	s	if AC > 0 then PrC:= s
jzero	s	if AC $= 0$ then PrC:= s
halt		

Note that j stands for a register number; T$[i]$ denotes the current content of tape cell i; Rj denotes the content of register Rj; c is any natural number (a constant); s denotes any instruction number in the program. All instructions increment PrC by one, unless stated otherwise.

Figure 4.19 Commands of RAM Machine

One can assume that a RAM machine has a control device (an analogue of the central processing unit (CPU) on computers), which contains registers and the *program*, which is a finite sequence of instructions $\alpha_1, \alpha_2, \ldots, \alpha_n$. Real computers, in accordance with the principles of the traditional von Neumann architecture, store the program and the data in the same RAM memory. This approach can be simulated by machines within the model we have adopted by encoding instructions as numerical codes, just like real computers. To complete the (informal) description of the machine, we assume that registers and cells of the RAM may contain any arbitrary natural number. At first, putting an arbitrarily large number into a single storage location appears totally unrealistic. However, the storage hierarchy of a modern computer (random access memory, hard disk, external disks) is based on rapidly changing technology and can really store arbitrarily large numbers. Unfortunately, with the current technology, you may have to have a lot of disk cartridges and a lot of time to change them to manipulate some really huge numbers. The machine starts to work with the first instruction. If it reaches the instruction `halt`, it halts, and the content of the RAM is considered its output.

Standard Turing machines input and output strings over some finite alphabets Σ, while, according to our informal definition, RAM machines write (and read) natural numbers in their memories. Since we want them to compute functions in the spirit of standard Turing machines, we will make the following assumption. Let Σ be some finite alphabet. Let $\mathbf{E}$ be some one-to-one function (bijection) from Σ to the set $\{0, 1, \ldots, |\Sigma| - 1\}$. We can consider $\mathbf{E}(a)$ as the numeric code of the symbol $a \in \Sigma$. Now, we will assume that, instead of input string $a_1 a_2 \ldots a_n \in \Sigma^*$, the RAM machine receives input $\mathbf{E}(a_1)\mathbf{E}(a_2)\ldots\mathbf{E}(a_n)$ in the first n cells of the tape. Accordingly, we can interpret the output as a string in Σ, translating numeric codes $\mathbf{E}(b)$ in the cells of the machine back to $b \in \Sigma$. Thus RAM machines can be viewed as computing functions over the same domains and with the same ranges as standard Turing machines.

As the reader may realize, our machines are practically equivalent to programs in any assembly language. This, in turn, makes it possible to implement any high-level programming language on such a machine. On the other hand, one can show that any random access Turing machine can be simulated by a standard Turing machine. This implies that the Turing machine, as originally defined in Section 4.1, is capable of doing anything a modern computer can. We are going to sketch the main details of this simulation (the details can be found in the book [Lewis and Papadimitriou]).

Let A be a random access Turing machine with k registers and a program counter (viewed as the separate register). We will describe a $k + 3$-tape standard Turing machine B that simulates A. In other words, B will compute the same partial Turing computable function as A. The machine B stores the current configuration of the machine A and, iteratively, carries out the transition from it to the next configuration.

First we describe how the tapes of machine B are used. On the first tape, B receives its input in some finite alphabet Σ and outputs the result (if it halts) in the same alphabet. The second tape is used to keep the content of the tape of the original machine A. Every integer r contained in a cell of A must be considered together with its *address*, that is, the number of this cell. Thus, machine B must actually store pairs (l, r), where l is the number of a cell and r is the number stored in this cell. Since B can use only the finite alphabet Σ, we can assume that Σ contains additional symbols $0, 1, (,), \mathbf{,}$, and A stores pairs (l, r) in the form $(1010, 100)$, where 1010 and 100 are binary codes of l and r, respectively. The pairs representing (l, r) can be located on the second tape in any order, and can be separated by an arbitrary number of blanks. This requires a special end-marker, say, $\ominus \in \Sigma$, on this tape that helps B figure out where the end of all the pairs (l, r) is.

The third tape of B is used as an auxiliary working tape. The last k tapes simulate registers of machine A. They store the values of the register in binary code. The current value of the program counter is memorized by states of machine B.

The simulation of machine A consists of three major phases. In the first phase, machine B translates the input string $w = a_1 a_2 \ldots a_n \in \Sigma^*$ on the first tape to the sequence of codes of $(1, \mathbf{E}(a_1))$, $(2, \mathbf{E}(a_2))$, $\ldots$, $(n, \mathbf{E}(a_n))$ on the second tape.

During the second phase B simulates execution of the instructions of A. Every step of machine A requires a number of steps by B. These steps depend on the specific instructions of A, which are represented by the values of the program counter. As we mentioned, these values are represented by states of machine B. This means that the set of states of the machine B is divided into pairwise distinct sets Q_i, one per each instruction α_i in the program α_1, α_2, $\ldots$, α_n of A. Now we consider some examples showing how B simulates various instructions of A.

Suppose that the instruction α_i is **add** 3. This means that the contents of register 3 is added to the accumulator (register 1) and the result is left in the accumulator. To perform binary addition, B uses the subset of states Q_i and working tape 3 for intermediate computations. The final result of the addition is stored on the tape reserved for the accumulator. If the instruction is, say, **subC** 20, machine B first writes the constant 20 on the working tape 3 and then performs subtraction.

Suppose now that the next instruction is **jump** 10. B copies the number 10 to the contents of the PrC, making sure that the next instruction of A to be simulated is α_{10}.

Now suppose that α_i is **write** 3. This instruction is supposed to copy the content of the accumulator to the cell on the tape of A pointed to by register 3. Suppose that the accumulator stores the number 5, and the register 3 points to cell 8. The binary codes of 5 and 8 are 100 and 111, respectively. Machine B writes the string (111,100) on the second tape: it finds the end marker $\ominus$, replaces it by (, then copies 111 from register 3, 100 from the accumulator, writes the closing parenthesis), and places the end marker $\ominus$ after the given string. The second tape may contain another string $(111, j)$, that is, cell 8 of A previously contained some number j. To preserve the integrity of the data, B scans the second tape backwards looking for such a string. If it finds one, B erases it.

We hope that we have convinced the reader that other instructions can be simulated similarly. If machine A ever reaches a **halt**, machine B enters the third phase of the simulation. In this final phase, B translates the output on the second tape back to the alphabet Σ and writes it on the first tape. Thus machine B computes the same function as A.

As we have shown earlier, multitape Turing machines are as powerful as one-tape machines. Thus, RAM machines are exactly as powerful as standard one-tape Turing machines.

4.4 Nondeterministic Turing Machines

In Section 4.3 we made several attempts to increase the computational power of Turing machines. We found out that none of the features considered — multiple tapes, multidimensional tapes, multiple heads, or random access memory — can increase the computational power of the basic model. However, all devices we have observed so far were deterministic. What if we allow Turing machines to use the power of *nondeterminism*? We learned in Chapter 2 that nondeterminism does not affect computational power of finite automata. However, nondeterministic pushdown automata turned out to be substantially more powerful than deterministic ones. In this section we are going to show that nondeterminism does not increase the power of Turing machines. We do this by showing that nondeterministic machines can be simulated by deterministic ones.

First we have to define **nondeterministic Turing machines**. As in our previous definitions of nondeterministic devices, the transition set of such a machine A can contain *multiple* transitions $((q, a), (p, \alpha))$ with the same left-hand part (q, a). Being in state q and observing the symbol a on the tape, machine A can apply any of these transitions. [As in case of pushdown automata, we will also assume that for some configurations (q, a) there will be no transitions $((q, a), (p, b))$; in these cases a nondeterministic machine crashes and, consequently, does not halt normally.]

It has been quite easy to define nondeterministic Turing machines. However, it is much more complex to define *what they compute*. The problem is that if a computational device is nondeterministic, it can produce multiple outputs, depending on the choice of transitions at every step. The definition of nondeterministic computability of functions is therefore somewhat clumsy and not too natural, so we concentrate on nondeterministic Turing machines deciding languages.

Thus we give the following definition of *semidecidability* by nondeterministic Turing machines. A Turing machine M **semidecides** a language L if, for any $w \in L$, at least one computation of M on the input w halts, and, for any $w \notin L$, no computation of M on w halts. Note that we do not require *all* computations on $w \in L$ to halt.

Despite the complexity of the definitions of computing and nondeterminism, as in the cases of finite and pushdown automata, nondeterminism can be utilized as a convenient programming tool that in many cases enhances clarity of algorithms solving complex problems. A popular example of a problem where nondeterminism can effectively be employed is the *composite number recognition problem*. A number is called **composite** if it is a nonprime greater than 1. In other words, a composite number can be represented as a product of two numbers greater than 1. For example, 4, 8, 9, and 24 are composite numbers, while 0, 1, 2, 3, 5, and 23 are not.

The composite number recognition problem is to determine if the number is composite, for example, can be represented as the product of two *factors* greater than 1. In other words, we must show that the composite number recognition problem is *decidable*. To do this, we must design a Turing machine that decides the problem. One way to solve this problem is to try all possible numbers p and q

smaller than the given number n, multiply them, and test if $p \times q = n$. (Actually, it is enough to try all p and q that are smaller than the square root of n.) We could implement this idea in the form of a deterministic Turing machine. However, the algorithm itself is very slow, and even slower when the Turing machine implements it. A nondeterministic machine, though, can *guess* the factors p and q (if any) and then just multiply them and test that $p \times q = n$, which is relatively easy and fast. Thus, we can design a relatively efficient nondeterministic Turing machine that *semidecides* the set of composite numbers.

Even though a nondeterministic algorithm for semideciding composite numbers is much more efficient, as previously discussed, one can design a deterministic algorithm solving this problem. In fact, we could directly convert our nondeterministic algorithm into a deterministic one. It turns out that *any* nondeterministic machine can be simulated by a deterministic one.

Theorem 4.4.1 *Any nondeterministic Turing machine semideciding a language can be simulated by a Turing machine semideciding the same language.*

Proof: The proof uses a computational technique called **Dovetailing**. This is a primitive form of timesharing the execution of several computations. In the first step, the first program is run for one step. In the second step, the first program is run for two additional steps and the second program is run for two steps. In general, at the ith step, the first $i - 1$ computations are run for i additional steps each and the ith computation is run for i steps. This situation can be represented graphically (see Figure 4.20), where row i lists the new computation to be started along with all the computations to be run for an additional i steps. A picture like the one of Figure 4.20 reminded someone of the tail of a dove, and the name has stuck to the technique.

$$1$$
$$1\ 2$$
$$1\ 2\ 3$$
$$1\ 2\ 3\ 4$$
$$1\ 2\ 3\ 4\ 5$$
$$1\ 2\ 3\ 4\ 5\ 6$$
$$1\ 2\ 3\ 4\ 5\ 6\ 7$$

Figure 4.20 Dovetailing

Let A be a nondeterministic Turing machine semideciding a language L. We describe a deterministic Turing machine B that also semidecides L. B will be derived only from the details of A. Given any input string w, machine B will try to simulate all computations of A on w. If *at least one* computation of A on w halts, B halts; otherwise B does not halt on w.

It is not a problem to simulate a particular computation of A. However, B must simulate *all* computations and must make sure that it halts if at least one computation of A halts. At any step of any computation, machine A may choose a transition from a finite subset Δ' of the set of all transitions Δ. Thus, at any step of computation, the size of the subset Δ' is bounded by the same number $|\Delta|$ that depends only on machine A and does not depend on the chosen computation. We can represent all possible computations in the form of a tree (see Figure 4.21) where every node in the tree has at most $k = |\Delta|$ children.

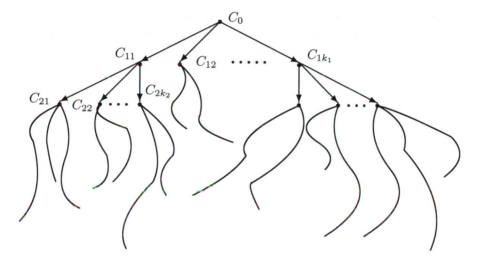

C_0 is the initial configuration. C_{11}, C_{12}, ..., C_{1k_1}, $k_1 \leq |\Delta|$ are all possible configurations obtained after application of one transition.

Figure 4.21 The Tree of Nondeterministic Computations

Machine B dovetails machine A, applying *every* applicable transition (there are at most k of them) to any configuration of A and memorizing every obtained configuration. To do this step-by-step, machine B can use two tapes to memorize configurations obtained on odd and even steps, respectively, of computation of A. Assume, for instance, that all configurations obtained by the tenth step of computation are stored on the second tape. Then, for any such *nonhalting* configuration C, machine B consecutively applies all applicable configurations from the set of transitions of A, writes resulting configurations on the first tape, and erases C. When all configurations on the second tape are erased, the machine B starts to simulate the eleventh step of the computation of A, using the configurations on the first tape and writing results on the second tape. Technically, machine B may use more tapes, for example, one tape to store the set of transitions of A. If, at some point, A reaches a halting state, B erases the contents of all tapes and halts. If no computation of A halts, the machine B will never halt as.

The above process can be visualized (and actually implemented) as the process of walking the tree of computations of A on w, visiting every vertex. This can be done using, for example, the well-known *breadth-first search* algorithm.

It is clear that machine B semidecides the same language as A. According to the results of Section 4.3.1, machine B can be transformed into a standard one-tape Turing machine semideciding the same language.

$$\boxed{\text{End Proof}}$$

Comparing the ways the one-tape machines simulate more complex machines in Section 4.3 and the way the deterministic machine B simulates A in the proof of Theorem 4.4.1, the reader can notice one important difference. Any "subprogram" of a standard Turing machine in Section 4.3 simulates just *one step* of a more complex machine, while one phase of the above construction potentially simulates *any finite number of steps* of the underlying machine A. As a result of this, while the standard machines in the previous sections work approximately as fast as the machines that they simulate, the number of steps the machine B uses to simulate n steps of the nondeterministic machine in the above construction expands to an exponent of n. Could we construct a deterministic machine that would simulate A more efficiently? Or, maybe, would any deterministic algorithm simulating A be inefficient? Is inefficiency the price that one has to pay when converting nondeterministic algorithms to deterministic ones? It turns out that this profound question is *open*. We discuss this issue further in Chapter 6.

4.5   Turing Enumerable Languages

In Section 4.2 we defined semidecidable and decidable (or Turing computable) languages. In this section we are going to take a closer look at these languages and their properties. First we establish the following simple property of decidable languages.

Theorem 4.5.1 *If a language L is decidable, then its complement $\overline{L}$ is decidable.*

Proof: Let A be a Turing machine that computes the characteristic function η_L. The machine B computing $\eta_{\overline{L}}$ simulates A. When A outputs 1, B outputs 0, and vice versa.

$$\boxed{\text{End Proof}}$$

Now, we introduce an equivalent term for semidecidable languages: We will call them **Turing enumerable**. A popular definition for Turing enumerable languages used in the literature is that a language is Turing enumerable if it is $Dom(f)$ for some partial Turing computable function f (recall Definition 4.2.2). This definition is clearly equivalent to the following one: A language is Turing enumerable if it is $Dom(f)$ for some partial Turing computable function f and $f(w) = 1$ for any $w \in Dom(f)$. If $L = Dom(f)$ for some f computed by a Turing machine A, we can easily construct a Turing machine B that outputs 1 on any input w whenever A outputs $f(w)$.

Still none of the equivalent definitions of Turing enumerable languages we have introduced so far relate to the word *enumerable* in the name. We are going to give yet another definition of Turing enumerable languages that directly connects this word to the notion.

Definition 4.5.1 *A language L is called* **Turing enumerable** *if $L = \{f(i)|i \in Dom(f)\}$ for some partial Turing computable function f. We say that f* **enumerates** *the language L (any number $i \in Dom(f)$ can be viewed as an* index *of a string in L).*

We can show that the above definition is equivalent to any of the definitions we introduced so far. Assume, for example, that we are given a machine A that halts whenever $w \in L$. Let us fix some natural ordering of all strings in the tape alphabet Σ of machine A. For example, we can use the ***lexicographic ordering*** of strings over Σ. For this ordering, the characters $a_1, a_2, \ldots, a_n$ in Σ are numbered, and any string $u = b_1 b_2 \ldots b_k$, $b_i \in \Sigma, 1 \leq i \leq k$ over Σ precedes another string $v = c_1 c_2 \ldots c_m$, $c_j \in \Sigma, 1 \leq j \leq m$ if for some $r \leq min(k, m)$ the number of b_r is smaller than the number of c_r and for any $i < r$ the numbers of b_i and c_i are the same. For example, if $\Sigma = \{0, 1\}$ and 0 and 1 have numbers 0 and 1, respectively, then the string 01101 will precede the string 01111. One can easily design a "successor" Turing machine S that, given any string in Σ, outputs its successor in the lexicographic ordering.

Now we can construct a Turing machine B that operates as follows. Using the lexicographical ordering of all strings over Σ, dovetail the computations of A on these strings (in the spirit of simulating the nondeterministic machine in Section 4.4). More precisely, make sure that, for any n, when n steps of computation of A on the *first* string w_1 (in the lexicographic ordering) have been simulated, B simulates $n - 1$ steps of A on the second string w_2, $n - 2$ steps on the third string w_3, ... and 1 step on the string w_n. B uses here as a "subprogram" the machine S computing w_{i+1} for every w_i. In this way, B ensures that computations on all strings will eventually be simulated. Consider what happens at some step i of the simulation. If some computation $A(w)$ halts at step i, then B writes the string (i, w) on a special output tape. We assume that $(,), \boldsymbol{\mathflat}$ are not present in the original alphabet Σ. If no computation $A(w)$ halts at step i, B writes $(i, \sqcup)$ on this tape. If two or more computations of A halt on the same step i of simulation, all of them but one may be artificially "delayed" for a few steps.

It is clear, that if $w \in L$ then a string (i, w) for some number i will eventually show up on the output tape of B. Machine B operates indefinitely (never halts), and its output is infinite. However, now we can design another machine M that will compute the function f enumerating L. To compute f on the input number i, the machine M simulates B until the string (i, w) shows up on its output tape. If $w = \llcorner$, $M(i) \uparrow$; otherwise, M outputs w and halts.

Now we have to show that if $L = \{f(i) | i \in Dom(f)\}$ for some partial Turing computable function f, then there exists a Turing machine that halts on any $w \in L$ and does not halt on any $w \notin L$. Let A compute f. The required machine B, given any input w, will dovetail the simulation of machine A on inputs 0, 1, 2, ... B uses a "subprogram" that for every number in N in binary computes the next number in sequence. If $w = f(i)$ for some i, machine A will output w eventually, and, accordingly, machine B will halt; otherwise, $B(w) \uparrow$.

Thus, being the *domain* of some partial Turing computable function is equivalent to being the *range* of some partial Turing computable function!

Now we are going to find out how decidable languages relate to Turing enumerable ones. First, it is easy to show that every decidable language is Turing enumerable.

Theorem 4.5.2 *If a language is decidable, it is Turing enumerable.*

Proof: Suppose a Turing machine M computes the characteristic function η_L of the language L. We can easily transform M so that, instead of outputting 0 (on $w \notin L$), it goes into an infinite loop and never halts. Thus, L is Turing enumerable.

$$\boxed{\text{End Proof}}$$

As we have already mentioned, it will be shown in Chapter 5 that not all Turing enumerable languages are decidable. Still, one can prove the following result.

Theorem 4.5.3 (Post's Theorem) *If a language L and its complement are Turing enumerable, then L is decidable.*

Proof: Suppose a Turing machine A semidecides L (halts on $w \in L$ and does not halt on $w \notin L$) and B similarly semidecides $\overline{L}$. Consider the Turing machine M that, given any w, simulates $A(w)$ and $B(w)$. If A halts, then M outputs 1, if B halts, M outputs 0. Note that A and B can never halt or fail to halt together on the same w. One can easily see now that M computes η_L. Thus, L is decidable.

$$\boxed{\text{End Proof}}$$

Exercises

Section 4.1

Exercise 4.1 Consider the following Turing machine:

$$((s, \sqcup), (h, \sqcup))$$
$$((s, a), (q, b))$$
$$((s, b), (q, a))$$
$$((q, a), (s, \rightarrow))$$
$$((q, b), (s, \rightarrow))$$
$$((q, \sqcup), (q, \sqcup))$$
$$((s, \triangleright), (s, \rightarrow))$$
$$((q, \triangleright), (s, \rightarrow))$$

with the initial state s and the halting state h.

a) Trace the machine when started in the configuration $(s, \triangleright\underline{a}bbabba)$.

b) Describe in English what this Turing machine does.

Exercise 4.2 This exercise is from [Lewis and Papadimitriou]. Consider the Turing machine

$$((s, a), (q, \leftarrow))$$
$$((s, \sqcup), (s, \sqcup))$$
$$((s, \triangleright), (s, \rightarrow))$$
$$((q, a), (p, \sqcup))$$
$$((q, \sqcup), (h, \sqcup))$$
$$((q, \triangleright), (q, \rightarrow))$$
$$((p, a), (p, a))$$
$$((p, \sqcup), (s, \leftarrow))$$
$$((p, \triangleright), (p, \rightarrow))$$

with the initial state s and the halting state h. Let $n \geq 0$. Describe carefully what the machine does when started in the configuration $(s, \triangleright \sqcup a^n \underline{a})$.

Exercise 4.3

a) Give a complete set of transitions for the Turing machine of Figure 4.6

b) Give a Turing machine that moves its head one cell to the left and writes a (if the symbol being observed is not the marker $\triangleright$).

Exercise 4.4 Using primitives L, R, and those of Figures 4.3—4.6, construct a Turing machine that enters a halting state on the strings from the language $L = \{a^i b^j | i, j \geq 0\}$.

Exercise 4.5 Give complete sets of transitions for the following Turing machines:

a) $R_{\sqcup}$

b) $L_{\sqcup}$

c) $R_{\overline{\sqcup}}$

d) $L_{\overline{\sqcup}}$

Exercise 4.6 ◆ Give a complete set of transitions for the Turing machine in the Example 4.1.3.

▬▬▬ Section 4.2 ▬▬▬

Exercise 4.7 Give a complete set of transitions for the Turing machine of Example 4.2.1.

Exercise 4.8

a) Give a complete set of transitions for the machine Shl (described in the Example 4.2.2) that shifts an input string one position to the left (assume that the first symbol on the input tape is blank).

b) Give a complete set of transitions for the machine Shr that shifts an input string one position to the right (assume that the first symbol on the input tape is blank).

Exercise 4.9 Construct a Turing machine that computes the function $f(k) = k+1$ (as described in Example 4.2.3).

a) Use primitives R,L, and so on defined in Section 4.1

b) Give a complete set of transitions.

Exercise 4.10 ◆ Using primitives L, R, and so on defined in Section 4.1, construct a Turing machine that decides the language $\{ww^R | w \in \{a,b\}^*\}$.

Exercise 4.11 Using primitives L, R, and so on defined in Section 4.1, construct a Turing machine that decides the language $\{a^n b^n | n \geq 0\}$.

Section 4.3

Exercise 4.12 Give a formal definition of a multitape Turing machine.

Exercise 4.13 Using primitives L, R, and so on defined in Section 4.1, construct a two-tape Turing machine that decides the language $\{a^n b^n | n \geq 0\}$.

Exercise 4.14 Using primitives L, R, and so on defined in Section 4.1, construct a three-tape Turing machine that decides the language $\{a^n b^n c^n | n \geq 0\}$.

Exercise 4.15 ◆ Using primitives L, R and so on defined in Section 4.1, construct a three-tape Turing machine that computes the function $f(x, y) = x + y$.

Exercise 4.16 ◆ Construct a one-tape two-head Turing machine that decides the language $\{a^n b^n | n \geq 0\}$ in two different ways:

a) Use primitives L, R and so on defined in Section 4.1

b) Give a complete set of transitions.

Exercise 4.17 Using primitives L, R, and so on defined in Section 4.1, construct a one-tape three-head Turing machine that decides the language $\{a^n b^n c^n | n \geq 0\}$.

Exercise 4.18 ◆ Construct a one-tape two-head Turing machine that decides the language $\{ww^R | w \in \{a, b\}^*\}$:

a) Use primitives L, R, an so on defined in Section 4.1

b) Give a complete set of transitions.

Exercise 4.19 Let L_1, L_2 be decidable languages. Let M_1, M_2 be Turing machines computing their characteristic functions. Prove or disprove

a) $L_1 \cup L_2$ is decidable.

b) $L_1 \cap L_2$ is decidable.

c) $\overline{L_1}$ is decidable.

d) ◆ $L_1 L_2$ is decidable.

e) ◆ $(L_1)^*$ is decidable.

Section 4.4

Exercise 4.20 Using primitives R, L, and so on defined in Section 4.1, construct nondeterministic one-tape one-head Turing machines semideciding the languages represented by the following regular expressions:

a) $a^* a b^* b$

b) $aab^* bba^*$

c) $ab^* ab^*$

Exercise 4.21 ◆ Construct a one-head one-tape nondeterministic Turing machine semideciding the language $\{ww | w \in \{a, b\}^*\}$.

a) Use primitives L, R, and so on defined in Section 4.1

b) Give a set of transitions.

Section 4.5

Exercise 4.22 ◆ Turing enumerability of languages can be defined slightly differently than in Definition 4.5.1: A language L is called *Turing enumerable* if L is either empty or $\{f(i)|i \geq 0\}$ for some Turing computable function f. Prove that this notion of Turing enumerability is equivalent to the one in Definition 4.5.1.

Exercise 4.23 Let L be an infinite Turing enumerable language. Show that the language can be enumerated *without repetitions*, that is, $L = \{f(i)|i \geq 0\}$ for some Turing computable function f such that if $i \neq j$ then $f(i) \neq f(j)$.

Exercise 4.24 Show that the class of Turing enumerable languages is closed under the following operations:

a) Union

b) Intersection

c) Concatenation

d) ◆ Kleene star.

Exercise 4.25 ◆ Show that every infinite Turing enumerable language contains an infinite decidable language.

Chapter 5

Undecidability

Chapter 5

Undecidability

5.1 The Church-Turing Thesis

In Chapter 4 we introduced the Turing machine as a computational device that was supposed to model any reasonable computational process. We noticed that, combining Turing machines to build new ones, one could implement practically all major instruments of conventional programming: sequence, conditional branching, and conditional loops. Still, in the beginning Turing machines seemed to be too clumsy to carry out really complex computational tasks. However, we showed that any attempts to enhance computational capacity of Turing machines would fail. They can simulate any assembly language programs runnable on modern computers. Since any program in any high-level programming language can be translated to an assembly language program, this means, in turn, that *any program* in *high-level programming language* can be simulated by a Turing machine.

This reasoning suggests that, by introducing Turing machines, we have reached the limit of what a computational device can do. In other words, Turing machines are able to implement *any algorithm* viewed as a computational procedure that is a sequence of simple steps carried out in accordance with a finite set of instructions. The notion of an algorithm, a finite program solving a computational task, can be traced back to our ancient ancestors, who often faced problems involving rather complex computations. The word *algorithm* itself is a slightly transformed version of the name of *Al-Khoresmi*, the great Middle-Asian mathematician who recognized the importance of special computational procedures solving mathematical problems in the Middle Ages. However, this notion, which nowadays is intuitively clear even to many people who are not related to computer science, did not have an adequate mathematical model until Turing invented his machines. Thus, we adopt the following principle: *Any algorithmic procedure that can be carried out by a human being or by a computer can be carried out by a Turing machine.* This principle, known as the **Church-Turing thesis**, was formulated first by an outstanding American logician Alonzo Church in 1936. Since then, the Turing machine has been viewed as a legitimate mathematical model of algorithms. Note that the thesis is not a mathematical result. An *algorithmic procedure* or an *algorithm* is an informal notion, a result of certain understanding between computer scientists. We could rather call the thesis a philosophical hypothesis. It is conceivable that it can be discarded in the future if someone can come up with a computational procedure widely accepted by the computer community as a legitimate algorithm that cannot be implemented as a Turing machine. The general opinion is that this will never happen.

There are two important practical implications of the Church-Turing thesis. First, according to this principle, if we have managed to come up with even informal, say, verbal, description of some computational procedure, this procedure can be implemented as a Turing machine, and, thus, as a computer program. Thus, to show that some function is computable (Turing computable) or some language is decidable, we do not have to write complete set of transitions for a Turing machine. It is enough to give an exact verbal description of an algorithm understandable by the computer community.

Another implication of the thesis is probably even more important. A Turing machine is a mathematically precise model. It opens a possibility to show that some problems *cannot* be solved by *any* algorithm. What we have to show is that there is no Turing machine that can solve the problem in question.

How can one show that a problem is *unsolvable*, that is, can be solved by no algorithm? Turing machines (or rather, sets of transitions representing them) are finite objects. We will find a way to *enumerate* all of them. Then, applying a *diagonalization* argument, we will show that the set of all functions *cannot* be enumerated. This *cardinality* argument will demonstrate that the set of all possible algorithms is, in a sense, *too small* to cover all computational problems.

The diagonalization idea is very powerful, yet does not provide any specific example of an unsolvable computational problem. In order to find such examples for the classes of algorithms represented by finite and pushdown automata, we applied "pumping" techniques. However, this technique is not applicable for Turing machines which represent all conceivable algorithms. Thus, we will develop a new powerful diagonalization technique that exploits the *power* rather than the *limitations* of Turing machines. Namely, assuming that Turing machines can compute *anything*, we will come to the conclusion that they are capable of recognizing their own properties. These machines operate on their *own codes*. Then, applying a certain diagonalization argument, we will be able to construct a Turing machine that halts and does not halt on the same input (its own code!). This diagonalization technique will expose a large class of nonalgorithmic computational problems: Algorithms *are not capable of recognizing properties of functions computable by algorithms.*

5.2 Universal Turing Machines

Every Turing machine is a finite "program." From this point of view the whole class of Turing machines can be viewed as a *programming language*. The same is true for the classes of finite and pushdown automata, though these classes represent much less powerful programming languages. The main feature of any reasonable programming language is that programs in this language can be *interpreted* and *run* on a computer. We have managed to come up with a mathematical model representing all programs in our programming language. Now the question is whether we can build a mathematical model for the desired computer that interprets and simulates an arbitrary Turing machine. Interpreting and running programs is a *computational task*, a hard one, but still manageable by an *algorithm*. This must be, as our programs run successfully on computers. Thus, according to the Church-Turing thesis, there exists a Turing machine that can solve this task. That is, there exists a Turing machine that can interpret *any* arbitrary Turing machine. Such a Turing machine is called **universal**. The universal machine exists, but building such a machine is a rather complex problem. We are going to devote the rest of the section to the details of this construction.

Our first problem is that the universal machine must be able to *input* Turing machines. Turing machines may have arbitrarily large numbers of states, tape symbols, and instructions, while the alphabet of a universal Turing machine, as well as any other Turing machine, is finite. Thus, we must find a way to encode any Turing machine by a string in some fixed finite alphabet. Moreover, the universal machine must be able to decode the code.

Let $A = \{a_1, a_2, \ldots, a_n, \ldots\}$ and $Q = \{q_1, q_2, \ldots, q_n, \ldots\}$ be infinite sets. We can assume that tape symbols and states of any Turing machine belong to A and Q, respectively. Since the sets are infinite, they contain enough tape symbols and, respectively, states for any Turing machine. What matters for any Turing machine is the *sizes* of the state and tape alphabets, rather than the *names* of the symbols. Changing the names of the symbols or the states does not change the actual set of transitions of the Turing machine. Now, we can encode every symbol a_i as $a\bar{i}$, where $\bar{i}$ is the binary code of the natural number i. For example, $a101$ stands for a_5. Similarly, $q\bar{i}$ encodes q_i. To make decoding easier, we can assume that a_1 always stands for the marker $\triangleright$, a_2 always stands for the blank and $q1$ is assumed to be the start state.

Thus, the alphabet Σ of our universal Turing machine U will contain symbols $a, q, 0, 1$. In addition, it will also contain the symbols $(,), \rightarrow, \leftarrow$, and comma. We also have to find a way to identify halting states. Hence, we will assume that halting states are represented by the *empty* string in the right-hand pairs of transitions. For instance, applying the transition $((q, a), (, a'))$ would mean that a Turing machine had entered a halting state. This will work out all right, as no more transitions will be applied after entering a halting state. Now every Turing machine can be represented as a sequence of codes of transitions $((q\bar{i}, a\bar{j}), (q\bar{k}, t))$ with t being some $a\bar{r}$ or $t \in \{\rightarrow, \leftarrow\}$ ($q\bar{k}$ may be empty). For example, a part of the code could be

$((q1100, a1010), (q101011, \rightarrow))$. We will assume that the sequences of transitions in these codes are lexicographically ordered. Given any Turing machine M, let $\langle M \rangle$ stand for its code as defined as above.

The same method can be used to code any strings in any finite alphabet Σ'. Namely, any Σ' of cardinality $k = |\Sigma'|$ can be considered as the subset $\{a_3, a_4, \ldots, a_{k+2}\}$. We begin with a_3 since a_1 and a_2 are reserved to represent the left marker and the blank. Thus, any string w over the alphabet Σ' can be encoded by the string $\langle w \rangle$ over the alphabet A.

The universal machine U is supposed to simulate any Turing machine M on any input string w over the alphabet of M. We will assume that machine U receives its input as a concatenation $\langle M \rangle \langle w \rangle$, halts if and only if M halts on w, and outputs the value $\langle M(w) \rangle$. We can use a three-tape version of a machine U since, as we know, it can be converted into a standard one-tape machine. Machine U gets its input $\langle M \rangle \langle w \rangle$ on the first tape. It copies the code $\langle M \rangle$ to the second tape, where it consults it whenever it must simulate a next transition of machine M. The code $\langle w \rangle$ is then shifted to the left border of the first tape. The first tape is used to simulate the data processing performed by M on input w. As the head on this tape cannot simultaneously observe the whole string $a\bar{i}$ coding the symbol a_i, we will assume that before simulating any step of M, the head is positioned on the first symbol of $a\bar{i}$, that is, on a. The third tape is used to memorize the code $q\bar{i}$ of the current state q_i of machine M. (see Figure 5.1.) To simulate one step of machine M, machine U uses the state q_j (or, rather, its code $q\bar{j}$) of machine M and the code of symbol a_i it observes on the first tape. It then finds the code of a transition with the left-hand pair (q_j, a_i) on the second tape and, simulating application of this transition, performs the necessary transformations (or just moves) on the first tape and writes the code of a new state on the third tape. This completes the description of the operation of U.

5.3   The Halting Problem

Consider the class of partial functions $f : N \rightarrow N$ with a domain aof ny subset of N. At least some of these functions are computable by Turing machines, or, equivalently, by algorithms. Is every partial function computable by an algorithm? We are going to show that the answer to this question is negative. Our proof will involve a *cardinality* argument. We will show that all Turing machines can be *enumerated*. On the other hand, we will establish using a *diagonalization* argument that the partial functions cannot be enumerated.

How can we enumerate all Turing machines? To accomplish this, we will encode every Turing machine M by a natural number, $n(M)$, so that the machine M can uniquely be restored from its code. The first part of our coding procedure will, given a machine M, find its code $\langle M \rangle$ as defined in Section 5.2. Now consider the code of some transition, say, $((q1010, a1110), (q101, \rightarrow))$. Our goal is to code this string in binary. Indices of states and tape symbols are already in binary. However,

Input Tape

$\langle w \rangle$	

↑

Input Tape

$\langle M \rangle$	

Current State

$\langle$initial state of $M\rangle$	

Figure 5.1 U after Initialization on $\langle M \rangle \langle w \rangle$

there are seven other symbols that must be coded: (,), →, ←, a, q, and comma. Let us code each of these symbols by a 5-bit string as follows: The symbol (is coded by 10000,) is coded by 10001, and successive symbols in the list are numbered by adding 1 to the prior binary number. Thus, the comma will be coded by 10110. Now, to differentiate indices from these seven symbols, we encode each 1 by the 5-bit string 11111 and each 0 by the string 00000. Thus, our transition above will be encoded as

10000 10000 10101 11111 00000 11111 00000 10110 10100 11111 11111 11111
00000 10001 10110 10000 10101 11111 00000 11111 10110 10010 10001 10001

We separated each 5-bit group by spaces to make the relationship between codes and what they code more transparent. In fact, the resulting string should not have any spaces. Now we can consider the binary string obtained this way from code $\langle M \rangle$ as the binary representation of the desired natural number $n(M)$. Note that it always begins with 1 (as the code of (in the beginning of any set of transitions is 10000). Moreover, machine M can easily be restored, given its code $n(M)$.

Now let k be any natural number. We can associate a Turing machine T_k with this number using the following agreement: let us fix some Turing machine T that does not halt on any input; if $k = n(M)$ for some Turing machine M, then T_k is M, otherwise T_k is T. Thus, we obtained a *numbering* of *all* Turing machines (known as **Gödel numbering**). We will use this numbering to prove the following result.

Theorem 5.3.1 *There exists a function $f : N \to N$ that is not partial Turing computable.*

Proof: Every partial Turing computable function is computed by some Turing machine. Let φ_k denote the one-argument function computed by the machine T_k. Some machines T_k may compute functions of multiple arguments; however, we can always assume that T_k computes one-argument function if we disregard the commas separating arguments. Next, consider the *diagonal* function f defined as follows:

$$f(x) = \begin{cases} \varphi_x(x) + 1, & \text{if } x \in Dom(\varphi_x) \\ 0, & \text{otherwise} \end{cases}$$

The construction of f is represented in Figure 5.2. Rows in this table represent the functions φ_i. Columns represent the arguments. The construction of f is designed to make f different from each function φ_x on argument x, for example, along the diagonal of Figure 5.2.

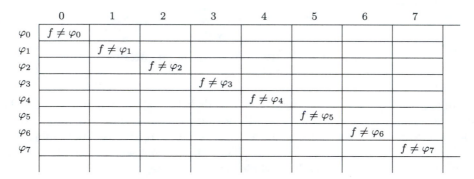

Figure 5.2 The Diagonal Function

Suppose by way of contradiction that f is computed by some machine T_i. As $Dom(f) = N$, T_i halts on the input i. Consider the value $f(i) = T_i(i)$. According to the definition of f, $f(i) = T_i(i) + 1$, a contradiction.

$$\boxed{\text{End Proof}}$$

Theorem 5.3.1 shows that some functions cannot be computed by algorithms. However, the diagonal function we "constructed" is too "abstract." We would like to find more "natural" examples of problems that cannot be computed by algorithms.

Consider the following computational task: Given the text of any program P (in any programming language, pick your favorite) and any input X, determine if P *halts* on X. Can we design an algorithm *Halt* that solves this problem? The positive answer to this question would be of utmost importance for designers of program debuggers. If your program P worked "too long" on some input X, you could apply the debugging software implementing *Halt* to determine if P looped on X, which would imply the presence of a "bug" in your design of P. However, the answer is negative; No such algorithm *Halt* exists. If such an algorithm *Halt* existed, it could then be implemented as a program, say, *HALT* in the *same programming language* as any other program P. This program $HALT(P, X)$ would take two inputs, P and X, and outputs 1 if P halted on X, and 0, otherwise. However, we can now slightly modify *HALT* to build another program $DIAGONAL(P)$ that, given the text of a program P as its input, calls *HALT* on the input (P, P). The program *DIAGONAL* is, in fact, a specific implementation of the diagonal argument used above to construct a *diagonal* function computable by no Turing machine. Finally, based on *DIAGONAL*, we build another program $CONTR(P)$ that calls *DIAGONAL* as a module and *does not halt* if and only if $DIAGONAL(P) = 1$ (that is, *HALT* determines in this case whether P halts on the input being *its own text*). The construction of the program *CONTR* is presented in Figure 5.3.

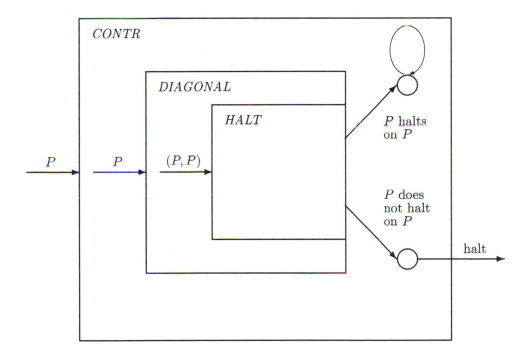

Figure 5.3 The Program *CONTR*

Now we examine the behavior of the program *CONTR* using *its own text CONTR* as input. Suppose *CONTR(CONTR)* halts. Notice that the result of the computation $HALT(CONTR, CONTR) = 0$, that is, *HALT* answers that *CONTR does not halt* on *CONTR*. Now suppose that *CONTR(CONTR)* does not halt. Then $HALT(CONTR, CONTR) = 1$, that is, *HALT* claims that *CONTR halts* on *CONTR*. We have a contradiction. What caused this contradiction was our assumption that the algorithm *Halt* could be programmed in the same programming language as any other program. However, this assumption is a consequence of a more general Church-Turing thesis stating that some programming languages (say, Turing machines) are *universal* mathematical models representing *all* conceivable algorithms. Since we have adopted the thesis, we are compelled to acknowledge that *Halt* cannot exist.

Our reasoning above was somewhat informal. We used such terms as *programming language* and *text of a program as input* that were not defined. Now we will formalize the above reasoning using the framework of Turing machines.

We agreed to adopt a Turing machine as a mathematical model for a "universal" programming language. Now, we have to address mathematically the problem of running Turing machines on their own "texts." This is where universal Turing machines come into the picture: They can manipulate other Turing machines given their *codes*. Thus, we consider the following **Halting Set**:

$$HALT = \{\langle M\rangle\langle w\rangle|\ \text{Turing machine } M \text{ halts on the input } w\}$$

Note that $HALT$ is semidecidable (or, in other words, Turing enumerable): Given the code $\langle M\rangle\langle w\rangle$, the universal Turing machine U can simulate M running on w and halt if M halts on w. That is, U halts on $\langle M\rangle\langle w\rangle$ if and only if M halts on w. Now we are going to prove the following fundamental result.

Theorem 5.3.2 *The halting set is not decidable (Turing computable).*

Proof: Suppose $HALT$ is Turing computable. Consider then the following set:

$$H_0 = \{\langle M\rangle|\ \text{Turing machine } M \text{ halts on the input string } \langle M\rangle\}$$

H_0 formalizes the restriction of the "program" $HALT(P, X)$ to the input (P, P) in the above informal argument. Since $HALT$ is decidable, H_0 is clearly decidable as well. A Turing machine T deciding $HALT$ can be modified to form the machine T_0 that decides H_0 as follows. T_0 converts any input $\langle M\rangle$ to the "pair" $\langle M\rangle\langle M\rangle$ and then calls the machine T. According to Theorem 4.5.1, if H_0 is decidable, then its complement $\overline{H_0}$ is decidable. However, we are going to show that $\overline{H_0}$ is not even *semidecidable.*

Suppose $\overline{H_0}$ is semidecidable. Then there exists a Turing machine M_0 that semidecides it. Run M_0 on its own code $\langle M_0\rangle$. Suppose M_0 halts on $\langle M_0\rangle$. This means that $\langle M_0\rangle$ is in $\overline{H_0}$. However, then $\langle M_0\rangle \notin H_0$, that is, M_0 *does not* halt on the input $\langle M_0\rangle$, a contradiction. Now, suppose M_0 does not halt on its code. This means that $\langle M_0\rangle \notin \overline{H_0}$, that is $\langle M_0\rangle \in H_0$. However, then, according to the definition of H_0, M_0 *halts* on $\langle M_0\rangle$ and we get a contradiction again. Thus, *no* Turing machine can semidecide $\overline{H_0}$.

$$\boxed{\text{End Proof}}$$

The above proof actually gives us two more results.

Theorem 5.3.3 *The class of all Turing enumerable languages is not closed under complement.*

Theorem 5.3.4 *There exist languages that are not Turing enumerable.*

5.4 Undecidable Problems

The halting set is a formalization of the so-called **Halting Problem**: to determine if an arbitrary Turing machine halts on an arbitrary input string. In the previous section we have shown that this problem cannot be decided by a Turing machine. Consequently, according to the Church-Turing thesis, *no algorithm can decide the Halting Problem.* In this section we will give many other examples of undecidable problems. In fact, we are going to describe a large class of "natural" undecidable problems related to *properties* of programs.

It will be convenient for us in this section to use the word *program* for a Turing machine. In any event, according to Church-Turing thesis, any *algorithm* can be implemented as a Turing machine. Since languages are just sets of strings, when considering sets of strings representing the texts of programs, we can call some languages *properties* of programs. From this perspective, a program P has the property defining the language L if $\langle P \rangle \in L$ and does not have this property if $\langle P \rangle \notin L$. For example, the two languages below obviously represent some properties of programs:

- $L_1 = \{ \langle P \rangle \mid P \text{ outputs } 1 \text{ on input } 0 \}$.

- $L_2 = \{ \langle P \rangle \mid P \text{ terminates (halts) on input } 0 \text{ in at most two steps} \}$.

Definition 5.4.1 *Let, for any function f, $\mathcal{P}_f$ stand for the set of all programs computing the function f. A property L of programs is called* **functional** *if*

1. *For any function f, either $\langle P \rangle \in L$ for all programs $P \in \mathcal{P}_f$, or $\langle P \rangle \notin L$ for all programs $P \in \mathcal{P}_f$; and*

2. *Neither L nor its complement $\overline{L}$ are empty sets.*

Consider the languages L_1 and L_2 defined above. L_1 clearly represents a functional property since, for any function f, either $f(0) = 1$, or $f(0) \neq 1$. If $f(0) = 1$, then the codes of all the programs P computing f are in L_1. If $f(0) \neq 1$, then no codes for programs P computing f are in L_1. Hence, the first condition in the definition of a functional property is satisfied. The second condition of the definition of functional property obviously holds as well. There are programs, say, for the constant 1 function, with codes in L_1, and programs, say, for the constant 0 function, with codes not in L_1.

On the other hand, L_2 is not a functional property. To demonstrate this, consider programs computing the function $f(w) = w$. To compute such a function, a program P may do nothing, or carry out some dummy actions, since the output is not different from the input. One can easily design a Turing machine computing f that halts in at most two steps on any input. Likewise, it is easy to design a Turing machine that does essentially nothing but halts in at least three steps.

As it turns out, functional properties of programs are the ones that are undecidable. To establish this fact, we are going to develop a general mechanism that relates computational problems to each other — the mechanism of *reduction*. Informally, a computational problem A is reducible to a computational problem B if a solution to the problem B can be "translated" to a solution to the problem A. Now, suppose we have established that

a) The problem A is reducible to B;

b) A is undecidable.

Then we must conclude that problem B is undecidable as well, since, if B were decidable, its algorithmic solution could have been "translated" to a solution for problem A.

Now we formalize the above reasoning.

Definition 5.4.2 *Let $L_1, L_2 \subseteq \Sigma^*$ be languages. We say that L_1 is reducible to L_2 if there exists a Turing computable function $r : \Sigma^* \to \Sigma^*$ such that, for any $x \in \Sigma^*, x \in L_1$ if and only if $r(x) \in L_2$.*

The computable function r provides the desired "translation" of the problem to decide L_1 to the problem of deciding L_2. That is, if you had an algorithm $\mathcal{B}$ deciding L_2 and the reduction r (or, rather, an algorithm computing r), then you could decide if $x \in L_1$ by the following algorithm $\mathcal{A}$:

Compute $r(x)$. Apply $\mathcal{B}$ to $r(x)$. If $r(x) \in L_2$, then $x \in L_1$; otherwise $x \in \overline{L_1}$.

Suppose you are surfing the Web and searching for a list of places selling some common item, like pizza, and your search returns thousands of hits. You decide to look for the cheapest pizza, but the list is too long, you will starve before looking at all the entries. However, if your search engine has a sort utility, you can sort the hits according to price and then the task becomes a matter of choosing the first place on the list. What you have just done is to reduce the problem of testing for the least cost entry in a list to the problem of testing for the first entry in a list.

Conversely, if L_1 were undecidable and reducible to L_2, it would imply the undecidability of L_2. For, otherwise L_1 would be decidable by the above algorithm $\mathcal{A}$. Now we will apply this idea to demonstrate the undecidability of any functional property.

Theorem 5.4.1 (Rice's Theorem) *Any functional property of programs is undecidable.*

Proof: We begin with the following remark. When we code Turing machines using the coding $\langle P \rangle$, some strings $w \in \Sigma^*$ may not code any Turing machine. It is reasonable to assume though that any such w actually codes a Turing machine that halts on no input [we made a similar assumption about the coding $n()$ in Section 5.3].Now according to this assumption, any string over the underlying alphabet Σ is the code of some Turing machine.

Let L be any functional property. Let $HALT$ be the halting set from the previous section. Let S be a Turing machine that halts on no input. Then either its code $\langle S \rangle$ is in L, or it is in $\overline{L}$. If $\langle S \rangle \in \overline{L}$, we will try to show that $HALT$ is reducible to L. If $\langle S \rangle \in L$, we can note that since L is a functional property, $\overline{L}$ is obviously a functional property as well, and we can similarly show that $HALT$ is reducible to $\overline{L}$. In the first case, it will imply undecidability of L; in the second case, we will thus demonstrate undecidability of $\overline{L}$. Since, obviously L is undecidable if and only if $\overline{L}$ is undecidable, in both cases our goal will be achieved. We are going to consider the second case, that is, $\langle S \rangle \in \overline{L}$.

As we have just mentioned, our aim in this case is to reduce the halting set $HALT$ to the language L. Let f be the function defined on no argument. Machine S obviously computes this function. Since $S \in \overline{L}$ and L is a functional property, $\mathcal{P}_f \subseteq \overline{L}$. Using the part 2 of the definition of a functional property (Definition 5.4.1), we conclude that there exists at least one program $R \in L$. Let g be the function computable by program R. Since L is a functional property, $\mathcal{P}_g \subseteq L$.

We are now ready to define a function r reducing $HALT$ to L. Given any Turing machine P, consider a Turing machine T that implements the following algorithm on any input $w \in \Sigma^*$.

Algorithm 5.4.1 Run P on its code $\langle P \rangle$. If P halts, run R on w and output $R(w)$.

> End Algorithm

There exists a simple algorithm that translates the code $\langle P \rangle$ of any Turing machine P into a code for the above machine T. According to the Church-Turing Thesis, this algorithm can be implemented as a Turing machine, say, A. Let r be the (Turing computable) function computed by A. We are going to show that r is the desired function reducing $HALT$ to L. That is, we have to show that

$$\langle P \rangle \in HALT \longleftrightarrow r(\langle P \rangle) \in L$$

Suppose $\langle P \rangle \in HALT$. Then P halts on its own code, and, according to the definition of $\langle T \rangle = r(\langle P \rangle)$, on any input w, T produces the same output as R. Thus, $\langle T \rangle$ is in $\mathcal{P}_g$, and, consequently, it is in L.

Now suppose that $\langle P \rangle \notin HALT$. Then P never halts on its code. Consequently, the machine T never halts on any input w. Thus, $\langle T \rangle \in \mathcal{P}_f$, and, therefore, $\langle T \rangle \notin L$.

We have established that $HALT$ is reducible to L. As we argued above, if L were decidable, it would imply the decidability of $HALT$. Thus, L must be undecidable.

$$\boxed{\text{End Proof}}$$

What Rice's theorem shows is that properties of programs are undecidable if they are, in fact, "about functions," rather than "about programs." It can be used as a powerful tool to show that a large variety of properties of programs are undecidable. Here are some examples of such properties:

- $K_1 = \{\langle P \rangle | P \text{ outputs 5 on the input 0 and does not halt on the input 5}\}$.

- $K_2 = \{\langle P \rangle | P \text{ does not halt on the input 5}\}$.

- $K_3 = \{\langle P \rangle | P \text{ halts on every input}\}$.

- $K_4 = \{\langle P \rangle | P \text{ is equivalent to a given program } P_0\}$.

- $K_5 = \{\langle P \rangle | \text{ the number of inputs on which } P \text{ halts is finite}\}$

- $K_6 = \{\langle P \rangle | P(x) = 1 \text{ if } x \text{ is even and } P \text{ does not halt on any odd input}\}$.

We can easily show that all these properties are functional and thus conclude that all of them are undecidable. Let us show that K_3 is a functional property. Let f be any function. If f is defined on all arguments (that is, $Dom(f) = \Sigma^*$) then $\mathcal{P}_f \subseteq K_3$. If f is undefined on at least one argument, then obviously no program P with the code in K_3 computes f, that is, $\mathcal{P}_f \subseteq \overline{K_3}$. Since there obviously exist programs that are in K_3 and that are not in K_3, the second part of the definition of a functional property is satisfied as well. Thus, K_3 represents a functional property. According to Rice's theorem, it is undecidable. Now we show that K_6 is a functional property (other examples can be found in Exercise 5.4). Let f be any function. First, let us assume that $f(x) = 1$ on every even x and f is undefined on every odd x. Then $\mathcal{P}_f \subseteq K_6$. If $f(x) \neq 1$ for some even x or $f(x)$ is defined for some odd x, then $\mathcal{P}_f \subseteq \overline{K_6}$. Thus, the first condition of the definition of a functional property is satisfied. There exist programs that are in K_6 and that are not in K_6. Thus, K_6 is a functional property, and, consequently, undecidable.

Now we present some examples of decidable properties of programs:

- $M_1 = \{\langle P \rangle | \text{ the program } P \text{ contains the transition } ((q, 0), (p, 1))\}$.

- $M_2 = \{\langle P \rangle | \text{ there exists a configuration of } P \text{ that yields a configuration of } P \text{ with the given state } q\}$.

- $M_3 = \{\langle P \rangle | \text{ starting on the empty tape, the program } P \text{ reaches the given state } q \text{ in at most five steps}\}$.

- $M_4 = \{\langle P \rangle | \text{ there exists a configuration of } P \text{ with the given state } p \text{ that yields a configuration with the given state } q\}$.

One can easily design a decision algorithms for all these properties (Exercise 5.5). In particular, it means that these properties are not functional — for, if they were, then, according to Rice's theorem, they would be undecidable. More examples of decidable and undecidable properties can be found in Exercise 5.6.

Exercises

Section 5.2

Exercise 5.1 Using the coding system described in Section 5.2, find the codes for the following transitions:

a) $((q_3, a_4), (q_4, \rightarrow))$

b) $((q_2, \sqcup), (q_3, a_4))$

c) $((q_1, a_1), (q_3, \rightarrow))$

Exercise 5.2 Using the coding system described in the Section 5.2, find the code $\langle w \rangle$ for the following strings w:

a) $a_3 a_4 a_5$

b) $a_3 \sqcup a_4 a_4$

c) $\triangleright \sqcup a_3 a_4$

Section 5.3

Exercise 5.3 ◆◆ A non-Turing computable function can be built without direct diagonal construction. Let us define a function g as follows. For every integer n, $g(n)$ is the largest number $k \geq 0$ such that there exists a Turing machine with the tape alphabet $\{\triangleright, \sqcup, a, b\}$ and at most n states which, when started on empty tape, halts at configuration $(h, \sqcup a^k)$. (Such a function is known as the *busy-beaver function*.)

a) Show that the function g is *monotone infinitely growing*, that is, for all $n \geq 0, g(n) \leq g(n+1)$ and for infinitely many n, $g(n) < g(n+1)$.

b) Let f be an arbitrary Turing computable function. Let m_f be the number of states of some Turing machine which, for any $n \geq 0$, when started on the blank tape, halts with the output $a^{f(n)}$. Show that, for any n, $g(n+m_f) \geq f(n)$. [In other words, for every Turing computable function f, one can find a constant m_f such that $g(n + m_f)$ is greater than $f(n)$.]

c) Show that the function g is not Turing computable. [Hint: If g is Turing computable, so is $f(n) = g(2n)$. Now apply the statements proved in 2) and 1) to get a contradiction.]

Section 5.4

Exercise 5.4 Show that the following properties defined in the Section 5.4 are functional:

a) K_1

b) K_2

c) K_4

d) K_5

Exercise 5.5 Briefly describe algorithms deciding the following properties defined in the Section 5.4

a) M_1

b) M_2

c) M_3

d) M_4

Exercise 5.6 ◆ Determine which of the following properties of programs are decidable. If a property is decidable, briefly describe an algorithm deciding it. If a property is undecidable, first show that it is functional.

a) $R_1 = \{\langle P \rangle | P$ terminates on all even numbers$\}$.

b) $R_2 = \{\langle P \rangle | P$ halts on no input$\}$.

c) $R_3 = \{\langle P \rangle | P$ reaches state q, when started on the blank tape, in at most 10 steps, or reaches the state p, when started on input a, in at most 20 steps $\}$.

d) $R_5 = \{\langle P \rangle | P$ contains no transition with the left-hand side $(q, \sqcup)\}$.

e) $R_6 = \{\langle P \rangle |$ state q can be reached from state p in at most three steps $\}$.

f) $R_7 = \{\langle P \rangle | P$ has fewer than 100 states and halts on input 0$\}$.

Chapter 6

Computational Complexity

Chapter 6

Computational Complexity

6.1 The Definition and the Class P

In Chapter 5 we observed numerous examples of problems that cannot be solved by algorithms. Now we are going to take a closer look at the class of problems that *can* be solved by algorithms, that is, the class of decidable problems. A large number of such problems have been presented in this book, and the reader with any experience in computer science can probably add many more to this list. While discussing the algorithmic solutions to some of the decidable problems, we tried to underline the feasibility of their algorithmic solutions by using the word "efficient." However, since this term is not formally (mathematically) defined, it is definitely too vague to yield a common understanding of what is meant. Now, having a universal model of algorithms, Turing machines, we are in a position to approach the problem of efficiency on a formal basis.

How can one naturally quantify efficiency of a computational process? Suppose a problem has at least two different algorithmic solutions. How can we judge which one is more efficient? A natural solution seems to compare their *running times*, that is, the number of steps they carry out to produce the output. We can define running time formally based on our mathematical model of algorithms — standard (one-tape one-head) Turing machines. Given a Turing machine M and an input w, its **running time** $t_M(w)$ is the number of steps M carries out on w from the initial configuration to a halting configuration.

Let us consider the running time of some of the algorithms that we have discussed. Finite automata are like Turing machines except that they do not write and do not move the head backwards. Hence, finite automata can be considered a type of Turing machine. Let A be any deterministic finite automaton. When A reads a character, it just changes its state and moves its head one position to the right. These actions correspond to the execution of two instructions of a Turing machine. Thus, the running time $t_A(w) = 2 \cdot |w|$ for any A and any input w.

Consider a simple deterministic Turing machine M that recognizes the palindromes $w = w^R$. This machine "memorizes" the leftmost symbol, runs to the right end, compares it with the rightmost symbol, then "memorizes" the second symbol from the right, runs back to the second leftmost symbol, compares it with memorized symbol, and so on. In the first phase, M performs $|w| + 2$ instructions as "hitting" the right delimiting blank and returning to the rightmost nonblank symbol requires two additional instructions. In the second phase M performs $(|w| + 2) - 2$ instructions, and $(|w| + 2) - 4$ instructions in the third phase, and so on. The total number of such phases is $|w|/2$ ($[|w|/2] + 1$ for a w of odd length). Summing the above numbers, we find out that $t_M(w) = c \cdot |w|^2$ for some constant number c. [The reader is encouraged to construct the exact expression for $t_M(w)$ as requested in Exercise 6.1.]

In these examples, the running time increases with the length of the input. There are many examples of computational problems (especially those using graphs), when the running time of solutions can vary dramatically even for inputs of the same length. Thus, we have to analyze two different types of running time:

1. *Worst-case* when we consider the longest running time for all inputs of any given length;

2. *Average-case* when we consider the average of all running times for inputs of a given length.

The following discussion below will address only the worst case analysis. For this case, we can view the running time of a Turing machine M as a function $f : N \to N$, where $f(n)$ is the maximum number of steps M uses on any input of the length n.

We are interested in comparing the running times of different Turing machines. A further consideration is to be able to establish if a running time of f can be *bounded* by some other (simpler to express) function g. In this analysis, we are interested in investigating how algorithms (implemented as Turing machines) behave on a variety of larger and larger inputs. This type of analysis is called *asymptotic*. Consider, for example, $f(n) = 2n^3 + 2n + 5$ and $g = 10n^2 + 3$. For the numbers $n \leq 4$, $f(n) \leq g(n)$, however, when n increases, f grows much faster than g. What defines the rate of growth of g is its highest term n^3. Asymptotic analysis disregards lower terms as well as the constant 2. To express the fact that the rate of growth of g is not greater than the rate of growth of f, we use the so-called *big-O* notation: $g(n) = O(f(n))$. $f(n)$ itself is $O(n^3)$.

How much can we learn about the real complexity of computational problems from the model of computational complexity we just introduced? As we have shown in Chapter 4, the computational power of standard Turing machines is the same as the computational power of, say, random access Turing machines that avoid moving the head back and forth unnecessarily by using direct memory access. Even a simple two-head one-tape machine can recognize palindromes faster than the above machine M. This machine just moves the second head to the right end of the input string w, of length n and starts moving the two heads toward each other, comparing the symbols they observe. The running time $t_K(n)$ of such a machine K is $c \cdot n$ for some constant c. Thus, running time depends on the model that we choose, and the immediate conclusion may be that we learn very little about the real complexity of a computational problem using running time to measure it.

However, careful examination of the simulations of one model of algorithms by another developed in Chapter 4 can bring the reader to the following conclusion: *If K is any deterministic Turing machine and M is a fancy Turing machine that simulates K with running time $t_M(n)$, then $t_K(n)$ is $O(p(t_M(n)))$ for some polynomial $p(x)$.* (We refer the reader to any book on computational complexity for details. For example, [Papadimitriou]). For instance, a two-head Turing machine K recognizing palindromes runs in time $t_K(n) = c \cdot n$. Simulating it by a standard one-tape one-head machine M, we get the running time $t_M(n) = c' \cdot n^2$. The polynomial $p(x)$ in this case is $d \cdot x^2$ for some constant number d. In other words, all formal models of the same algorithm are *polynomially related to each other* as far as their computational complexity is concerned. When we translate an algorithm to a different formalism, its running time can increase, but the rate of growth is bounded by a polynomial.

How important is this fact for practical computer scientists? To answer this question, we consider the following class of Turing machines.

Definition 6.1.1 *We say that a Turing machine M is **polynomially bounded** if there exists a polynomial $p(x)$ such that, for any postive integer n, $t_M(n) \leq p(n)$.*

Based on the above definition we can define the following class of computational problems.

Definition 6.1.2 *A language is called **polynomially decidable** if there exists a polynomially bounded Turing machine that decides it.*

The class of all polynomially decidable languages is denoted by $\mathcal{P}$.

Examples of languages in $\mathcal{P}$, as we have just observed, are all regular languages and the language of palindromes.

Consider any language L in $\mathcal{P}$. It is decided by a polynomially bounded standard (one-head one-tape) Turing machine. In light of our reasoning, this means L can be decided by a polynomially bounded machine *within any formal paradigm of algorithm.*

Can any algorithm be implemented as a polynomially bounded machine? Consider the following computational problem known as the TRAVELING SALESMAN PROBLEM: Given a weighted undirected graph G and a vertex a_0 in G (Figure 6.1), find the path of minimum cost that begins and ends in a_0 and visits every vertex in G. One can interpret this problem as the task of finding the shortest distance for a salesman who must visit a number of cities. The cities are represented by the vertices of the graph and the distances between the cities are represented by weights assigned to the edges of the graph.

There is a simple algorithmic solution to this problem. Let n be the number of vertices of G. For every sequence of vertices, $a_{i_1}, a_{i_2}, \ldots, a_{i_k}, k \leq n$, determine

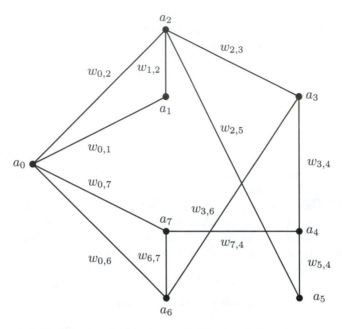

Figure 6.1 An Undirected Weighted Graph

if it is a path visiting every vertex, and then find the path that has the minimum weight. While being formally correct, this algorithm looks somewhat suspicious. The problem with this algorithm is that there are too many paths to inspect. The total number of sequences a_{i_1}, a_{i_2}, ..., a_{i_k}, $k \leq n$ is obviously $(n-1)!$, and even for such a small number as $n = 11$, the algorithm has to inspect $10! = 3,628,800$ paths. For a number n such as 50, the task extends far beyond the computational capabilities of the most powerful computers. It would take billions of billions of years to inspect all paths in such a graph!

The algorithm for the TRAVELING SALESMAN PROBLEM is obviously infeasible from a practical perspective. Any machine implementation of this algorithm is definitely not polynomially bounded. The number of possible paths to be inspected is at least exponential in n. Our last example makes clearer the value of the class $\mathcal{P}$ that has been widely accepted by computer science community: *Problems in $\mathcal{P}$ are the ones that may have practically feasible algorithmic solutions.* In a certain sense, this statement can be interpreted as a *quantitative* version of the Church-Turing thesis. While all Turing machines solve all potentially solvable computational problems, polynomially bounded Turing machines solve all practically feasible computational problems.

How sound is this new version of the Church-Turing thesis? Suppose we designed an algorithm that runs in time x^{1000}. One can argue that this algorithm is not practically feasible at all. Even an algorithm that runs in time $100^{100}x^2$ can hardly be viewed as practically feasible. However, when a polynomial-time algorithm for a hard problem is found, it often clears a way to find a practical solution to the problem. Polynomials that bound the running times of practical algorithms usually have a very low degree and relatively small constant coefficients. This can be regarded as a strong empirical argument supporting the quantitative version of the Church-Turing thesis.

The reader may have noticed that we avoided the question of whether the TRAVELING SALESMAN PROBLEM is in $\mathcal{P}$. The algorithm solving this problem was definitely not polynomially bounded. However, this does not mean that the problem is not in $\mathcal{P}$. There may still exist a more efficient polynomially bounded solution to the problem. As we will discuss in Section 6.2, the question of whether the TRAVELING SALESMAN PROBLEM is in $\mathcal{P}$ is *open*.

We have still not answered the fundamental question: Do there exist decidable languages that are not in $\mathcal{P}$, that is, that cannot be decided by polynomially bounded algorithms? To demonstrate that there exist undecidable problems, we exhibited a problem (the halting set) for which no solution could be found by a Turing machine. A similar idea can be applied to show that there are decidable problems not in $\mathcal{P}$. To do so, one can define a decidable problem with no polynomially bounded solution. To formally establish this fact, we need the following simple property of the class $\mathcal{P}$, which is interesting on its own right.

Theorem 6.1.1 *The class $\mathcal{P}$ is closed under complement.*

Proof: Suppose a Turing machine decides a language $L \in \mathcal{P}$. Then, $\overline{L}$ is decidable by the polynomially bounded machine M', which outputs 0 if M outputs 1, and vice versa.

$$\boxed{\text{End Proof}}$$

Now we can exhibit a decidable language that is not in $\mathcal{P}$. Consider the language

$$H_{\mathcal{P}} = \{\langle M \rangle \langle w \rangle | M \text{ accepts (outputs 1 on) } w \text{ in at most } 2^{|w|} \text{ steps}\}$$

This language can be viewed as a $\mathcal{P}$ "version" of the halting set we observed in Chapter 5. $H_{\mathcal{P}}$ is easily decidable. Given any $\langle M \rangle$ and any input $\langle w \rangle$, the decision algorithm can simulate machine M on w for at most $2^{|w|}$ steps and find out if M outputs 1 on w. On the other hand, we can prove the following.

Theorem 6.1.2 *The language $H_{\mathcal{P}}$ is not in $\mathcal{P}$.*

Proof: Our proof mimics the proof of undecidability of the halting set H (Theorem 5.3.2). Only this time we must show that $H_{\mathcal{P}}$ is beyond the reach of the polynomially bounded rather than all Turing machines.

Suppose $H_{\mathcal{P}} \in \mathcal{P}$. Then we can easily transform a polynomially bounded Turing machine that decides the language $H_{\mathcal{P}}$ to a polynomially bounded Turing machine that decides the language:

$$L = \{\langle M \rangle | M \text{ accepts } \langle M \rangle \text{ within at most } 2^{|w|} \text{ steps}\}$$

According to Theorem 6.1.1, the complement of this language $\overline{L}$ is in $\mathcal{P}$ as well. Thus, there exists a polynomially bounded machine M_0 that decides the language $\overline{L}$. That is, M_0 accepts all codes of Turing machines M that fail to accept their own codes $\langle M \rangle$ within $2^{|\langle M \rangle|}$ steps. Let $p(x)$ be a polynomial that bounds the running time of machine M_0.

Whatever polynomial $p(x)$ is, its rate of growth is smaller than the rate of growth of the function 2^x. That is, there exists a positive integer x_0 such that $p(x) \leq 2^x$ for all $x \geq x_0$. We can assume that the length of the code $\langle M_0 \rangle$ is at least x_0. One can always add dummy instructions to M_0 that do nothing, but just increase the length of the encoding.

Now, given its own code $\langle M_0 \rangle$ as the input, M_0 must output either 1 or 0. However, in both cases we will get a contradiction. Suppose M_0 outputs 1 on $\langle M_0 \rangle$. This means that M_0 does not accept $\langle M_0 \rangle$ within $2^{|\langle M_0 \rangle|}$ steps. However, the running time of M_0 on $\langle M_0 \rangle$ is bounded by $p(|\langle M_0 \rangle|) \leq 2^{|\langle M_0 \rangle|}$. Thus, if M_0 does not accept its code within $2^{|\langle M_0 \rangle|}$ steps, it must output 0, a contradiction. Now suppose that M_0 outputs 0 on $\langle M_0 \rangle$. Then M_0 accepts $\langle M_0 \rangle$ (within $2^{|\langle M_0 \rangle|}$ steps, which does not matter in this case), a contradiction.

$$\boxed{\text{End Proof}}$$

6.2   The Class $\mathcal{NP}$

In this section we consider many problems about graphs. We briefly review the terminology related to them. Every graph G is a pair (V, E), where V is a finite set of vertices, and $E \subseteq V \times V$ is the set of edges. A *path* is a sequence of vertices, v_1, v_2, ..., v_n such that (v_i, v_{i+1}) is an edge of G for each i with $1 \leq i < n$. A *cycle* in G is a path that begins and ends with the same vertex. A cycle is *simple* if it contains every vertex (except the initial one) at most once. An undirected graph is called *complete* if each pair of vertices in it is connected by an edge.

In Section 6.1 we built a decidable analogue of the halting set that was not in $\mathcal{P}$. Whatever the theoretical importance of this example is, one can hardly agree that it represents a "real" computational problem. Our claim that class $\mathcal{P}$ represents the practically feasible computational problems will be better justified if we can exhibit practical computational problems that are not polynomially bounded.

Our first candidate for such a problem is obviously the TRAVELING SALES-MAN PROBLEM. However, before we try to make a judgment about whether this problem is in class $\mathcal{P}$, we must make sure that this natural computational problem can formally be represented in form of a *language*, that is, a set of strings. The original formulation of the problem is an example of an *optimization problem*, since it requires the finding of the *optimal* (minimal) solution among many possible ones. To convert this problem into a language, we will change it slightly, introducing a bound B and dividing all graphs into two groups:

- Those that have a simple cycle with the total weight not exceeding B, and

- Those that do not have such a cycle.

We will also pay attention to only simple cycles that contain all vertices in G. We will call such a cycle a *tour*. Note that it does not matter where the tour begins and ends. The total weight of a tour does not change if we change the starting vertex. In order to formulate the language version of the TRAVELING SALESMAN PROBLEM, we first give a more formal version of the problem:

> Given an integer $m \geq 2$, the weight matrix $(w_{i,j})$ of some graph G, and a bound $B \geq 0$, determine whether there is a tour $v_{i_0}, v_{i_1}, \ldots, v_{i_m}$ with the total weight $w_{i_0,i_1} + w_{i_1,i_2} + \ldots + w_{i_{m-1},i_m} \leq B$.

Still, the formulation is not presented as a language. To complete our formalization, we have to represent every input in the form of a string over some finite alphabet. The input for the given problem consists of a graph G, the weight matrix $(w_{i,j})$, and the bound B. The graph G can be encoded by its *adjacency matrix* of size $n \times n$, where $n = |V|$. The adjacency matrix has a 1 in position (i, j) if there is an edge from v_i to v_j in G, and 0 otherwise. This matrix can be represented in a linearized form as a string (of length n^2). Let $c(G)$ stand for this code of G. Similarly, the weight matrix can be represented as a string of binary codes of $w_{i,j}$. Let $c(w_{i,j})$ stand for this code of the weight matrix. Finally, B can be represented by its binary code $c(B)$ as well. Thus, we can consider the concatenation $c(G)c(w_{i,j})c(B)$ as an input string. Now, the TRAVELING SALESMAN PROBLEM can be represented as the language

$$TSP = \{c(G)c(w_{i,j})c(B)| \text{ there is a tour } v_{i_0}, v_{i_1}, \ldots, v_{i_m} \text{ in } G \text{ with the total}$$
$$\text{weight } w_{i_0,i_1} + w_{i_1,i_2} + \ldots + w_{i_{m-1},i_m} \leq B\}$$

We chose the TRAVELING SALESMAN PROBLEM as a candidate for a computationally complex problem because of its obvious practical value. However, the formal variant of the problem is not that simple. Thus, to take a closer look at the nature of the underlying computational complexity of this and other problems, we will consider a number of other somewhat less "practical" computational problems that, nevertheless, shed more light on the problem under discussion.

Our next example is a somewhat simplified version of the TRAVELING SALESMAN PROBLEM. Let G be any undirected graph (with no weights). We will call a tour in such a graph a **Hamiltonian cycle**. (The graph of Figure 6.2 has a Hamiltonian cycle $v_1, v_2, v_6, v_3, v_5, v_4, v_1$.)

The HAMILTONIAN CYCLE PROBLEM is, given a graph G, to determine if it has a Hamiltonian cycle. More formally, it can be defined as the language

$$HC = \{c(G)|G \text{ has a Hamiltonian cycle}\}$$

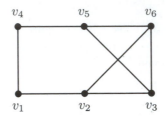

Figure 6.2 A Graph with a Hamiltonian Cycle

This problem does not look any easier than the TRAVELING SALESMAN PROBLEM. To solve it, one should probably try all possible paths in G and check if they form Hamiltonian cycles. However, the total number of different paths in G may be $|V|!$.

Now we consider one more computational problem on graphs. A **clique** in an undirected graph G is a subset $V' \subseteq V$ such that all vertices in V' are connected to all the other vertices in V'. In other words, a clique is a complete subgraph of G. The *size* of a clique is the number of vertices in it. The CLIQUE PROBLEM can be formulated as an optimization problem: Given a graph G, find a clique in G of maximum size. For example, the maximum size of a clique in the graph of Figure 6.3 is 4. The language version of the problem, similar to the TRAVELING

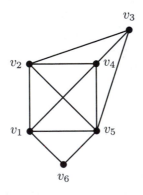

Figure 6.3 A Clique of Size 4

SALESMAN PROBLEM, requires some bound k on the size of a clique, or rather its binary code $c(k)$. The language version of the CLIQUE PROBLEM can be represented as

$$C = \{c(G)c(k)|G \text{ has a clique of size } k\}$$

An obvious algorithm for solving this problem is to list all the subsets of V of size k and, for each of them, determine if they form a clique. When k is proportional to $|V|$, the number of all subsets of size k is a function that grows faster than any polynomial. The reader will probably agree that it would not be easy to find a faster algorithm for this problem.

All three hard computational problems observed in this section dealt with graphs. In fact, problems of similar computational complexity can be found in many other areas of computer science, mathematics, economics, and so on. Our next example, the SUBSET-SUM PROBLEM, is an arithmetic problem. Given a set of integers S and a number t (so-called *target*), determine if there is a subset $S' \subseteq S$ whose elements add up to t. For example, if $S = \{15, 4, 7, 3\}$ and $t = 11$, then the desired subset S' is $\{4, 7\}$. The problem can be represented in the form of the language

$$
\begin{aligned}
SS \quad = \quad & \{c(k_1)c(k_2)\ldots c(k_n)c(t) | \text{there exist numbers} \\
& k_{i_1}, k_{i_2}, \ldots, k_{i_r} \in \{k_1, k_2, \ldots, k_n\} \\
& \text{such that } k_{i_1} + k_{i_2} + \ldots + k_{i_r} = t\}
\end{aligned}
$$

As in prior examples, there is a simple algorithm solving this problem. List all subsets of $\{k_1, \ldots, k_n\}$ and check if any of them sums up to t. However, the total number of subsets of the given set is 2^n. It does not seem to be likely that a more efficient algorithm could exist.

Our list of computationally complex problems in this section concludes with a problem concerning formulas of the propositional (Boolean) logic. To formulate this problem, we first define (somewhat informally) these formulas. A **clause** is composed of

- Boolean variables $x_1, x_2, \ldots$;

- Logical (Boolean) connectives: $\neg$ (applied to variables) and $\vee$ (applied to variables x_i and their negations $\neg x_i$).

Examples of clauses are

$$x_1 \vee \neg x_2 \vee \neg x_3 \vee x_4$$

and

$$\neg x_3 \vee x_1 \vee \neg x_5$$

A Boolean formula in conjunctive normal form (or, simply, *a **Boolean formula***) is a sequence of clauses in parentheses connected by logical connectives $\wedge$. Examples of formulas are

$$f_1 : (\neg x_1 \vee x_2 \vee x_3) \wedge (x_2 \vee \neg x_4 \vee \neg x_3) \wedge (\neg x_2 \vee x_4)$$

and

$$f_2 : (x_2 \lor x_3 \lor \neg x_4) \land (x_1 \lor x_4 \lor \neg x_2)$$

(Logical connectives $\lor$ and $\land$ in formulas stand for *or* and *and*, respectively.) Plugging in 0's or 1's for variables in the formulas evaluates them to 0 or 1, in accordance with truth-tables for the logical connectives $\lor, \land$, and $\neg$. If the formula evaluates to 1, the set of values for the variables $x_1, x_2, \ldots$ is called a *satisfying assignment*. A formula having a satisfying assignment is called a **satisfiable formula**. For example, formula f_1 is satisfied by the assignment $x_1 = 0, x_2 = 1, x_3 = 1, x_4 = 1$. The SATISFIABILITY problem is, given a formula, to determine if it satisfiable. Suppose $c(f)$ is an appropriate coding of a formula f. Then the problem can be represented in form of the language

$$SAT = \{c(f) | f \text{ is a satisfiable formula}\}$$

A simple algorithm deciding this language plugs in all possible assignments for variables in f and tests if the assignment is satisfying. If the number of variables in a formula f is n (and the length of f largely depends on this number), then the total number of assignments to inspect is 2^n. As in the prior cases, no faster algorithm seems to exist.

As we have hinted, it is unlikely that any polynomially bounded solution exists for any of the above computational problems. This argument is far from being mathematically correct. It has not been proved yet that polynomially bounded algorithms do not exist for the above problems. The major reason why such a proof is hard to find is that all the above computational problems *can* be solved in polynomial time by *nondeterministic* machines.

Definition 6.2.1 *We say that a nondeterministic Turing machine M is* **polynomially bounded** *if there is a polynomial $p(x)$ such that, for any input string w, at least one computation of M on input w halts in at most $p(|w|)$ steps.*

Recall how a nondeterministic machine M decides a language L. For any $w \notin L$, *all* computations of M on w must reject it. For any $w \in L$, at least one computation of M on w accepts it, however, some other computations may reject w. When it comes to polynomially bounded computations, this way to decide languages seems very peculiar. One computation accepts a string, another one rejects it. However, as we will demonstrate, there will be nothing peculiar about nondeterministic algorithms solving our computational problems.

Note that any of the above complex computational problems can be solved as follows. Form a finite sequence of strings and for every string in the sequence test if it satisfies the conditions of the problem. If such a string is found, the input is accepted; otherwise it is rejected. The testing part in all the algorithms we observed was fairly easy. In other words, the test could be performed by a polynomially bounded *deterministic* algorithm. One can conceive a nondeterministic algorithm that, given any input string w, operates in two phases:

1. *Guess* a string u to be tested;

2. *Verify* that the string u satisfies the conditions of the problem (if the guess was wrong, u would not satisfy the conditions).

The first part of such an algorithm is obviously nondeterministic. However, the verification phase for the problems in this section, as we will see, can be carried out in polynomial time by a deterministic algorithm. Then the combination of the two phases becomes a polynomial-time nondeterministic algorithm.

Now we concentrate on the verification phase. As our discussion suggests, a **verification algorithm** A takes two arguments w and u. The string u is called a **certificate**. The language L is said to be **verified** by a deterministic verification algorithm A if

$$L = \{w| \text{ there exists a certificate } u \text{ such that} A(w, u) = 1\}$$

Now we can define a class of languages containing all the problems we have observed.

Definition 6.2.2 *A language L is said to belong to the **class** $\mathcal{NP}$ if there exists a deterministic polynomial-time algorithm A and a polynomial q such that*

$$L \quad = \quad \{w| \textit{there exists a certificate } y \textit{ such that}$$
$$|y| \leq q(|w|), \textit{ and } A(w, y) = 1\}.$$

*In other words, A **verifies** L **in polynomial time** ($\mathcal{NP}$ stands for* nondeterministic polynomial*)*

Note, that we used the term *algorithm* rather than a *Turing machine* in this definition. As we discussed in the previous section, polynomial time does not depend on the formal model within which algorithms are formalized. Different formalizations result just in different polynomial bounds on the running time.

An important technical issue that we have not addressed so far is how the choice of the coding of the input data can affect polynomial-time algorithms. To demonstrate the importance of this issue, we can compare the *unary* and *binary* codes for an integer n. The length of n in unary code is n, while the binary code for n has the length $\log n$, an exponentially shorter value. However, if we choose representations of data in alphabets that have *at least* two symbols, it turns out that they are *polynomially related*. That is, the length, say, of the binary code of any data, is a polynomial of the length of the code, of the same data, in base 8, and vice versa. It is reasonable to consider only encodings of data in base 2 (binary) or greater. Then the fact that all reasonable encodings are polynomially related implies that, if a problem is solvable in polynomial time with one encoding of the input data, it is solvable in polynomial time with any other encoding. In other words, the type of encoding *does not matter as far as polynomial-time computability is concerned*. This observation gives us the opportunity to describe polynomial-time algorithms in somewhat abstract terms, omitting some coding and decoding technicalities.

Now it is easy to demonstrate that all the problems discussed in this section are in the class $\mathcal{NP}$. Consider, for example, the SATISFIABILITY problem. Given any assignment $x_1 = a_1$, $x_2 = a_2$, ..., $x_n = a_n$, a_1, a_2, ..., $a_n \in \{0,1\}$ for the Boolean variables in a formula f, a verification algorithm A just plugs them in and then, scanning the formula from left to right, determines if every clause contains at least one 1 (then the whole formula evaluates to 1, otherwise; it evaluates to 0). The running time of this algorithm can be bounded by the polynomial $d \cdot |w|$, where $w = c(f)$ is the input code of a formula f and d is some constant. Thus, A, being applied to the inputs $c(f)$ and a_1, a_2, ..., a_n, runs in polynomial time. The length n of the assignment vector (the certificate) does not exceed the length of $c(f)$ (the number of variables in a formula f is not greater than the length of f). Thus, $SAT \in \mathcal{NP}$.

The HAMILTONIAN CYCLE PROBLEM is shown to be in $\mathcal{NP}$ by exhibiting a verification algorithm A that, given the input encoding $c(G)$ of a graph G and the code u of a path $v_{i_1}, v_{i_2}, \ldots, v_{i_k}$, in G, determines if the path forms a simple cycle containing $|V| + 1$ vertices. The algorithm can scan the code of the path and, for each pair (i_r, i_{r+1}), "consult" the code of G to determine if this pair is an edge in G. In addition, A must make sure that $v_{i_1} = v_{i_k}$ and that $v_{i_r} \notin \{v_{i_1}, \ldots, v_{i_{r-1}}\}$ for all $r < k$. Even if we use a "clumsy" one-head one-tape Turing machine to implement this algorithm, it will run in time $d \cdot (|c(G)| + |u|)^2$. The length of the certificate u does not exceed the length of the code $c(G)$ (if it does, then it must be rejected, because a Hamiltonian cycle cannot contain more that $|V| + 1$ vertices). Thus we have established $HC \in \mathcal{NP}$. The problems TSP, C, and SS are covered in Exercise 6.4.

Note that $\mathcal{P} \subseteq \mathcal{NP}$. A polynomial-time algorithm A deciding $L \in \mathcal{P}$ can easily be converted to a two-argument polynomial-time verification algorithm A' that just ignores the second argument and simulates A.

Now we can address the question we failed to answer so far: Do deterministic *polynomial-time algorithms* exist for the problems TSP, HC, C, SS, and SAT? A more general question is if all problems from $\mathcal{NP}$ are in $\mathcal{P}$, or, in other words, if $\mathcal{NP} = \mathcal{P}$. The answer to this question is *unknown*, and it is one of the most challenging open problems in computer science. The widely shared opinion among computer scientists is that the classes $\mathcal{P}$ and $\mathcal{NP}$ are different. The intuitive reasoning behind this point of view is that while finding solutions and verifying their correctness can be done quickly for the problems in $\mathcal{P}$, only the verification part can be performed quickly for the problems in $\mathcal{NP}$.

In the next section we will provide another powerful argument to support the conjecture that $\mathcal{P}$ and $\mathcal{NP}$ are different. There are many open problems related to relationships between classes $\mathcal{P}$, $\mathcal{NP}$, and classes that cover decidable problems even more complicated than in $\mathcal{NP}$. It is not known, for example, if the class $\mathcal{NP}$ is closed under complement.

6.3 $\mathcal{NP}$-Completeness

The reader probably noticed certain similarities among the various nondeterministic polynomial-time solutions to all five of the problems that we discussed in Section 6.2: A nondeterministic "guess" is followed by a (relatively) simple deterministic verification algorithm. As we will demonstrate in this section, there is a formal mathematical basis for this similarity. All five of the problems are *polynomial-time related*, that is, a polynomial-time deterministic solution to any of them would provide polynomial-time deterministic solutions to all of them. In other words, if any of them were in $\mathcal{P}$, then the rest of them would be in $\mathcal{P}$. In fact, an even more powerful result is true. If any of these problems had a polynomial-time deterministic solution, then any other problem in $\mathcal{NP}$ would have a polynomial-time deterministic solution! Not every problem in $\mathcal{NP}$ has this property. Thus, we call our five problems $\mathcal{NP}$-*complete* problems. These five problems actually form a very small portion of thousands of important computational problems in many areas of computer science, mathematics, economics, manufacturing, communications and so forth. that are $\mathcal{NP}$-complete in the above sense.

To formally define the notion of completeness, we must introduce the notion of *polynomial-time reductions* between computational problems. The notion of reductions between languages was introduced in Chapter 5. Polynomial-time reduction differs from the general type of reduction in one important aspect: The reducing algorithm must be polynomially bounded. Based on this, we will be able to claim that if we managed to translate a language L to some language $L' \in \mathcal{P}$, then the language L itself would be in $\mathcal{P}$. We will play out this property of polynomial-time reductions to establish completeness of our five (and some other) $\mathcal{NP}$ problems. Now we proceed formally.

Definition 6.3.1 *A function $f : \Sigma^* \to \Sigma^*$ is called **polynomial-time computable** if there is a polynomially bounded Turing machine computing it.*

Definition 6.3.2 *Let L and $R \subseteq \Sigma^*$ be two languages. We say that the language L is **polynomial-time reducible** to R if there exists a polynomial-time computable function r such that, for any $w \in \Sigma^*$, $w \in L$ if and only if $r(w) \in R$. The function r is called **polynomial-time reduction**.*

Polynomial-time reductions make possible polynomial-time solutions to computational problems based on efficient translations of these problems to other problems whose polynomial-time solutions have already been found. More specifically, suppose we are to design a polynomial-time decision algorithm for the language L, which is polynomial-time reducible to a language R. Suppose we have an algorithm B that decides R in polynomial time. Then the following algorithm A decides L: given any input string w, compute $r(w)$ (in polynomial time), then call the polynomial-time algorithm to determine whether $r(w) \in R$. If $r(w) \in R$, then $w \in L$; otherwise $w \notin L$ (a "flowchart" of A is given in Figure 6.4). Note that since

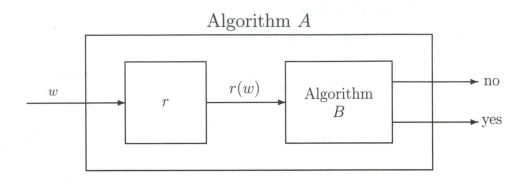

Figure 6.4 Algorithm A

$r(w)$ is computable in time that is bounded by a polynomial p of $|w|$, the length of the result $|r(w)|$ cannot exceed $p(|w|)$ [otherwise, the algorithm computing r would be unable to complete even writing $r(w)$ on the output tape in time $p(|w|)$]. Suppose a polynomial q bounds the running time of algorithm B. Then B's running time on the instance $r(w)$ is bounded by $q(p(|w|))$. However, any composition of two polynomials is a polynomial itself (consider, for example, $(x^2)^3 = x^5$). Thus, the running time of A is bounded by a polynomial. In other words, A is a desired polynomial-time algorithm.

This result can be turned around. Suppose it requires more than polynomial (say, exponential) time to decide a language L that is polynomial-time reducible to R. Then it would require at least exponential time to decide R. If R were decidable in less than exponential time, then the polynomial-time reduction of L to R would provide us a less than polynomial-time algorithm deciding L (the composition of a polynomial and a function growing slower than exponential would result in a function growing slower than exponential), a contradiction. In other words, R is *at least as hard as* L.

The five problems we discussed in Section 6.2, among many other important computational problems in $\mathcal{NP}$, are known to be polynomial-time reducible to each other. Some of these problems, such as the HAMILTONIAN CYCLE and the TRAVELING SALESMAN PROBLEM, are very similar to each other and designing a polynomial-time reduction for these problems is relatively easy. However, in many cases, when problems are very different, designing such a reduction has been an act of real "algorithmic" creativity. Accordingly, some polynomial-time reduction algorithms are very complex. In this section we present three polynomial-time reductions, from HAMILTONIAN CYCLE to TRAVELING SALESMAN PROBLEM, from SATISFIABILITY to its restricted version, 3-SATISFIABILITY, where every clause contains at most three variables or their negations, and finally from 3-SATISFIABILITY to CLIQUE. The first reduction is fairly simple; the second and the third are relatively sophisticated. Many other polynomial-time reductions between problems in $\mathcal{NP}$ can be found in [Garey and Johnson].

Theorem 6.3.1 *HC is polynomial-time reducible to TSP.*

Proof: We must design a polynomial-time algorithm that, given any undirected graph G, constructs an undirected weighted graph G' and a bound B such that G has a Hamiltonian cycle if and only if there is a tour in G' with the total weight bound by B. The desired algorithm operates as follows: Given $G = (V, E)$, choose the bound $B = 0$ and define $G' = (V, E')$ as the *complete* graph with the same set of vertices V and with the following weights assigned to edges

$$w_{i,j} = \begin{cases} 0 & \text{if } (v_i, v_j) \in E \\ 1 & \text{if } (v_i, v_j) \notin E \end{cases}$$

It is quite clear that the algorithm we have described works in polynomial time. Now we have to show that G has a Hamiltonian cycle if and only if G' has a tour with the total weight 0. First, suppose G has a Hamiltonian cycle. Suppose this cycle is given by path h. Each edge in h is present in the graph G' and hence has weight 0. Thus, h is a tour in G' with the total weight 0. Conversely, let h be a tour in G' with the total weight 0. Then this tour contains only edges from G, for, otherwise, its total cost would be greater than 0. Thus, h corresponds to a Hamiltonian cycle in G.

End Proof

Now we consider the problem of reducing SAT to its restricted version, 3-SAT. In this version, every clause contains at most three variables or negated variables.

Theorem 6.3.2 *SAT is polynomial-time reducible to 3-SAT.*

Proof: The polynomial-time algorithm A transforming boolean formulas with clauses of arbitrary length to the formulas with clauses containing at most three variables or negated variables per clause operates as follows: Let $f = C_1 \wedge C_2 \wedge \ldots \wedge C_n$ be a formula in SAT. Let $C \in \{C_1, \ldots, C_n\}$. Suppose $C = l_1 \vee l_2 \vee \ldots \vee l_k$, where $k > 3$. Given C, introduce a new set of boolean variables $y_1, \ldots, y_{k-3}$ (a new set for each clause C) and substitute C by the following conjunction of short clauses:

$$(l_1 \vee l_2 \vee y_1) \wedge (\neg y_1 \vee l_3 \vee y_2) \wedge (\neg y_2 \vee l_4 \vee y_3) \wedge \ldots \wedge (\neg y_{k-4} \vee l_{k-3} \vee l_k)$$

The new formula, $A(f)$, contains at most three elements per clause. It is easy to see that the above convertion can be carried out in polynomial time. We have to show that f is satisfiable if and only if $A(f)$ is satisfiable.

Suppose that some assignment T satisfies the formula f. Note that every clause C in f must be satisfied by T. If C is a "short" clause (at most three variables or negated variables) in f, then it is present in $A(f)$ and is thus satisfied. If $C = l_1 \vee l_2 \vee \ldots \vee l_k$ is a "long" clause ($k > 3$); then let i be the smallest index for which l_i is evaluated to true value by T (such an index must exist since C is evaluated to true). Now we extend the assignment T to the new variables $y_1, y_2, \ldots, y_{k-3}$ associated with C as follows: If $j \leq i - 2$ then y_j is set to true; otherwise it is set to false. Under this new assignment T', $(l_1 \vee l_2 \vee y_1)$ and every clause

$$(\neg y_{j-1} \vee l_{j+1} \vee y_j)$$

for $j \leq i - 2$ evaluates to true since y_j is true. Then, $(y_{i-2} \vee l_i \vee y_{i-1})$ is true since l_i is true. Finally, all $(\neg y_{j-1} \vee l_{j+1} \vee y_j)$ for $j > i - 2$ and $(\neg y_{k-3} \vee l_{k-1} \vee l_k)$ evaluate to true since all $\neg y_{i-1}, \neg y_i, \ldots, \neg y_{k-3}$ are true. Thus the whole subformula of $A(f)$ obtained from C is satisfied.

Now suppose that $A(f)$ is satisfied by some assignment T. We show that T satisfies every clause C in f. Indeed, every "short" clause (up to three variables or negated variables) is trivially satisfied. Now, suppose C is a "long" clause and C' is the corresponding subformula of $A(f)$. Note that C' is satisfied. We intend to show that at least one l_i in C' must have the value true under the assignment T. Indeed, otherwise y_1 should be true, and, therefore, all $y_2, \ldots, y_{k-3}$ should be true. However, then the last clause $(\neg y_{k-3} \vee l_{k-1} \vee l_k)$ is not satisfied. Since at least one l_i gets the value true under T, it also satisfies the clause C. Thus, T satisfies all clauses in f.

> End Proof

Now we show that 3-SAT is polynomial-time reducible to CLIQUE.

Theorem 6.3.3 *3-SAT is polynomial-time reducible to C.*

Proof: Let $f = C_1 \wedge C_2 \wedge \ldots \wedge C_n$ be an instance of a formula in 3-SAT with n clauses $C_1, C_2, \ldots C_n$. Given f, we are going to construct a graph G such that f is satisfiable if and only if G has a clique of size n.

For each clause $C_r = (l_1^r \vee l_2^r \vee l_3^r)$ in f, we create a triple v_1^r, v_2^r, v_3^r of vertices in the graph G. Then we connect different vertices v_i^r, v_j^s by an edge if and only if the following two conditions hold:

1. v_i^r and v_j^s are in different triples $(r \neq s)$;

2. l_i^r is not the negation of l_j^s (or vice versa).

(An example of the construction for the formula

$$f = (x_1 \vee x_2 \vee x_3) \wedge (\neg x_1 \vee \neg x_2 \vee x_3) \wedge (\neg x_1 \vee x_2 \vee x_3)$$

is given in Figure 6.5). The transformation of f to G can obviously be accomplished in polynomial time. Now we have to show that it is in fact a reduction. Suppose that, for some assignment of values to variables, f evaluates to 1. Then each clause C_r must contain at least one variable or negated variable l_i^r that has the value 1. Pick the corresponding vertex v_i^r for each such l_i^r. Let V' be the set consisting of all such vertices v_i^r. Note that $|V'| = n$, since we picked one v_i^r for every clause C_i. We

$$C_1 = x_1 \vee x_2 \vee x_3$$

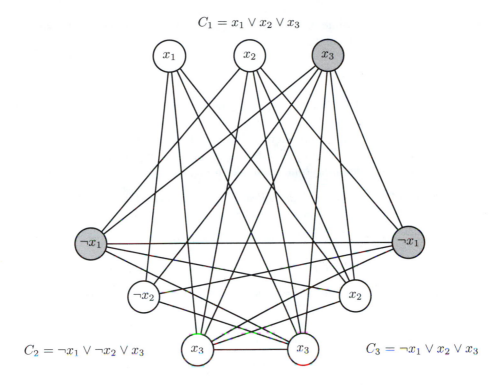

$C_2 = \neg x_1 \vee \neg x_2 \vee x_3$
$C_3 = \neg x_1 \vee x_2 \vee x_3$

Figure 6.5 The Graph Derived from a Boolean Formula f

are going to show that any two vertices $v_i^r, v_j^s \in V'$ are connected with each other. Indeed, according to the definition of V', neither of l_i^r or l_j^s can be the negation of the other, since both of them get the same value for the same assignment of 0's and 1's to variables. Thus, according to the definition of G, they are connected by an edge. In other words, the subgraph of G with the set of vertices V' is a clique of size n.

Now suppose that G has a clique G' of size n with the set of vertices V'. No edges in G connect vertices in the same triple. As the size of the clique is $n = |V'|$, V' must contain exactly one vertex v_i^r per triple. Let us assign 1 to every corresponding l_i^r. Since no l_i^r in our set can be the negation of another l_j^s in this set, according to the definition of the graph G, this will not result in assigning 0 and 1 to the same variable. The given assignment satisfies every clause, and, therefore, the whole formula f. The values of variables that are not present in the above set can be set arbitrarily as they cannot affect the result of evaluation for f.

In the example of Figure 6.5 a clique of size 3 connects the vertices corresponding to x_3 from the first clause, $\neg x_1$ from the second clause, and $\neg x_1$ from the third clause. A corresponding satisfying assignment for f is $(x_1 = 0, x_2 = 1, x_3 = 1)$. We have chosen to set the value of $x_2 = 1$, as this can be chosen arbitrarily without changing the satisfiability of f.

$$\boxed{\text{End Proof}}$$

Many other examples of polynomial-time reductions between problems in $\mathcal{NP}$ can be found in [Garey and Johnson]. It is suggested that the reader design a few polynomial-time reductions from Exercises 6.6,6.7, 6.8, 6.9, and 6.10.

The five problems in $\mathcal{NP}$ we exhibited have another important property. *Any language in $\mathcal{NP}$ is polynomial-time reducible to any of them.*

Definition 6.3.3 *A language L is called $\mathcal{NP}$-complete if $L \in \mathcal{NP}$ and every language $L' \in \mathcal{NP}$ is polynomial-time reducible to L.*

Historically, the language *SAT* was the first one discovered to be $\mathcal{NP}$-complete.

Theorem 6.3.4 (Cook's Theorem). *The language SAT is $\mathcal{NP}$-complete.*

Cook's theorem has been one of the most important discoveries in theoretical computer science. Its proof is based on a meticulous polynomial-time mapping of accepting Turing machine computations to satisfiable Boolean formulas. The complete proof of this theorem can be found in [Garey and Johnson, Lewis and Papadimitriou].

Since SAT, TSP, HC, C, SS are polynomial-time reducible to each other, all of them are $\mathcal{NP}$-complete. Many other important $\mathcal{NP}$-complete problems can be found in other books on the theory of computation and computational complexity. Some other $\mathcal{NP}$-complete problems are presented in Exercise 6.5.

We will mention just one more of them that is relevant to the topics discussed in this book, the INEQUIVALENCE OF *-FREE REGULAR EXPRESSIONS. A regular expression is called *-free if it does not contain Kleene stars. The INEQUIVALENCE OF *-FREE REGULAR EXPRESSIONS problem is to determine for two given *-free regular expressions R_1 and R_2, if $L(R_1) \neq L(R_2)$. It is interesting that it is unknown whether the problems of equivalence of regular expressions and nondeterministic finite automata (discussed in Chapter 2) are even in $\mathcal{NP}$.

$\mathcal{NP}$-completeness of many computational problems is considered as a powerful argument supporting the conjecture that classes $\mathcal{P}$ and $\mathcal{NP}$ are different.

Designing computer solutions to many $\mathcal{NP}$-complete problems is an important practical problem. It has been possible to design a variety of such solutions that, still being formally slow, work in polynomial time on practically important instances of the problem. More information about this area of theoretical computer science can be found in [Lewis and Papadimitriou, Papadimitriou].

Exercises

Exercises

━━━━━ **Section 6.1** ━━━━━

Exercise 6.1 ◆ Find the exact polynomial $p(x)$ such that $t_M(w) = p(|w|)$ for the Turing machine described in the Section 6.1 that decides the language $\{w|w = w^R, w \in \{a, b\}\}$.

Exercise 6.2 Show that the language $L = \{udu|u \in \{a, b\}\}$ can be decided by a Turing machine M with the running time $t_M(w) = c \cdot |w|^2$ for some constant c.

Exercise 6.3 Show that the class $\mathcal{P}$ is closed under the following operations:

a) Union

b) Intersection

c) Concatenation

━━━━━ **Section 6.2** ━━━━━

Exercise 6.4 Show that the following languages defined in Section 6.2 are in $\mathcal{NP}$:

a) TSP

b) C

c) SS

Exercise 6.5 Formulate every computational problem in this exercise in the form of a language. For every language, show that it is in $\mathcal{NP}$ (briefly describe a polynomial-time verification algorithm for the language). For every language, briefly describe a deterministic algorithm deciding it.

a) Given a graph $G = (V, E)$, a subset $V' \subseteq V$ is called an **independent subset** of vertices if every edge of the graph G is incident to at most one vertex in V' (in other words, no vertex in V' is connected to any other vertex in V'). The **Independent Set Problem** is to find an independent set of vertices of a given size k.

b) The **Partition Problem** is: Given a finite set of integers $S = \{a_1, a_2, \ldots, a_n\}$, determine if the set can be partitioned into two sets S_1, S_2 such that the sum of all elements of the first set equals the sum of all elements of the second set.

c) The **Two-Machine Scheduling Problem** is: Given a finite set of integers $S = \{a_1, a_2, \ldots, a_n\}$, partition it into two subsets S_1, S_2 such that the sums of elements in each set do not exceed a given bound D. (The problem relates to scheduling n tasks on two machines. Both machines have the same speed, and the order of task execution does not matter. $a_1, a_2, \ldots, a_n$ are execution times of the tasks. The question is, given a deadline D, determine if all tasks can be distributed between two machines so that all of them can be completed before the deadline).

d) Let U be a finite set and $\mathcal{A} = \{S_1, S_2, \ldots, S_n\}$ be a collection of subsets of U. The **Exact Cover Problem** is to determine if there exist *disjoint* (mutually nonintersecting) subsets $S_{i_1}, S_{i_2}, \ldots, S_{i_m}$ in the collection $\mathcal{A}$ such that their union is U.

e) Let $G = (V, E)$ be an undirected graph. A set $V' \subseteq V$ of nodes is called a **cover** of the graph G if every edge in G is incident to at least one vertex in V'. The **Node Cover Problem** is, given a graph G and a number $k > 1$, determine if there exists a cover C of the graph G such that $|C| \leq k$.

f) Let A be an m-by-n integer matrix and b be an integer m-vector. The **Integer Programming Problem** is, given such a matrix A and a vector b, determine if there exists a Boolean n-vector x (that is, x contains only 0's and 1's) such that $Ax \leq b$.

g) The **Subgraph Isomorphism Problem** is: Given graphs G_1 and G_2, to determine if G_1 is a subgraph of G_2.

Section 6.3

Exercise 6.6 ◆ Show that the language IS representing the INDEPENDENT SET PROBLEM as defined in Exercise 6.5 is $\mathcal{NP}$-complete. (Hint: Show that the language C representing an $\mathcal{NP}$-complete CLIQUE PROBLEM defined in Section 6.2 is reducible to IS in polynomial time.)

Exercise 6.7 ◆ Exhibit a polynomial-time reduction from the language P representing the PARTITION PROBLEM as defined in Exercise 6.5 to the language SS representing the SUBSET-SUM PROBLEM defined in Section 6.2 (The PARTITION PROBLEM is known to be $\mathcal{NP}$-complete. The reduction will show that the SUBSET-SUM PROBLEM is also $\mathcal{NP}$-complete.)

Exercise 6.8 ◆ ◆ Show that the language P representing the PARTITION PROB-LEM as defined in Exercise 6.5 is $\mathcal{NP}$-complete. (Hint: Show that the language SS representing an $\mathcal{NP}$-complete SUBSET-SUM PROBLEM defined in Section 6.2 can be reduced to P in polynomial time.)

Exercise 6.9 ◆ Exhibit a polynomial-time reduction from the language P representing the PARTITION PROBLEM as defined in Exercise 6.5 to the language TMS representing the TWO-MACHINE SCHEDULING PROBLEM defined in Exercise 6.5. (The PARTITION PROBLEM is known to be $\mathcal{NP}$-complete. The reduction will show that the TWO-MACHINE SCHEDULING PROBLEM is also $\mathcal{NP}$-complete.)

Exercise 6.10 ◆ ◆ Show that the language IP representing the INTEGER PRO-GRAMMING PROBLEM as defined in Exercise 6.5 is $\mathcal{NP}$-complete. (Hint: Show that the $\mathcal{NP}$-complete language $3 - SAT$ defined in Section 6.3 is reducible to IP in polynomial time.)

References

Garey M., and D. Johnson.

Computers and Intractability: A Guide to NP-Completeness.
W. H. Freeman & Co, San Francisco, CA, 1979.

Lewis H., and C. Papadimitriou.

Elements of the Theory of Computation. Prentice Hall, Inc.,
Upper Saddle River, NJ, 1981.

Papadimitriou C.,

Computational Complexity. Addison-Wesley Co., Reading,
MA, 1994.

List of Symbols

Index

203